The Palgrave Lacan Series

Jacques Lacan is one of the most important and influential thinkers of the 20th century. The reach of this influence continues to grow as we settle into the 21st century, the resonance of Lacan's thought arguably only beginning now to be properly felt, both in terms of its application to clinical matters and in its application to a range of human activities and interests. The Palgrave Lacan Series is a book series for the best new writing in the Lacanian field, giving voice to the leading writers of a new generation of Lacanian thought. The series will comprise original monographs and thematic, multi-authored collections. The books in the series will explore aspects of Lacan's theory from new perspectives and with original insights. There will be books focused on particular areas of or issues in clinical work. There will be books focused on applying Lacanian theory to areas and issues beyond the clinic, to matters of society, politics, the arts and culture. Each book, whatever its particular concern, will work to expand our understanding of Lacan's theory and its value in the 21st century.

Meera Lee
Editor

Lacan's Cruelty

Perversion beyond Philosophy, Culture and Clinic

palgrave
macmillan

Editor
Meera Lee
Asian American Studies Program
Hunter College, CUNY
New York, NY, USA

The Palgrave Lacan Series
ISBN 978-3-031-06237-7 ISBN 978-3-031-06238-4 (eBook)
https://doi.org/10.1007/978-3-031-06238-4

Cover illustration: cbording/Getty Images

This Palgrave Macmillan imprint is published by the registered company Springer Nature Switzerland AG.
The registered company address is: Gewerbestrasse 11, 6330 Cham, Switzerland

Acknowledgments

I am grateful to those friends and colleagues who helped me bring this book to publication. Derek Hook graciously suggested that I consider putting something together on Lacan after the Écrits Conference at Duquesne University in 2019. I extend my gratitude to the series editors Calum Neill and Derek Hook for offering me this opportunity and for their confidence. The contributors of this book have maintained commitment to the project during challenging times in the past two years. Jean-Michel Rabaté has been an insightful interlocutor and has provided me with invaluable support and comments throughout the entire process. My understanding of "Lacan's cruelty" is greatly indebted to him. Gregg Lambert has shown me an exceptional way to think in psychoanalysis and philosophy. My warm thanks go to Azeen Khan, whose superb reading of Freud and Lacan has been a great source of inspiration—and for being such a dear friend and companion *inside* and *outside* psychoanalysis. I cannot express enough my deepest gratitude to Jean Jonassaint and Romita Ray for their ceaseless and loyal support and for their extraordinary care both professionally and personally.

Finally, and most of all, I thank my parents for still believing in me, with love.

Meera Lee

I am grateful to those friends and colleagues who [illegible] this book to publication. Derek Hook graciously [illegible] that I consider putting something together [illegible] after the [illegible] [illegible] [illegible] Neill and Derek Hook [illegible] the [illegible] their [illegible]. The contributors of [illegible] have [illegible] [illegible] with [illegible] My understanding of "[illegible]" [illegible] indebted to him [illegible] Lambert [illegible] shown me [illegible] think [illegible] and philosophy. My warm thanks [illegible] [illegible] friend and I [illegible] has been a great source of inspiration—and for being such a dear friend and companion [illegible] [illegible] for their [illegible] [illegible] both professional [illegible]

Finally, and most of all, I thank my parents for [illegible]

[illegible]

Contents

Notes on Contributors

Frédéric Baitinger is an associate researcher at the Research Chair in Philosophy at the Saint-Anne Hospital and a psychoanalyst working in private practice in Paris, France. He is also the author of numerous articles on Lacanian psychoanalysis, feminism and French theory and is completing a manuscript titled *Decolonizing the Unconscious.*

Arka Chattopadhyay teaches literature, philosophy and psychoanalysis in the Department of Humanities and Social Sciences in IIT Gandhinagar, India. He is also a fiction writer in Bengali. He is the author of the monograph, *Beckett, Lacan and the Mathematical Writing of the Real* (Bloomsbury, 2018), the Bengali novel *Uponyosto* (Boibhashik 2018) and a collection of Bengali short stories (2021). He is the founding editor of *Sanglap* and has co-edited volumes on Beckett and Nabarun for Bloomsbury, Roman and Brill. He is working on his second monograph on Posthumanism and two co-edited volumes on affective ecology and Badiou and modernism.

Derek Hook is Associate Professor of Psychology and clinical supervisor in the Department of Psychology at Duquesne University. He received clinical training in Freudian/Lacanian psychoanalysis in London. He is the author of "Six Moments in Lacan" and "A Critical Psychology of the Postcolonial" and, along with Calum Neill, is editor to Palgrave Lacan Series. His most recent publication is a book edited with Sheldon George, entitled *Lacan and Race*. Along with Stijn Vanheule and Calum Neill, he is the editor of the four-volume series Reading Lacan's Ecrits. He runs a YouTube channel with 60+ filmed introductory lectures on Lacanian theory.

Gregg Lambert is Dean's Professor of Humanities at Syracuse University. His most recent books are *The World Is Gone: Philosophy in Light of the Pandemic* (2021), *The People Are Missing: Minor Literature Today* (2021), *Toward a Geopolitical Image of Thought* (2021) and *The Elements of Foucault* (2020). Author of nineteen books and critical editions, and over eighty articles, Lambert is internationally renowned for his writings on the contemporary Humanities, as well as critical theory and philosophy, especially for his writings on Gilles Deleuze and Jacques Derrida.

Meera Lee is on the faculty of the Asian American Studies Program at Hunter College, CUNY, and a psychoanalyst in New York City. Her writings have appeared in *Positions: Asia Critique*, *Verge: Global Asias*, *Telos*, *Symposium* and *Tamkang Review*, as well as the edited book *Psychoanalyzing Cinema: A Productive Encounter with Lacan, Deleuze and Žižek*. She is working on two book projects, a monograph titled *Of Cruelty: The Superego Today in Freud and Lacan* and a co-authored book (with Jan Jagodzinski) on the film director Kim Ki-duk.

Tracy McNulty is Professor of Comparative Literature at Cornell University and a psychoanalyst in private practice. She is the author of *The Hostess: Hospitality, Femininity, and the Expropriation of Identity* (2007) and *Wrestling with the Angel: Experiments in Symbolic Life* (2014). She is completing a book titled *Emancipation by Relay: Psychoanalysis and Historical Transmission*.

Jean-Michel Rabaté is Professor of English and Comparative Literature at the University of Pennsylvania, co-editor of the *Journal of Modern Literature*, co-founder of Slought Foundation, and a fellow of the American Academy of Arts and Sciences. He is the author or editor of more than forty books on modernism, psychoanalysis, philosophy and literary theory. Rabaté's recent titles include *Rust* (2018), *Kafka L.O.L.* (2018), *After Derrida* (2018), *Rire au Soleil* (2019), *New Beckett* (2019), *Understanding Derrida/Understanding Modernism* (2019), *Knots:*

Post-Lacanian Readings of Literature and Film (2020), *Beckett and Sade* (2020), *Rires Prodigues* (2021), *Historical Modernisms: Time, History and Modernist Aesthetics* (co-edited with Angeliki Spiropoulou, 2021) and *James Joyce Hérétique et Prodige* (January 2022).

Benjamin Strosberg is a clinical practitioner and scholar who trained at Duquesne University. His work brings together Lacanian psychoanalysis and Adorno's critical theory focusing on the relevance of philosophical questions for psychotherapy.

Stephanie Swales is Associate Professor of Psychology at the University of Dallas, a practicing psychoanalyst, a licensed clinical psychologist, and a clinical supervisor located in Dallas, Texas. Along with numerous articles and book chapters in the area of Lacanian psychoanalysis, she has authored two books: *Psychoanalysing Ambivalence with Freud and Lacan: On and Off the Couch* (, 2019), co-authored with Carol Owens, and *Perversion: A Lacanian Psychoanalytic Approach to the Subject* (2012). She also serves as a book review editor for the journal *Psychoanalysis, Culture & Society*.

List of Figures

1

Introduction: Psychoanalysis in the Bedroom

Meera Lee

"There is no equivalence…in which what is known as sexual relation in the parlêtre in the human being finds a support. Isn't this what a demonstrated for us in what is known as the clinic, which is another use of the *bed*"[1] (my emphasis), Jacques Lacan proclaimed in his last teaching of Seminar XXIII in which Lacan famously formalized his provocative idea of human sexuality. In this seminar, Lacan more firmly urged us to rethink the traditional conception of the sexual-body outside the frame of biologism and naturalism, pushing it to what he called "the speaking body." His much-celebrated axiom of the "non-sexual relation," as a result, disturbed the order of the knowledge of human reproduction and civilization in the domains of science, philosophy and religion, as well as in the epistemic regime of Freud—this notion of the non-sexual rapport continues to puzzle many readers of Lacan and has also become arguably the most favorite quote of Lacan's in the contemporary Lacanian clinic.

M. Lee (✉)
Asian American Studies Program, Hunter College, CUNY,
New York, NY, USA
e-mail: ml6732@hunter.cuny.edu

M. Lee (ed.), *Lacan's Cruelty*, The Palgrave Lacan Series,
https://doi.org/10.1007/978-3-031-06238-4_1

But what does the non-sexual rapport mean when two (or more) bodies encounter? More specifically, what does the non-sexual mean in perversion to where sex or sexuality is inherently attached? How do we understand Lacan's metaphor of the clinic as another "bed" with respect to perversion when human sexuality exists only in a non-sexual form?

This edited volume attempts to expand on the discourse and clinical praxis of perversion in Lacanian psychoanalytic theory. In contemporary society, perversion is a precarious, if not controversial, concept. An understudied and often misconceived topic in the cultural domain perversion is conceived as an aberrant sexual behavior that engages in non-conventional or deviant sexual activities, causing a physical infliction to the partner. In the practice of psychoanalysis, perversion's status has remained unresolved between theory (the law of desire) and practice (clinical diagnosis). Some Lacanian theorists have also argued that, to an extent, perversion does not exist in a clinical setting, while others have limited it to the Freudian theory of a polymorphous infantile sexuality. In academia, many queer studies scholars have attempted to salvage the term "perversion" or "pervert" from the clinical category as they see it as unjustly stigmatized and associated with homosexuality. The most notable and comprehensive exploration of perversion remains the work of Élisabeth Roudinesco, a historian of psychoanalysis and biographer of both Sigmund Freud and Lacan. In her book, *Our Dark Side: A History of Perversion*, Roudinesco firmly states that perversion exists. But she distinguishes perversion from "perversity," arguing that the latter typically involves dehumanization or cruelty.[2] Her book emphasizes the necessity of the study of perversion within the domains of "the historical, political, cultural and anthropological" that breaks from not only a former DSM categorization of perversion but also the current culture of paraphilia that leaves no differentiation between the practices of perversity (e.g., concentration camps) and perverse fantasies.[3] Her argument alerts us to the danger of the domestication of our imaginary and also the "perverse effect" that makes us blind to the problems of a "perverse system" like capitalism or positivist scientism due to its immediate productivity.[4] Echoing this sense, this collection of essays intends to examine perversion on the non-domesticated and non-pathological levels.

While Lacan firmly establishes his psychoanalytic thinking on the clinical structures of neurosis and psychosis in his return to Freud, his theoretical formulation of perversion remains relatively sparse in his seminars and writing. Despite this paucity, Lacan's essay "Kant with Sade" remains one of the most crucial and, at the same time, impenetrable texts in his oeuvre. Seldom discussed in the clinical setting, the essay underscores the impact of perversion in European history. Originally written as a preface to Marquis de Sade's novella, *Philosophy in the Bedroom* (1795), "Kant with Sade," which Lacan had intended to include in a 15-volume edition of Sade's complete works, instead first appeared in 1963 in the literary journal, *Critique*. It has been assumed that the "unintelligibility"[5] of Lacan's text might have been the reason for the volume editor's rejection of his essay. If "Kant with Sade" is considered one of Lacan's most impenetrable texts, this is due less to his arguably obscure prose style than to his odd coupling of the moral philosopher Kant with the libertine, pornographic, aristocratic novelist Sade. Composed mostly of philosophical reflections, which already sets the tone of Lacan's seemingly radical if not unsettling approach to psychoanalysis, sadism and perversion, in this essay, Lacan stresses that perversion initiated a shift not only in the intellectual domains of literature, law, philosophy and psychoanalysis but also in the ideological domain of ethics, giving rise to "the great revolutionary crisis of morality."[6] If Lacan had called his essay "Freud with Sade" instead, representing a Freudian "catalogue"[7] of perversion as Lacan himself sarcastically alluded to in the opening paragraphs of "Kant with Sade," might have French literary and psychoanalytic circles reacted differently to his essay? In fact, Lacan noted that Freud's "radical" concept of pleasure, namely, his beyond the pleasure principle, which was distinct from the conventional ethics of the good, was accepted because of the legacy that Sade had left in the theme of "delight in evil [*bonheur dans le mal*]."[8] In short, according to Lacan there could not have been a Freud beyond the pleasure principle or perversion had it not been for Sade. If Sade had called his writing "Psychoanalysis in the Bedroom," what sort of "psychoanalysis" was there in "the Sadean bedroom?"

Presumably influenced by writing about Sade by Simone de Beauvoir, Maurice Blanchot and Georges Bataille, Lacan highlights that "cruel reason" is the foundation of Sadean perversion, or in other words, that sadism follows in the spirit of Kantian apathy. Here, we must distinguish the explicit sexual content of Sade's writing from the system at work in his texts, just as his writings must be separated from Sade the individual. This is not to say that the content and text are antithetical to one another. Rather they are complementary in the sense that the distinction between content and method in Sade echoes Kant's formalism in law-making, which subsequently explains why in his earlier teaching Lacan turned to Kant to establish the logic of psychoanalysis through the effects, and not meanings, of language. How then does Lacan couple Kant's universal law to Sadean pleasure?

If we turn to Freud to explain Kantian pleasure in Sade, especially since it was, as Lacan noted, Sade who gave a free pass for Freud's non-conventional theory of pleasure, we see it is not arbitrary. The question of pleasure has to do with the question of "well-being" (*das Wohl*). In the classical sense, well-being is manifested when the subject experiences a pleasure in its relationship to objects, for example, food or sex. In this philosophical tradition, empirical well-being is the measure of happiness. In contrast, for Kant, feeling "good" (*bien*) is conceived as a pathological phenomenon of the purely subjective investment in the object, which Kant defines as opposed to universalist ethics. For Kant, happiness remains outside the empirical objects to which the subject is attached. It is here, in *alienation*, that Kantian happiness lies. Kant's well-being is manifested when the subject represses its right to pleasure, and is absolutely void of any personal pleasure. For Kant (and Freud to some extent), therefore, the *holiness* of the subject occurs when the subject is *cruelly* alienated from what it feels is truly its own. Paradoxically, the subject gains true freedom through the repression (*Verdrängung*) of freedom—or unfreedom—to ultimately disavow good feelings. Kant's system of the moral law is founded on this *perverse* form of distantness to empirical experience, and it is here that subjective experience becomes universal (or "common" in Lacan's translation of the German word, *allgemeine*) ethics.[9] It is this apathy in Kant's categorical imperative that Lacan found at work in Sade's system of writing, namely, the Sadean universe. In a similar vein, in his essay "Masochism: Coldness and Cruelty," Deleuze also illuminates apathy as an essential constituent of Masoch's perversity, highlighting the coldness in masochism. In spite of their opposed positions, marked in Freudian terms by activity and passivity, both Sadean and Masochian perversions exhibit a *cruel* unfeeling or coldness directed to the other at the level of the psyche.

On this point, this volume intends to examine Lacan's idea of perversion from the perspective of *cruelty*: cruelty not associated with physical violence or torture in a broader sense but as a signifier capable of attracting varied approaches to perversion. It should come as no surprise that even though his theory intended to account for libidinal economies of sexuality, Freud's "Three Essays on the Sexuality" and "The Child is Being Beaten," for example, were an implicit discussion of cruelty in connection with the drive. Furthermore, in his essays "Group Psychology," "The Ego and the Id," "Group Psychology" and "Civilization and Its Discontents," Freud's main concern was to address psychical cruelty caused by aggression beyond the pleasure principle. One might also recall Freud's young patient, the Rat Man, whose face expressed horror with enjoyment when he heard about the inhumane physical torture (using rats) narrated by his senior officer, which obviously indicates a certain kind of perversity and cruelty encapsulated in his psyche.

In his address to the States General Psychoanalysis, entitled "Psychoanalysis Searches the States of its Soul: The Impossible Beyond of a Sovereign Cruelty," Jacques Derrida emphasizes that "cruelty without blood" mutated from the Latin world *crudus*, which is associated with blood, that is "bloody cruelty" (the French word *cruor* implicating *sang*).[10] To suffer for the sake of suffering or to make the other suffer in pure delight in evil in order to take a psychical pleasure that cannot be determined or delimited, in the Derridean sense, implies "a cruelty of the *psyche*," which is to say, "nonbloody cruelty" (original emphasis).[11] Stressing this invisibility of blood or "a cruel mutation of [bloody] cruelty" (e.g., a transformation of the methods of the death penalty from quartering or cutting to lethal injection or electrocution), Derrida asserts, despite his ambivalence toward psychoanalysis, that psychoanalysis is the only possible discipline that can search for the soul of the living.[12] He remarks:

> The only discourse that can today claim the thing of psychical suffering as its own affair would indeed be what has been called, for about a century

> psychoanalysis…'[P]sychoanalysis' would be the name of that which, without the biological or other alibi, would be turned toward what is most *proper* to psychical cruelty.[13]

Here, he gives another status to psychoanalysis, which he calls "without alibi." Whether the meaning of "without alibi" is purely "physical suffering as its own affairs" or a judicial mechanism against the crime, as Elizabeth Rottenberg explains, both registers (the physical or the judicial) cannot be conceived without invoking cruelty.[14] Moreover, "[c]ruelty not only exists, but it insists and resists—it looms out, unsurmountable, that nagging mixture of aggression and pleasure found in pain," as Jean-Michel Rabaté puts it.[15] *Without* alibi is thus only possible *not without* cruelty. Hence: "no psychoanalysis without cruelty."[16]

I have organized this collection of essays on Lacan's perversion on the foundation that cruelty is a mutation, and insistence and persistence. Despite the "stunning" appearance of Sade's and Masoch's literary works and their peculiar sexual practices in eighteenth- and nineteenth-century Europe—one may remember that what led Sade to prison was not his peculiar sexual rituals but his writing—this volume intends to avoid a reductive discourse of perversion within the domain of the historiography or historicity of sexuality, or as abnormal sexual acts that deviate from "normative" sexual practice, akin to images of bestiality or sin. Instead of reducing the notion of perversion to cultural representations or a historical discourse, the splendid essays in this collection, written by leading Lacanian theorists and practitioners, aim to investigate the varied signifiers of cruelty fundamental to the concept of perversion in Lacan's psychoanalytic theory. Specifically, the contributors interrogate perversion in connection with cruelties linked to various registers of the Oedipus complex, the-Name-of-the-Father, the law, desire, fantasy, jouissance, anxiety, fetishism and capitalism at both the theoretical and clinical levels. In this volume, on the cruelties of perversion, therefore, psychoanalysis is in dialogue with literature, philosophy, culture and the clinic *without alibi.*

In this manner, each author has taken their own stance on the relation of perversion and cruelty with respect to Lacan. The collection opens with the notion of cruelty, beginning with a magnificent essay by

Jean-Michel Rabaté's, "Cruelfictions of Psychoanalysis: Freud, Derrida, Mignotte," which establishes a conceptual frame for the entire volume. Rabaté masterfully explores the ways that "blood" has been theorized, taking us from philosophy (Hegel, Nietzsche and Derrida) to psychoanalysis (Freud, Lacan and Mignotte), from Greek myth (Prometheus) to modern literature (Kafka and Joyce). He enlightens the transformation of cruelty from bloody to bloodless (hence *sang sang*), between Derrida on *cruor* and Freud on *Grausamkeit*, and connects this new form of non-bloody cruelty to Mignotte's idea of void as the primal psychical cruelty. The reader will be struck by the way he explores bloodless cruelty without disregarding the drive, that is, the vitality of the bodily organs, and without disconnecting their bodily symptoms from psychical manifestations. Drawing on Hegel's concept of blood as creating its own line of flow, his essay further examines how blood (emphasizing it is not the heart) remains the core force of life, just as it was for Prometheus, whose life depended on the flood of blood in his liver. When this substance of life-blood lacks, argues Rabaté, there is a psychical void that causes suffering. In a deconstructive turn that echoes Mignotte, however, he maintains that this psychical void is a force of regeneration, a remainder "from the ground," to borrow Kafka's words, where humans are born to love and hate, a psychic residue that enabled Joyce to continue to write. Rabaté calls this the "cruelfiction of psychoanalysis." Framed in this way, Rabaté's essay reasserts the important principles of psychoanalysis: the inseparability of the psyche and the body (Freud), and the real of the body (Lacan).

Arka Chattopadhyay's essay that follows, "Intimate Cruelties: Perversions, Sexuality and the Human Animal," bridges psychoanalysis and literature as a splendid rendition of Rabaté's idea of the "cruelfiction of psychanalysis." Chattopadhyay carefully guides us through the multiple paradigms of perversion dispersed throughout Lacan's teachings. He outlines Lacan's ideas of perversion, ranging from its formulation as a structure to its link to perverse fantasies of the neurotic, the perversity of the drive that perpetually misses its object, sexuality as intrinsically perverse, and, finally, *père-version* or varying versions of the father in an increasingly disintegrating take on the father-function. The chapter leads to a major and important shift in Lacan's construction of perversion by altering its index from the desire-of-the mother within the pre-Oedipal to the-Name-of-the-Father within the Oedipal. Chattopadhyay shows the way this indexical transformation from the mother-function to the father-function in Lacan's perversion is consistent with a paradigmatic shift in his "topology" from the imaginary to the symbolic, a turn that was more firmly established in his late theory of *père-version* and sinthome. On this theoretical foundation, Chattopadhyay subsequently offers an intriguing reading of the Indian writer Sandipan Chattopadhyay's untranslated Bengali novel, *Kukur Shamparke Du-Ekti Katha Ja Ami Jani* (*The One or Two Things I Know About Dogs*, 1991), underlining specifically that implications of incest, animality and possession are a phantasm of the Other and highlighting the intimate relation between perverse sexuality and cruelty. The reader will appreciate the essay's thought-provoking conclusion that literature is a "sinthomatic invention" in the domain of perversion.

Next is Gregg Lambert's essay "On the Right to Jouissance," which offers a political reading of Lacan's notion of jouissance. If Rabaté set a conceptual tone of cruelty, for this volume, Lambert provides, through his thorough exploration of Kant's *The Critique of Reason* and *Philosophy of Law* with respect to Sade's *Philosophy in the Bedroom*, a theoretical framework of law and desire extracted from Lacan's text "Kant with Sade," which serves as both a direct and an indirect reference point for many of the essays that follow. Reversing Slavoj Žižek's logic of the Sadean perversion—that is, shifting the order from Sade as the truth of Kant to Kant as the truth of Sade—which brings the original order of between Kant and Sade, Lambert examines the "legal" aspect of jouissance in Kant's system of the Moral Law. He meticulously takes us through Kant's universal belief in the moral exchange of property, which declares one's right to exchange one's body with others' bodies, on the hypothesis that the community has ownership of individual bodies, including the sexual organs. Lambert contends that this Kantian universal ethics is therefore the purest expression of the moral Good, which marks the ideology of the Republic. What the reader will consequently find in this chapter is Lambert's remarkable claim that Lacan's logic of the "instrumentalization" of one's body for the Other's jouissance was already in Kant's system, and the latter was to intensify that very "legal" right to enjoyment in multiplicated bodies. Lambert's rethinking jouissance within the original chronological and philosophical order of Kant to Sade suggests that the right to jouissance is the *duty* to enjoy, and the Sadean universe was, in fact, a criticism of the Bourgeois society that promoted these moral feelings. Argued in this way, his essay bears the provocative implication for the superego that its command to "enjoy!" is, in fact, a liberal duty, and that the right to jouissance may be as oppressive as the "no right to enjoyment." It is the cruelty of the superego.

Jouissance is a crucial topic throughout this collection. Fred Baitinger's essay, "Perverse Fascination for Death and Jouissance: Bataille, Lacan and the Anti-social Turn in Queer Theory," investigates the problematics of jouissance between Bataille and Lacan. Baitinger thoroughly explores the paradox of Bataille's idea of "inner experience," defined as an inarticulable experience invoking the impossible, by claiming that this "cold," impossible mode of being is achievable only through the recognition of being as a possibility in the experience of jouissance. By way of the paradoxical dialectics of the impossible and the possible at work in Bataille, Baitinger first critiques the way in which "anti-social" queer studies have reduced Lacan's jouissance to the right to "opt out" of "cruel optimism" or "reproductive futurism." Tackling the ethics of this absolute indulgence in the impossible, his essay makes the further claim that Bataille's idea of "inner experience" actually, and perhaps even quite ironically, influenced Lacan's formulation of Sadean apathy and his resultant idea of ethics. Baitinger investigates that by recognizing the limitations of Bataille's excessive expenditure of the impossible, Lacan actually takes into account the ethics of the extreme nature of jouissance and thus aims to limit the perversity and the cruelty contained in jouissance by grounding the subject in an experience of love and desire, which implies the existence of the Other, even if degraded at the level of a semblant. In this chapter, the reader will see that jouissance for Lacan is primarily linked to the superego's cruelty and the apathy, coming to split the subject and thereby create some kind of "meaningless" in jouissance. At the end of the essay, Baitinger explores the meaning of the "meaninglessness" of jouissance in relation to the sinthome, showing how the latter teaches the subject a *know-how* (*savoir*) to understand his or her symptom(s).

Meera Lee's essay, "Perversion After Freud: From the Cruel Father to the Joycean Clinic," rethinks perversion from the register of language instead of sexuality. Specifically, Lee's essay conceptualizes perversion in connection with the Name-of-the-Father. Lee first investigates the way the father-function produces what Freud calls "desexualization," a particular outcome that occurs after the dissolution of the Oedipus complex. Her examination discovers the psychic cruelty intrinsic to the father's desexualizing effects designated as both prohibiting and permitting. Contrary to the conventional understanding of the Oedipus complex, in this essay, we see that the cruelty of the father is not the threat of castration but, on the contrary, his permission of the son's primal desire for the mother. Lee stresses that this permitting by the father is, nevertheless, not without its severity, that is, without warranting the offspring's instinctual (or incestual) wishes, which she attributes to the perversity of the Oedipal law. Discussed in this way, she argues that this perversity of the father-function in the Oedipal structure parallels the disparity between speech and its invocation in Lacan's theory, and that furthermore this equivocation reinforces the discrepancy between the law and desire. Through this theoretical elucidation, Lee allows us to consider perversion as a linguistic perversity which gives rise to psychical cruelty. On this postulate, in her essay, the subject's *dependence* on the father is connected to *père-version* (*a version toward the father*); perversion is thus a *sinthomic* manifestation of cruelty. Drawing on this knot of the symbolic and sinthome developed in Lacan's late seminar, Lee concludes her chapter with what she calls "the Joycean clinic" as a new "version" of perversion, a space of everyday perverseness where the guaranteed meaning of the signifier (S1) fails to produce jouissance.

The essay that follows, "The Anxiety at the Heart of Perverse Experience: A Clinical Perspective" by Tracy McNulty, is a meticulous exploration of perversion in both theory and clinical practice from the perspectives of disavowal, fetishism and jouissance. If the other chapters of this volume link perversion to the structure of psychosis, McNulty situates the pervert within the clinic of neurosis, navigating artfully from Freudian to Lacanian theory. Her theoretical tour de force centers around a Belgium psychoanalyst Serge André's clinical case of "Dany," classified as a sadist, a first-ever introduction in the English-speaking world. Given the paucity of clinical cases of perversion and the skepticism around the clinical existence of perversion, her "analysis" of Dany is particularly valuable as it provides insight into the way the transvestite and the transsexual are connected to masochism within a fantasy structure. Through this investigation, McNulty maintains that the pervert's anxiety is the effect of the child's avowal of the mother's desire, which is only the inverted appearance of the disavowal of castration, that is, the castration of the mother's desire. Anxiety in her term is thus at the core of the pervert, originating in the child's phantasmatic desire to satisfy the mother's jouissance. Drawing on this theoretical and clinical formulation of anxiety and perversity, her essay continues on to discuss the implication of the "contract" in the practices of sadism and masochism (e.g., Sade and Sacher-Masoch). She proposes the thought-provoking argument that the contract regulates the pervert's anxiety and serves as a "perverse form" to generate the (feminine) jouissance for the Other.

Derek Hook's and Benjamin Strosberg's "'The Pornography of His Eyes': A Vignette of Perversion" is another superb clinical examination of perversion with respect to anxiety and jouissance. Hook and Strosberg systematically and creatively explore the specific perverse form of exhibitionism via what they call a "clinical vignette." Hook as the first author presents "an encounter" he had with an inmate in a corridor when he worked as a volunteer-counselor in a prison in West London. He remembers this moment, when his eyes were met with those passive yet invasive eyes of inmate's, a look he describes as a *pornographic* gaze, as quite horrifying but not without a sense of fascination. Analyzing carefully this "clinical vignette," which was reconstructed from his personal/non-clinical encounter with the other ("the patient") outside his regular clinical contact in the prison—a form different from the complete clinical case—Hook and Benjamin shed light on the role of the gaze in perverse acts. In their investigation, the authors show how the pervert's scopic drive can be read as a phallic gaze and that the gaze itself thereby functions as an instrument of exhibitionism. They define this gaze as the "third gaze," an imagined or fantasized gaze of the Other. It is a unique kind of the Other, identified as the social witness or social authority (e.g., the prison guard in the context of their clinical vignette) where jouissance is invoked. Advancing this logic of "third" with respect to jouissance, Hook and Strosberg maintain that the Other is the law, and the exhibitionist makes sure that the Other-law is seduced and derided for being a third witness. The essay concludes with the thought-stimulating argument that while perversion is the subversion of the law at one level, at another level, its transgression paradoxically reasserts the law.

The volume closes with "Neoliberalism and Liminality: Perverse Cruelties in the Age of the Capitalist Discourse" by Stephanie Swales, which is a compelling demonstration of what happens to the subject when capitalism replaces S1 the signifier considering Lacan's four discourses. Through an extensive array of media and culture, Swales methodically investigates the ways in which capitalism produces what she calls a "liminal creature" or "liminal being" in neoliberal society. She posits that the capitalist discourse, distinguished from Lacan's master discourse produced by S1, where a certain agent mends the split in the subject and therefore annihilates the lack in the Other, pushes the subject to the unlimiting proliferation of identity. As a result, Swales' essay shows how such a schizoid, machinic becoming of the subject, caused by neoliberal capitalism (a subject formation that one might associate with Deleuze and Guattari), threatens the *parlêtre*, "the speaking being," instituted by the signifier, which is an important theoretical construction in Lacan's late teaching. Through this investigation, she points to the problematics of the superego in the everyday life of contemporary society. In Swales' essay, the reader will see another side of the severity of the superego. The superego's endless imperative of "enjoy!" reduces desire to demand and, subsequently, prohibits the renewed satisfaction in the subject that the drive seeks to guarantee. Instead of satisfaction from the drive, what the subject ends up receiving is an endless surplus-jouissance, which she calls the "perverse cruelties" of neoliberal capitalism.

Summarized in this way, this collection studies perversion in an unprecedentedly enriching manner, offering a unique exploration of the novel aspects of perversion, and emphasizing the key role played by psychical cruelty, a psychoanalytic approach that has not been sufficiently addressed in the English-speaking world. As the reader of this volume will discover, in their rendering of the relationship of perversion and cruelty, each chapter is a tour de force of theoretical and clinical suppleness in the Lacanian psychoanalytic tradition. Through each contributor's superlative study of the *cruel* persistence of perversion, the reader will appreciate not only psychoanalysis' newly shaped idea of perversion but also the psychoanalytic implications of cruelty beyond the domains of history and culture. Framed and theorized in this way, this edition reaffirms anew the value of perversion in psychoanalysis and, accordingly, offers a new direction for the clinical treatment of perversion.

Notes

1. Jacques Lacan, *The Seminar of Jacques Lacan Book XXIII: The Sinthome*, ed. Jacques-Allain Miller, trans. Adrian Price (Cambridge: Polity, 2016), 84.
2. Élisabeth Roudinesco, *Our Dark Side: A History of Perversion*, trans. David Macey (Cambridge: Polity, 2009), 4–5.
3. Ibid., 4 & 159.
4. Ibid., 139. For more discussion of perversion and Roudinesco, see Jean-Michel Rabaté's Chapter Seven "From the History of Perversion to the Trauma of History." In *The Cambridge Introduction to Literature and Psychoanalysis* (Cambridge: Cambridge University Press, 2014), especially 177–82.
5. Dany Nobus, *The Law of Desire: On Lacan's 'Kant with Sade'* (London: Palgrave Macmillan, 2017), xvii.
6. Jacques Lacan, *The Seminar of Jacques Lacan, Book XVII: The Other Side of Psychoanalysis*, ed. Jacques-Alain Miller, trans. Russell Grigg (New York: W.W. Norton & Co., 2007), 70.
7. Jacques Lacan, "Kant with Sade." In *Écrits: The First Complete Edition in English*, trans. Bruce Fink (New York: W.W. Norton, 2006), 765.
8. Ibid.
9. Jacques Lacan, *Seminar of Jacques Lacan Book VII: The Ethics of Psychoanalysis, 1959–1960*, ed. Jacques-Alain Miller, trans. Dennis Porter (London: Routledge, 1992), 76–7.
10. Jacques Derrida, "Psychoanalysis Searches the States of Its Soul: The Impossible Beyond of a Sovereign Cruelty." In *Without Alibi*, trans. Peggy Kamuf (Stanford: Stanford University Press, 2002), 238–9.
11. Ibid., 239.
12. Ibid., 240 & 270.
13. Ibid., 240.
14. Elizabeth Rottenberg, *For the Love of Psychoanalysis: The Play of Chance in Freud and Derrida* (New York: Fordham University Press, 2019), 112.

15. Rabaté's remarks here, which are restated in his chapter for this volume, are from his Preface to Touria Mignotte's *Cruelty, Sexuality, and the Unconscious in Psychoanalysis: Freud, Lacan, Winnicott, and The Body of the Void*, trans. Andrew Weller (London: Routledge, 2020), xiii.
16. Ibid.

Bibliography

Lacan, Jacques. *Seminar of Jacques Lacan Book VII: The Ethics of Psychoanalysis, 1959–1960*. Edited by Jacques-Allain Miller. Translated by Dennis Porter. London: Routledge, 1992.

———. "Kant with Sade." In *Écrits: The First Complete Edition in English*. Translated by Bruce Fink. New York: W.W. Norton, 2006.

———. *The Seminar of Jacques Lacan Book XVII: The Other Side of Psychoanalysis, 1959–1960*. Edited by Jacques-Allain Miller. Translated by Russell Grigg. New York: W.W Norton, 2007.

———. *The Seminar of Jacques Lacan Book XXIII: The Sinthome*. Edited by Jacques-Allain Miller. Translated by Adrian Price. Cambridge: Polity, 2016.

Nobus, Dany. *The Law of Desire: On Lacan's 'Kant with Sade.'* London: Palgrave Macmillan, 2017.

Rottenberg, Elizabeth. *For the Love of Psychoanalysis: The Play of Chance in Freud and Derrida*. New York: Fordham University Press, 2019.

Roudinesco, Élisabeth. *Our Dark Side: A History of Perversion*. Translated by David Macey. Cambridge: Polity, 2009.

2

Cruelfictions of Psychoanalysis: Freud, Derrida, Mignotte

Jean-Michel Rabaté

In one of his most searching essays on psychoanalysis, Jacques Derrida asserts that the main problem it encounters as a discourse and a clinical praxis is the existence of cruelty.[1] Cruelty not only exists, but it insists and resists, which presents unsurmountable problems. The term refers to a mixture of aggression and pleasure found in pain, a heady cocktail hard to conceptualize. It is such a problem that Touria Mignotte addresses in her book *Cruelty, Sexuality, and the Unconscious in Psychoanalysis*. The notion of cruelty that she deploys is not cultural but psychoanalytical, which sends us on the path of specific genealogies and different terminologies. "Cultural" cruelty would refer to the domain competently explored by Maggie Nelson in her 2011 bestseller, *The Art of Cruelty*.[2]

This essay expands and modifies the Preface I wrote for Touria Mignotte, *Cruelty, Sexuality, and the Unconscious in Psychoanalysis: Freud, Lacan, Winnicott, and The Body of the Void*, trans. Andrew Weller (London: Routledge, 2020), xiii–xxii.

J.-M. Rabaté (✉)
Department of English, University of Pennsylvania, Philadelphia, PA, USA
e-mail: jmrabate@english.upenn.edu

M. Lee (ed.), *Lacan's Cruelty*, The Palgrave Lacan Series,
https://doi.org/10.1007/978-3-031-06238-4_2

There Nelson tackles the proliferating manifestations of cruelty and highlights wanton displays of violence in media, literature and art.

Both Marquis de Sade's *120 Days of Sodom* and *Saló*, the filmic equivalent produced by Pier Paolo Pasolini in 1975 keep their power to shock. They repulse and fascinate. A radical artist like Thomas Hirschhorn has attempted to critique this perverse attitude in his show "De-Pixelation" at New York Gladstone Gallery (October 2017 to January 2018). The huge billboards covered with a montage of images taken from recent conflicts showing dead bodies spliced with publicity images has a startling effect of the viewer. Maggie Nelson and Thomas Hirschhorn force readers, viewers and consumers to adopt a critical position, discovering ethical stakes facing the society of cruel spectacles in which we live.

Mignotte does not tackle these issues directly although she is aware of what has been invested in them. She situates her investigation at a foundational level and within the specific discourse of psychoanalysis. I will first sketch the theoretical context of her approach by comparing it with Derrida's argument about psychoanalysis. I will then underline points of convergence in their approaches, which include readings of Freud, Nietzsche and Hegel. I will conclude with a discussion of cruelty in the myth of Prometheus revisited by Freud and Kafka.

Psychoanalysis, the Death Penalty and Cruelty

In July 2000, Derrida gave the opening lecture for the Paris *Etats généraux de la psychanalyse*. René Major, the main convener and a friend of Derrida, had asked psychoanalysts and intellectuals from all parts of the world to assess the situation of psychoanalysis. They were required to offer predictions for the future, outline tasks and orientations. Speaking in the main amphitheater of the Sorbonne to some 1200 psychoanalysts and academics, Derrida took stock of a particular political situation, and began by stating a personal complaint about his own pain and suffering. Major and his friends had planned this historical parallel by evoking the moment when the "estates-general" had been convoked by king Louis XVI. In June 1789, there was a split between the third estate made up of bourgeois and commoners and the representatives of the clergy and nobility.

The third estate refused to associate with them and created a National Assembly. This was the beginning of the French revolution. However, no revolution came from the four days of discussions held from July 8 to July 11, 2000. No common resolution led to a program for the new century. Division reigned and tensions cropped up between various groups, nationalities and specialties. In such a contentious context, Derrida had been right to focus on two terms he saw linked, sovereignty and cruelty.

Twice Derrida alluded to the French revolution, as when he wondered who could be the king in such an assembly,[3] but he did not want to restrict the meaning of cruelty to an etymology connected with blood because he wanted to include psychic cruelty. He asked: "Would such cruelty, if there is any and if it is properly psychical, be one of the horizons most proper to psychoanalysis?"[4] The ambition of Mignotte's book is to respond to such a question, expand it and reframe it within the concepts of psychoanalysis. She accomplishes this complex task in a non-partisan manner by moving between the theories of Freud, Lacan and Winnicott, the three interlocutors with whom she dialogues skillfully.

In his Paris lecture, Derrida began with the old Jewish joke explaining how one becomes a psychoanalyst: it is a Jewish surgeon who cannot stand the sight of blood.[5] This issue recurs in the two volumes of the Seminar on the Death Penalty, both of which take their point of departure in American law, namely the Eighth Amendment to the United States Constitution prohibiting the infliction of "cruel and unusual punishments." That sentence prevents the government from imposing penalties deemed either barbaric or too severe for the crimes committed. It has been operative in cases when the method used, like the electric chair, seemed to torture the sentenced person rather than kill efficiently. Derrida asks pointedly: have we avoided cruelty by choosing faster and more efficient ways of killing? He considers at some length the rhetoric of the quasi-painless cutting of the neck that accompanied the invention and use of the guillotine.

At a theoretical level, Derrida noted that by shifting from the Latin *cruor* to Freud's *Grausamkeit*, we move from bloody cruelty to bloodless cruelty, which generates an echolalic *sans sang*, as Derrida puns in French. It is not by replacing the bloody decapitation of the guillotine by a jolt from the electric chair, a lethal injection or the gas chamber that we have abolished cruelty. As Derrida repeats in "Psychoanalysis Searches the States of Its Soul," the end of bloody cruelty does not signal the end of cruelty: it merely corresponds to a social modification the codes and norms that affect the visibility of cruelty. But an invisible cruelty can be as ethically reprehensible. In German, *grausam* keeps no association with blood, its etymology being closer to that of "gruesome" in English, namely whatever can create horror, fear and shudder.

Freud's "Three Essays" unfolds a theory of cruelty stated quite clearly: "the history of human civilization shows beyond any doubt that there is an intimate connection between cruelty (*Grausamkeit*) and the sexual drive (*Sexualtrieb*); but nothing has been done towards explaining the connection, apart from laying emphasis on the aggressive factor in the libido."[6] Freud quotes authors who insist on relics of cannibalism in sexuality, others who stress the link between pain and pleasure: "every pain contains in itself the possibility of a feeling of pleasure." In a footnote added in 1926, he explains that he reserves a special place to the couple of sadism and masochism, and decides to "place them outside the class of remaining perversions."[7] Then Freud lists neurotic symptoms that include "the active and passive forms of the drive to cruelty (*Trieb zur Grausamkeit*),"[8] adding that this would be the root of the transformation of love into hate that is so common in paranoia.

Freud observes that cruelty appears early in children:

> The cruel component of the sexual drive develops in childhood even more independently of the sexual activities that are attached to erotogenic zones. Cruelty in general comes easily to the childish nature, since the obstacles that bring the drive to mastery (*Bemächtigungstrieb*) to a halt at another person's pain—namely a capacity for pity—is developed rather late.[9]

Freud links the drive to cruelty with a more intense erotogenic activity. He cautions educators against using corporal punishments that will be experienced as sources of perverse pleasure by the child. "Three Essays" provided Freud's foundation for his later insights, even if he introduced many nuances to his analyses. In *Beyond the Pleasure Principle*, the main philosophical statement of his maturity, he still insists on the links between sadism and the death drive.

Once and for all, Gilles Deleuze has deconstructed the idea that sadism and masochism should be considered as linked like the two sides of one single coin. Deleuze has questioned the reversibility posited by Freud between activity (sadism) and passivity (masochism) in the essay "Coldness and Cruelty" that serves as a preface to Sacher-Masoch's *Venus in Furs.*[10] Deleuze reminds us of the key fact that for Freud, the main site of cruelty is not the drive but the super-ego. The main difference between Deleuze and Freud is that the former looks at the texts written by Sade and Sacher-Masoch, whereas the latter attempts to understand sadism and masochism as two forms of perversions. Hence, for Deleuze, there is no sado-masochism as an entity, although there is, of course, cruelty: it reigns half-way between the "apathy" that the Sadean libertines want to conquer through a multiplication of crimes, and the "coldness" that the Masochist hero will gain after his many humiliations.

Like Deleuze, Mignotte appeals to principled monism, which is why she pushes the issue in the direction of a conceptual unity that she calls "destruction." Thus, she quotes Freud's treatment of the young man whom he called the "Ratman" because his main symptom was an obsession with a horrible torture of pushing a rat into a victim's anus. Freud names the young man "the Ratman" because of his fascination for the punishment, which had already appeared at the end of Sade's *120 Days of Sodom.* He had heard it explained by a "cruel" officer who "obviously took pleasure in cruelty."[11] Freud manages to make the young man disclose in words the torture that horrifies him. When Lanzer confesses that the torture entails rats boring their way into the victim's insides via the anus, he almost faints." At all the more significant moments of his narration, a very strange compound expression is visible on his face, which I can only interpret as *horror at the pleasure he does not even know he feels.*[12] At this moment, Freud witnesses what Lacan later called "jouissance," an excessive and unspeakable pleasure. It is so strong that it is almost painful, and of course totally unconscious, thus creating the paradox of a feeling one is not aware of feeling. Besides, there are other resources for a cruelty applied to oneself than in the rat torture. The real or metaphorical pain inflicted by the rat in the anus is less destructive than the cruelty of the super-ego. Here is why poor Lanzer must endlessly pay for a debt he already paid for.

What Lanzer brought to Freud was a notion that exceeded the economic logic that he had been relying on. It is the curious logic of jouissance, an excess that suddenly shifts from the plus to the minus. As Lacan reminds us, it was only later that Freud understood this, in *Civilization and Its Discontents*, when jouissance appeared in its dimension of negativity and evil, namely when it entails enjoying making others suffer, which ushers in the issue of cruelty: "those who like fairy stories turn a deaf ear to talk of man's innate tendencies to 'evil, aggression, destruction, and thus also to cruelty.'"[13] Lacan keeps quoting the famous passage from *Civilization and Its discontents* in which Freud mentions that humans need to humiliate, torture and kill other persons. Lacan quips that the sentences seem to come from Marquis de Sade's writings. Jouissance is closer to evil than to good, which is why Lacan will go on by developing a well-known parallel between Kant and Sade. In the end, he shows how Sade's Libertines become hostages of a fantasy of divine power, trying to emulate the terrifying exactions committed by a cruel and ferocious anti-God, that *Dio boia*, or "hangman god" mentioned by Stephen Dedalus in *Ulysses*.[14] Cruelty would be the stumbling stone for all ethics, as Lacan proves when reading Sade and Kant side by side, for its very existence negates the belief in reciprocity which is the foundation of humanitarian rules of non-aggression. Having moved beyond the pleasure principle and the morality principle, we have to appeal to a more archaic and foundational substance. Let's follow Mignotte's injunction that we need to dig deeper and tackle the issue of substance and its containers. As Lacan repeated in the 1970s, the only substance known to psychoanalysis is jouissance. Here, I would like to suggest that it has to confront itself to another physiological substance, namely blood. Hence we need to address the vexing issue of blood.

Is There a Future for Blood?[15]

To confront the substance bequeathed to us by the etymology of the word "cruelty," we need to examine the meaning of blood, which goes from representations of the friend and the enemy (for Carl Schmitt, as we know, what counts as "friend" is above all the blood-relative[16]) to images of racist discrimination. Latin was rather refined in that it distinguished between *sanguis* and *cruor*. *Cruor*, closer to "gore," signifies blood seen flowing from a wound, and thus one can distinguish the "crude" (the Latin *crudus* comes from *crūrus* in Indo-European, linked with *kruhrós*, from *krewth*, meaning "raw meat, fresh blood") from the "raw" and the "cruel." Freud understood the mechanism of psychical cruelty, the pleasure taken in making someone else or oneself suffer, or otherwise by watching suffering, as a pleasure born from our bodies and their cycles.

In English as in French, the term of "cruel" keeps a link with blood. How to make sense of blood? I suggest we take a look at Hegel's *Philosophy of Nature*,[17] because it is the most systematic attempt at providing a theory of blood linking the elements of natural life to the concept and hence to "Spirit." Hegel sees nature as a huge body in which dissolution is not negative but a relay generating further productions and reproductions. In his groundbreaking book on Hegel,[18] Markus Semm observes that the deployment of the Spirit in Nature adopts a general rhythm and follows the tempo of a vital pulse. Rhythmic exchanges are underpinned by a pulsation that runs through all phenomena. The pulsating beat enacting regenerative negativity finds a double exemplification in breathing and in the circuit of blood:

> This dissolution of this persistence is the pulmonary system, the true, ideal process with the outer world of inorganic Nature, with the element of air; it is the organism's own self-movement which, as elasticity, draws air and expels it. The blood is the result, the organism which through its own interior process returns into itself, the living individuality which makes members (*Glieder*) into viscera. The blood as axially rotating, self-pursuing movement, this absolute interior vibration, is the individual life of the whole in which there is no distinction—animal time.[19]

Hegel describes the process by which blood is formed:

> The blood elaborates itself from the air, the lymph, and the digestion, and is the transformation of these three moments. From the air, it takes pure dissolution, the light of the air, oxygen; from the lymph, the neutral fluid; from digestion, the moments of singularity, the substantial moment. And

> as thus the whole individuality, the blood opposes itself to itself afresh and generates shape.[20]

Blood combines dissolution, neutrality and singularity, all this tied together in a unique substance. We follow successive transformations by which this substance ends up characterizing the individuality of the living subject. It is marked by a pulsation obeying a universal law. Blood thus allegorizes the logical progression of the Concept or Notion (*Begriff*): "The endless process of division and this suppression of division which leads to another division, all this is the immediate expression of the Notion which is, so to speak, here visible to the eye."[21] One factor accounts for the rhythm of these successive negations, it is the essential "irritability" evinced by blood:

> Blood in general, as the universal substance of every part, is the irritable (*irritable*) concentration of everything into the interior unity: it is heat, this transformation of cohesion and specific gravity—but not merely the dissolution produced by heat but the real, animal dissolution of everything. Just as all food is converted into blood, so, too, blood is dispensed as the source from which everything takes its nutriment. That is what pulsation (*Pulsieren*) is in complete reality.[22]

The picture of blood drawn by Hegel is that of a life cycle repeating itself to constitute a *perpetuum mobile*.[23] Blood, not the heart, appears as the agent of the dynamic process. The heart is just a muscle that pumps, a material cause, whereas blood allegorizes the dynamism of life itself: "This is the blood, the subject, which no less than the will initiates a movement. As the whole movement, the blood is the ground and the movement itself."[24] Hegel notes that if an invalid remains immobile too long, he develops ankylosis:[25] this banal example leads to a discussion of the difference between arterial blood, redder because it contains more oxygen, and venous blood, bluish because it contains carbon. A section devoted to breathing discovers the rationale for the endless movement: it deploys the term that Hegel had found in Albrecht von Haller, this same "irritability." Blood is "irritable" in itself, there is no other cause for its dialectical mobility. Hegel rejects theories that reduced the workings of the heart to a mechanical force:

> But all these mechanical explanations of the physiologists are inadequate. From whence comes this elastic pressure of the walls and the heart? "From the irritation (*Reiz*) of the blood" they reply. According to this, therefore, the heart moves the blood, and the movement of the blood is, in turn, what moves the heart. But this is a circle, a *perpetuum mobile*, which would necessarily at once come to standstill because the forces are in equilibrium. But, on the contrary, this is precisely why the blood must be regarded as itself the principle of the movement; it is the "leaping point" (*punctum saliens*), in virtue of which the contraction of the arteries coincides with the relaxation of the ventricles of the heart.[26]

Indeed, in 1628, Harvey had discovered the circulation of the blood in the body. Harvey describes the heart of the embryo as a *punctum sanguinem saliens*, a tiny pulsating point which is the first spot in which can one recognize that any heart begins beating. It is also a point of fire, a notion that will be important for Freud, an *ignis scintillula.*[27] Refusing to ascribe the cause of blood circulation to a reflex action, which would lead to an endless hen-and-egg exploration (the heart cannot beat without blood but blood needs the heart to circulate: here would be an argument *ad infinitum*),[28] Hegel concludes that the "self-movement of blood" is the cause of the organic life cycle, which makes blood literally turn into the "subject." Thus, blood has a will of its own, a will that initiates and regulates the movement of the whole.[29]

After Harvey, Francis Glisson had introduced the concept of "irritability" in 1650 when analyzing psychosomatic diseases. His *De Natura Substantiae Energetica* (1672) describes a natural energy going through the body. This blind energy called "irritability" differentiates itself into sensations. "Irritable" reactions of organs like the intestines or the heart derive from their ability to be excited the cause of bodily actions. Glisson generalized this to include the whole living dynamism, in a *biousia*, which would explain why substance of bodies react to stimuli without requiring any mind, consciousness or sensation. This notion reappears when we speak of "irritable bowel syndromes," or in any other manifestation of classical hysteria.

One century later, the Swiss physician Albrecht von Haller took up the concept in his 1752 "Dissertation on the Sensible and Irritable Parts of Animals." Trying to refute the materialist suggestion that there might be something like a blind animating all living substances, Haller differentiated between sensation and irritability. Sensation belonged to nerves and irritability to muscles. Haller discussed the link between blood and the heart and restricted irritability to the muscle of the heart: for him, the heart was "irritated" by an influx of blood, and then it responded with systolic contractions. In *Philosophy of Nature*, Hegel criticizes Haller who would have fallen into the trap of an *ad infinitum* causal reasoning. Irritability entails a *Reiz* but to evoke a "response." Haller mentioned a *Reitzleitung* as the "conduction of impulses," forgetting that *Reiz* suggested "appeal," "charm," "attraction," "excitement" and "stimulation." Thanks to the semantic series, we understand how irritability can generate a principle of subjectivity: it ushers in the endless negativity at work in blood. The negativity of a blood-fire turns into thirst, hunger and desire.

This same principle applies to the process of breathing: "The respiratory process is a spontaneously interrupted continuity. Exhalation and inhalation are a volatization (*Verdunsten*) of the blood, a volatizing irritability (*verdunste Irritabilität*)."[30] The general operation of the lungs resembles the spontaneous mechanism of the heart, and therefore one can link this movement with the way to blood circulates:

> Now why is the blood connected with this ideal assimilation of the abstract Element? The blood is this absolute thirst *(absolute Durst)*, its unrest (*Unruhe*) within itself and against itself; the blood craves to be ignited (*hat Hunger nach Befeurung*), to be differentiated. More exactly, this assimilation is at the same time a mediated process with air, namely a conversion of air into carbon dioxide and venous (dark, carbonated) blood, and into arterial, oxygenated blood.[31]

Like fire, blood is a living being perpetually consuming itself: "Air is in itself the fiery and negative element; the blood is the same thing, but as a developed unrest—the burning fire of the animal's organism which not only consumes itself but also preserves itself as fluid and finds in air its *pabulum vitae*."[32] At work here is the "restlessness of the negative" that Jean-Luc Nancy has identified as Hegel's main conceptual discovery.[33] Blood allegorizes subjective negativity in the most concrete terms. Therefore, blood is "cruel." Its restless "cruelty" derives from the main law of all life: regeneration presupposes destruction, division, negation; then, even if there is a recombination, the cruelty will not have been evacuated.

To these insights, Mignotte adds the concept of the void: there is, she claims, a void preceding all division, a void which appears already in Plato's concept of the *khora* launched in *Timaeus* taken over and developed by Derrida and Kristeva. For both, *khora* refers to a receptacle, an unnamable material substratum, a pure dehiscence ready to accept any "fulfilment," an empty grail ready to capture bitter drippings of blood from the sacred wound. Mignotte sends us back to Freud's unflinching analysis of the origins of human societies founded on collective murder. The murder was as soon forgotten as committed. It would return in the collective unconscious as guilt leading to the subsequent deification of the father killed by the sons. In "thoughts for the times on war and death," Freud contends that not only is "the primaeval history of mankind filled with murder" but that "if we are to be judged by our unconscious wishful impulses, we ourselves are a gang of murderers,"[34] we can be comforted by recent Darwinian theory that this is not such a bad thing.

The groundbreaking book of *The Paradox of Goodness*[35] by Richard Wrangham argues that Homo Sapiens evolved by a practice of social cooperation required for the preemptive killings of the dominant males of each group, a process by which the need for communication, planning and strategy would lead to the need for language, sociability and tools. The worst and the best would thus have been entangled since the origins of human culture, language and religion. Even if Freud is not quoted in Wrangham's solidly documented book, he would have approved this sweeping thesis about our constitutive "paradox." Here is the paradox of cruelty: our most esteemed foundations, those archaic impulses slowly leading to useful inventions like the institutions of democracy and tolerance, are founded on cunningly planned collective murder.

The Cruel Foundation Myth: Prometheus

Freud had found similar ideas in the works of Nietzsche, who more than any philosopher made "cruelty" a key value in his deconstruction of morality. Indeed, Maggie Nelson begins her book on cruelty with a quote by Nietzsche: "One should open one's eyes and take a new look at cruelty."[36] Nietzsche knew the classical myth displaying pure cruelty: it was the cruel punishment of a Titan like Prometheus; here was and a first step in the rebellion of humanity against the power of the gods. Nietzsche discussed Prometheus in one early fragment from 1874, when he imagines that the ancient struggle will be forgotten after the gods have died out:

> Prometheus and his vulture were *forgotten* when the old world of the Olympians and their power were destroyed.
>
> Prometheus expects his redemption to come from human beings.
>
> He did not betray his secret to Zeus, Zeus perished because of his son.[37]

A paradoxical obsolescence derives from our modern lack of belief in the divinity of the gods or of God. Nietzsche suggests that Prometheus created more than the human race: he was the creator of the gods as well:

> Did Prometheus have to *fancy* first that he had *stolen* the light and then pay for that—before he finally discovered that he had created the light *by coveting the light* and that not only man but also the *god* was the work of his own hands and had been mere clay in his hands? All mere images of the maker—no less than the fancy, the theft, the Caucasus, the vulture, and the whole tragic *Prometheia* of all the seekers after knowledge?[38]

Prometheus would be a Titan who moves forward and begins the transformation of humanity into Overhumanity. Prometheus is not helpless: as all the myths concerning him aver, he has a hidden weapon: he knows Zeus's secret, the oracle announcing that Zeus will be dethroned or killed by a son, as he had done to his father. Prometheus is tortured so cruelly because he knows the secret of the gods: the gods are mortal too, or they can die of their own immortality.

Mignotte has seen this clearly when she posits the need for an intermediary like Prometheus who is presented by Aeschylus as a true god who suffers for men when punished by Zeus. Aeschylus presents also a political drama: Zeus is excessively cruel and bent on making the Titan suffer because his rule has just begun. As he is being chained to the rock and pierced through with an iron stake, Prometheus gets this explanation from Hephaistos, who seems reluctant to accomplish his grim task:

> This never-ending burden / of your present agony will wear you down, / for the one who is to rescue you someday / is not yet even born. This is your reward / for acting as a friend to human beings. / Though you are a god, you were not deterred / by any fear of angering the gods. / You gave men honors they did not deserve, / possessions they were not entitled to. / Because of that, you will remain on guard, / here on this joyless rock, standing upright / with your legs straight, and you will never sleep. / You will often scream in pain and sorrow, / for Zeus' heart is pitilessly harsh, / and everyone whose ruling power is new / is cruel and ruthless.[39]

Aeschylus uses the word τραχύς meaning *rough, hard, inflexible, cruel.* Zeus is a newcomer on the throne, he has just dispatched his own father. Like an African dictator, he starts his rule by killing and torturing all those who resist him. He is also petty, full of envy and fury. One of the surprises of the play is to see Prometheus later visited by Io who suffers even more: she screams each time she is stung by the gadfly sent by a jealous Hera. A similarly relentless display of cruelty is exhibited in equal measure by the two main gods of the Greek pantheon. Zeus is jealous of Prometheus, Hera is jealous of Io whom Zeus tried to seduce.

These political or psychological considerations should be brought back to a more archaic substratum. As we saw, Mignotte called upon the myth of Prometheus as an intermediary between the humans and the gods because his mediation was predicated on the power of fire:

> In this external conflict between men and Zeus, Prometheus is the intermediary who closes the gaping hole of the devouring fire of the angry Zeus: he nourishes it with his own materialized fire by consuming his own body, reducing the latter to a substance of purified fire, the liver. I would say that Prometheus nourishes the gaping hole of Zeus with his own "deep blood"

> which passes through, without abolishing it, the gap that he has created and that he wants to maintain between the two parts of his being: the divine part and the human part.[40]

When Salomon Reinach discussed the "Resurrection of Gods and Heroes," he took Prometheus as a model. He argued that all Greeks stories of metamorphosis were in fact resurrection myths:

> Prometheus was a cunning Titan who stole fire from heaven and presented it to man. Zeus punished the thief by nailing him to a rock where an eagle devoured his liver, which was perpetually renewed. But in primitive mythologies, the eagle was the bird who mounted to the sun and took fire from it to give to man; on the other hand, the eagle was immune from thunderbolts, and was nailed to the summits of buildings to serve as a lighting conductor. Hence the name of eagles (*actoi*) given to the pediments of Greek temples; hence also the legend of Prometheus, which corresponds to the following ingenuous dialogue: 'Why was this eagle crucified?'—'To punish him for stealing fire from heaven.' Originally, the legend was that of the eagle's chastisement. When for the eagle, *prometheios* (the far-seeing, a name given to the eagle as a bird of augury), men substituted the Titan, Prometheus, the eagle remained in the legend, but as executioner instead of victim.[41]

Reinach, an excellent Hellenist like Nietzsche, knew that the name "Prometheus" derives from "*prometheia,*" "foresight." Prometheus sees the future of humanity and his own resurrection or unbinding, but here the theme of resurrection migrates from the bird to the hero's liver:

> A divine animal when sacrificed never died completely; for after a few days of mourning a successor was found, another animal of the same kind, which remained sacred and intangible for a year. This explains the resurrection of so many gods and heroes, the fact that their tombs were shown, that they were honoured in a ritual, and represented as living among the gods.[42]

These immortal birds can also offer an image prefiguring the immortality of machines with endlessly replaceable parts, in which the world of technology consists, and that, we cannot forget, is what we owe to Prometheus's gift.

Freud quotes Reinach in the 1912 postscript to his analysis of the Schreber case. In most legends concerning Prometheus, the hero's regenerated liver is gnawed endlessly by an eagle, while in other versions, it is a vulture. If the eagle comes day after day to feed from this bloody substance, it is also because, as Salomon Reinach had explained, the Greeks would associate eagles with the heavens, with the sun and with lightning. Eagles were distinguished by one feature: their ability to look at the sun without being dazzled—a point remembered by Freud in his 1912 Postscript to his book on Schreber.[43]

Eagles were rumored to test their offspring: if they were unable to withstand the glare of the sun, the little ones would be cast out of the net in a premonition of the medieval "ordeal," as Freud writes. There cannot be a starker contrast than darkly pulsating viscera linked with divination and a paternal "truth" so blinding that almost nobody will be able to withstand it.

However, when Freud went back to the Prometheus myth in 1932 in his dense and strange paper on "The Acquisition and Control of the Fire," he insists on one detail of the legend: Prometheus would have hidden the stolen fire in fennel stalks, in which one can recognize penis-like objects. This is sufficient to send Freud to the many legends about micturition used to quench fire and extinguish flames. The acquisition of fire calls up images of homosexual urination as the exact opposite of the generous theft by the Titan. What matters is that the act is at root criminal—the crime being directed at Zeus, the main god. Freud continues:

> We know that in myths the gods are granted the satisfaction of all the desires which human creatures have to renounce, as we have learnt from the case of incest. Speaking in analytic terms, we should say that life of the drive (*Triebleben*)—the id—is the god who is defrauded when the quenching of fire is renounced: in the legend, a human desire is transformed into a divine privilege. But in the legend the deity possesses nothing of the characteristics of a super-ego, he is still the representative of the paramount life of the drives (*Trieblebens*).[44]

If the jealous and cruel gods allegorize the unleashing of the drives, the myth conveys clearly that the renunciation to the pleasures they enjoy, a renunciation demanded by culture, cannot but be painful. This is why the liver has to be chosen as the point of impact of the cruel punishment:

> In ancient times the liver was regarded as the seat of all passions and desires; hence a punishment like that of Prometheus was the right one for a criminal driven by the drives, who had committed an offence at the prompting of evil desires. But the exact opposite is true of the Bringer of Fire: he had renounced a drive and had shown how beneficent, and at the same time how indispensable, such a renunciation was for the purposes of civilization. And why should the legend treat a deed that was thus a benefit to civilization as a crime deserving punishment? Well, if, through all its distortions, it barely allows us to get a glimpse of the fact that the acquisition of control over fire presupposes a renunciation to the drive, at least it makes no secret of the resentment which the culture-hero could not fail to arouse in men driven by their drives.[45]

What has been renounced in this case? Not just the fire of love, a "symbol of the libido" but also a more transgressive fire. Freud goes on:

> When we ourselves speak of the 'devouring fire' of love and of 'licking' flames—thus comparing the flame to a tongue—we have not moved so very far away from the mode of thinking of our primitive ancestors. One of the presuppositions on which we based our account of the myth of the acquisition of fire was, indeed, that to primal man the attempt to quench fire with his own water had the meaning of a pleasurable struggle with another phallus.[46]

He then needs a third element beyond the binary opposites:

> In the antithesis between fire and water, which dominates the entire field of these myths, yet a third factor can be demonstrated in addition to the historical factor and the factor of symbolic phantasy. This is a physiological fact, which the poet Heine describes in the following lines:—

Was dem Menschen dient zum Seichen
Damit schafft er Seinesgleichen.

(With what serves a man for pissing,
He creates creatures in his image).

The sexual organ of the male has two functions; and there are those to whom this association is an annoyance. It serves for the evacuation of the bladder, and it carries out the act of love which sets the craving of the genital at rest. The child still believes that he can unite the two functions. According to a theory of his, babies are made by the man urinating into the woman's body. But the adult knows that in reality the acts are mutually incompatible—as incompatible as fire and water.[47]

Heine rediscovers here what had amused Hegel when he saw how Nature combined the high and the low in an outrageous combination of fire and urine: "the same conjunction of the high and the low which, in the living being, Nature naïvely expresses when it combines the organ of its highest fulfilment, the organ of generation, with the organ of generation."[48] In his turn, Freud offers us an almost grotesque image of drive-based enjoyment presented as the mindless interaction of mutually masturbating Titans who have not even discovered the difference between urination and ejaculation! Re-reading Freud's interpretation of the legend with Winnicott as a guide, Mignotte counters this version with a feminist twist: for her, Prometheus's liver is an equivalent of the placenta, "an interface between the matrix void and the void that is intrinsic to the egg."[49] But of course, even in the male version, this is not the end—as we know, *Prometheus Unbound* follows *Prometheus Bound*.

Kafka's Solution

These considerations explain why the Prometheus myth kept such an appeal for Franz Kafka. As a seeker for autonomy who considered love a form of torture by other means (mostly epistolary, as we see in his notorious letters to Felice), he found in the bound Greek Titan a model for his doomed struggle against a domineering and powerful father. More often than not, his Oedipal struggle would abort or be lost in perverted or sado-masochistic games similar to the twists he saw underpinning the master and slave dialectic. Some self-hate helps if one wants to achieve the freedom required to be a writer. This freedom will unmoor him from the ground of the family, it is a freedom from the blood links reminding him of a disgusting proximity smacking of the parents' abhorred sexuality, a thought almost unbearable for Kafka:

> Sometimes this bond of blood (…) is the target of my hatred; the sight of the double bed at home, the used sheets, the nightshirts carefully laid out, can exasperate me to the point of nausea, can turn me inside out; it is as if I had not been definitively born (*als wäre ich nicht endgültich geboren*), were continually born anew into the world out of the stale life in that stale room, had constantly to seek confirmation of myself there, were indissolubly joined with all that loathsomeness, in part even if not entirely, at least it still clogs my feet which want to run, they are still stuck fast in the original pulp.[50]

Like the good lawyer he is, Kafka attempts to argue that he has some ground to hate his family (*es gibt übergenug Grund zu zolchem Haß*).[51] Hate is then accompanied by shame, the shame of not having been born once for all. This generates another torture, the torture of having to be born again and again.

Günther Anders, one of the best early commentators of Kafka, has described at some length the "Promethean shame" in an essay that praises Freud's idea of the "birth trauma":

> Philosophically speaking, Sigmund Freud's discovery of the 'Trauma of Birth' cannot be rated highly enough: for what more incisive event could

> happen to life than being torn from the 'ground?' The feelings Freud brought into view ('Oceanic Feeling;' 'Death Drive') are metaphysical in every respect, even if Freud's language was masked by the scientific vocabulary of his century. This is equally true of the "Trauma of Birth" with which he described the *shock of individuation*, no matter how well he disguised it. In an analogy with our question 'who is ashamed?' the question to ask in relation to this trauma is the following: '*Who* is actually shocked here?'[52]

The death drive refers to the individual's wish to get rid of the "agony of being an individual."[53] For Anders, it underpins a deeper and hidden link between shame, birth and original trauma. The shock of individuation should be compared with "being torn from the ground." Prometheus, who is responsible for the creation of tool-making humanity against the wishes of the higher gods like Zeus, can relinquish his individuality and merge with the ground, the rock he has been chained to. Kafka's rewriting of Prometheus was originally without a title. It was not absurd for Max Brod to want to change the original order and turn the last paragraph into the first, because he thought that examples should conclude and not begin with a general law. Kafka had thought his parable somewhat differently. Here is my rather literal translation:

> The legend tries to explain the inexplicable; as it comes out of the ground of truth (*Wahrheitsgrund*), it has return to the inexplicable in the end.
>
> There are four legends concerning Prometheus: According to the first he was clamped to a rock in the Caucasus for betraying the secrets of the gods to men, and the gods sent eagles to feed on his liver, which was perpetually renewed.
>
> According to the second Prometheus, goaded by the pain of the tearing beaks, pressed himself deeper and deeper into the rock until he became one with it.
>
> According to the third his treachery was forgotten in the course of thousands of years, forgotten by the gods, the eagles, forgotten by himself.
>
> According to the fourth everyone grew tired of the groundless affair. The gods grew tired, the eagles grew tired, the wound closed tired.
>
> There remains the inexplicable mass of rock.[54]

Kafka planned to begin with a statement about the role of legends in general. Their function is to explain natural phenomena: as we know, any spring, tree, river, can be a pretext for a Greek myth, and account for a metamorphosis: Niobe wept and turned into stone, Io jumped and created the Ionian sea and so on. Kafka's riddle posits a link between myth and nature on the one hand, myth and human suffering on the other. The story of Prometheus provides an example of a universal principle following a sequence of four moments and describing a process of gradual exhaustion. The hero turns into stone, all the participants have forgotten what has happened, including the hero. All have been affected by the exhaustion of the myth. If no reason can be given for the cruelty of the gods and the indifference of Nature, then what explanation can be valid?

What remains unshakeable for Kafka is a principle of truth, in which he finds an indisputable *Wahrheitsgrund*. The positive side is that some truth can be found; truth needs a secure grounding to be valid. In the end, it will be only found in the ground of the rocky mountain; this substratum does not need any explication, it is just there. All the rest has been invented to make sense of the mountain. Kafka prevents us from believing in the possibility of grounding ourselves in the natural world, while suggesting that the mass of rock that we call a mountain can also function as a primordial void—which would send us back to Winnicott and Mignotte. She shows that the void leaves an organic remainder, whether it be called blood or liver, but a remainder that generates endless torture: life itself as eternal torture. If the liver survives, so as to allow for a torture predicated on Prometheus' immortality, the immortality of an endless suffering, we understand better Kafka's desire for a cessation of this living immortality: only by turning into stone and making one with the mountain will the absurd torture end. The liver has turned to stone but somehow lives on.

Among the parts of the human body, the skin and the liver share a common feature: they heal by reconstituting their tissues. However, if the Greek *hepar* keeps a link with the seat of pleasure and affects, the Germanic *lifere* that gave *liver* is cognate with "life," and also calls up "courage." Another writer, James Joyce, also connected the courage to write with the ability to face a never-ending torture. He had a tendency to identify with "crying Jesus," which is why he mentions the city of

Trieste in which he spent many years writing *Ulysses* in connection with rampant alcoholism and a decaying liver: "And Trieste, ah Trieste ate I my liver!"[55] Such a partial autophagy seems to have been the precondition required for the monumental generation of *Finnegans Wake*, a work written over seventeen years and that he would call his "cruelfiction," to blend crucifixion, cruelty and fiction: "O, you were excruciated, in honour bound to the cross of your own cruelfiction!"[56]

Notes

1. Jacques Derrida, "Psychoanalysis Searches the States of Its Soul: The Impossible Beyond of a Sovereign Cruelty." In *Without Alibi*, trans. Peggy Kamuf (Stanford: Stanford University Press, 2002).
2. Maggie Nelson, *The Art of Cruelty: A Reckoning* (New York: W.W. Norton, 2011).
3. Derrida, *Without Alibi*, 246 & 248.
4. Ibid., 239.
5. Ibid.
6. Sigmund Freud, "Three Essays." In *The Standard Edition Volume VII*, trans. James Strachey (London: The Hogarth Press, 1953–1974), 159, modified.
7. Ibid., Note 3.
8. Ibid., 166, modified.
9. Ibid., 192–3.
10. Gilles Deleuze, *Coldness and Cruelty* and Leopold von Sacher-Masoch, *Venus in Furs*, trans. Jean McNeil (New York: Zone Books, 1991).
11. Sigmund Freud, "A Case of Obsessive-compulsive Neurosis (the Ratman)." In *The "Wolfman"* and *Other Cases*, trans. Louise Adey Huish (London: Penguin, 2002), 134.
12. Ibid.
13. Jacques Lacan, *The Seminar of Jacques Lacan Book VII: The Ethics of Psychoanalysis, 1959–1960*, trans. Dennis Porter (New York, Norton, 1992), 185.
14. James Joyce, *Ulysses*, edited by Hans Walter Gabler (New York: Random House, 1986), 175.

15. This is Derrida's question. *The Death Penalty, Volume II*, edited by Geoffrey Bennington and Marc Crépon (Chicago: University of Chicago Press, 2017), 219.
16. "Friend is … originally only the blood brother, the blood relation, or one who has been made related through marriage…" Carl Schmitt, *The Concept of the Political*, trans. Matthias Konzett and John P. McCormick (Chicago: University of Chicago Press, 2007).
17. G. W. F. Hegel, *Philosophy of Nature*, trans. A. V. Miller (Oxford: Oxford University Press), 1970.
18. Markus Semm, *Der springende Punkt in Hegels System* (München: Boer, 1994).
19. Hegel, *Philosophy of Nature*, 366.
20. Ibid., 367.
21. Ibid., 368.
22. Ibid.
23. Ibid., 369.
24. Ibid.
25. Ibid.
26. Ibid.
27. See Semm's chapter "Blut und Puls in der Naturphilosophie" in *Der springende Punkt in Hegels System*, 17–47.
28. Hegel, *Philosophy of Nature*, 369.
29. Ibid.
30. Hegel, *Philosophy of Nature*, 392.
31. Ibid.
32. Ibid., 392–3.
33. Jean-Luc Nancy, *Hegel: The Restlessness of the Negative*, trans. Jason Smith and Steven Miller (Minneapolis: University of Minnesota Press, 2002).
34. See Freud "Thoughts for the Times on War and Death." In *The Standard Edition Volume XIV* (1923), trans. James Strachey (London: The Hogarth Press, 2001), 292 & 298.
35. Richard Wrangham, *The Goodness Paradox: The Strange Relationship Between Virtue and Violence in Human Evolution* (New York: Pantheon Books, 2019).
36. Nietzsche's *Beyond Good and Evil* is quoted by Maggie Nelson in *The Art of Cruelty*, 3.
37. Friedrich Nietzsche, *Unpublished Writings from the period of Unfashionable Observations*, trans. Richard T. Gray (Stanford: Stanford University Press, 1995), 387.

38. Friedrich Nietzsche, *The Gay Science*, trans. Walter Kaufmann (New York: Random House, 1974), 240–1.
39. Aeschylus, *Prometheus Bound*, trans. Ian Johnston. http://johnstonia-texts.x10host.com/aeschylus/prometheusboundhtml.html. Accessed February 2, 2020. The slashes indicate line endings.
40. Mignotte, *Cruelty, Sexuality and the Unconscious in Psychoanalysis*, 78.
41. Salomon Reinach, *Orpheus: A general History of religions*, trans. Florence Simmonds (London: W. Heinemann, 1909), 84–5. The German translation was published in 1910.
42. Ibid., 85.
43. Sigmund Freud, *The Schreber Case*, trans. Andrew Weber (New York: Penguin Books, 2003), 68–70. Freud quotes Reinach several times, see 70.
44. Sigmund Freud, "The Acquisition of Fire." In *The Standard Edition Volume XXII*, trans. James Strachey (London: The Hogarth Press, 1964), 189. I have modified the translation of *Trieb*, rendered as "instinct" by Strachey.
45. Ibid.
46. Ibid., 190.
47. Ibid., 192.
48. G.W. Hegel, *The Phenomenology of Spirit*, trans. A. V. Miller (Oxford: Oxford University Press, 1977), 210.
49. Mignotte, *Cruelty, Sexuality, and the Unconscious in Psychoanalysis*, 79.
50. Franz Kafka, *Diaries 1910–1923*, trans. Martin Greenberg (New York: Schocken, 1948), 371.
51. Franz Kafka, *Tagebücher 1910–1923* (Frankfurt: Fischer, 1998), 375.
52. Quoted in Christopher John Müller in *Prometheanism: Technology, Digital Culture and Human Obsolescence* (London: Rowman and Littlefield, 2016), 93, note 33.
53. Ibid.
54. I translate from Kafka's *Oktavheft* G., III (18 October 1917–January 1918), MS. Kafka 25, MLR reference A (ii) XXXVII, KKA reference: KBod AIII, 7. The slashes indicate paragraph breaks. See also Kafka, "Prometheus" in *The Complete Stories*, trans. Willa and Edwin Muir (New York: Schocken, 1971), 432.
55. James Joyce, *Finnegans Wake* (London: Faber, 1939), 301.
56. Ibid., 192.

Bibliography

Aeschylus. *Prometheus Bound.* Translated by Ian Johnston: http://johnstonia-texts.x10host.com/aeschylus/prometheusboundhtml.html.

Deleuze, Gilles. *Coldness and Cruelty*, and Leopold von Sacher-Masoch, *Venus in Furs*. Translated by Jean McNeil. New York: Zone Books, 1991.

Derrida, Jacques. *Without Alibi*. Translated by Peggy Kamuf. Stanford: Stanford University Press, 2002.

———. *The Death Penalty, Volume II*. Edited by Geoffrey Bennington and Marc Crépon. Chicago: University of Chicago Press, 2017.

Freud, Sigmund. "Three Essays" In *The Standard Edition Volume VII*. Translated by James Strachey. London: The Hogarth Press, 1953–1974a.

———. "Thoughts for the Times on War and Death." In *The Standard Edition Volume XIV*. Translated by James Strachey. London: The Hogarth Press, 1953–1974b.

———. "A Case of Obsessive-compulsive Neurosis (the Ratman)." In *The "Wolfman" and Other Cases*. Translated by Louise Adey Huish. London: Penguin, 2002.

———. *The Schreber Case*. Translated by Andrew Weber. New York: Penguin Books, 2003.

Hegel, G. W. F. *Philosophy of Nature*. Translated by A. V. Miller. Oxford: Oxford University Press, 1970.

———. *The Phenomenology of Spirit*. Translated by A. V. Miller. Oxford: Oxford University Press, 1977.

Joyce, James. *Finnegans Wake*. London: Faber, 1939.

Kafka, Franz. *Diaries 1910–1923*. Translated by Martin Greenberg. New York: Schocken, 1948.

———. *The Complete Stories*. New York: Schocken, 1971.

———. *Tagebücher 1910–1923*. Frankfurt: Fischer, 1998.

———. *Oktavhefte*. Online at PDF Download Die Acht Oktavhefte (German Edition).

Lacan, Jacques. *The Seminar of Jacques Lacan Book VII: The Ethics of Psychoanalysis 1959–1960*. Translated by Dennis Porter. New York: Norton, 1992.

Mignotte, Touria. *Cruelty, Sexuality, and the Unconscious in Psychoanalysis: Freud, Lacan, Winnicott, and The Body of the Void*. Translated by Andrew Weller. London: Routledge, 2020.

Müller, Christopher John. *Prometheanism: Technology, Digital Culture and Human Obsolescence*. London: Rowman and Littlefield, 2016.

Nancy, Jean-Luc. *Hegel: The Restlessness of the Negative*. Translated by Jason Smith and Steven Miller. Minneapolis: University of Minnesota Press, 2002.

Nelson, Maggie. *The Art of Cruelty: A Reckoning*. New York: Norton, 2011.

Nietzsche, Friedrich. *The Gay Science*. Translated by Walter Kaufmann. New York: Random House, 1974.

———. *The Gay Science*. Translated by Walter Kaufmann. New York: Random House, *Unpublished Writings from the period of Unfashionable Observations*. Translated by Richard T. Gray. Stanford: Stanford University Press, 1995.

Reinach, Salomon. *Orpheus: A General History of Religions*. Translated by Florence Simmonds. London: W. Heinemann, 1909.

Schmitt, Carl. *The Concept of the Political*. Translated by Matthias Konzett and John P. McCormick. Chicago: University of Chicago Press, 2007.

Semm, Markus. *Der springende Punkt in Hegels System*. München: Boer, 1994.

Wrangham, Richard. *The Goodness Paradox: The Strange Relationship Between Virtue and Violence in Human Evolution*. New York: Pantheon Books, 2019.

3

Intimate Cruelties: Perversions, Sexuality and the Human Animal

Arka Chattopadhyay

Is perverse fantasy the same as perverse structure?[1] Is perversion as *père-version* (versions of the father) more of a complex than a structure, with its link to the Oedipus? There are multiple contexts and paradigms in which the Lacanian teaching on perversion appears. I will trace these paradigms by going through the shifts from the desire-of-the-mother to the *Name(s)-of-the-Father*. These threads range from perverse structure, neurotic's perverse fantasies, perversion of the drive, sexual non-rapport and perversion to perverse sexuality and *père-version.* After establishing the Lacanian paradigms, I will offer a reading of Sandipan Chattopadhyay's Bengali-Indian novel *Kukur Shamparke Du-Ekti Katha Ja Ami Jani* (*The One or Two Things I Know About Dogs*, 1991) to deepen perversion through a literary text that is aware of both its perverse vision of human sexuality and its psychoanalytic footprints. The reading connects some of the Lacanian nuances with the novel without applying psychoanalysis to

A. Chattopadhyay (✉)
Department of Humanities and Social Sciences, IIT Gandhinagar, Gandhinagar, Gujarat, India
e-mail: arka.chattopadhyay@iitgn.ac.in

M. Lee (ed.), *Lacan's Cruelty*, The Palgrave Lacan Series,
https://doi.org/10.1007/978-3-031-06238-4_3

literature. The point is to compare and co-invoke the psychoanalysis and literature, as Lacan himself does with his literary scaffolding around discussions of perversion.

Lacanian Perversions: Between the Mother and the Father

In his seventh annual seminar, Lacan says, "we have restored full civil rights to perversion."[2] He links perversion with the transgressive drives that approach the gap between pleasure and *jouissance* and associates it with the drive that misses its object. There is a transgressive *jouissance* that resonates with the perversion of drives. He accords civil rights to perversion by making it into a "component drive" that "harmonizes with a totality."[3] In *Seminar VIII*, talking about transference-love in Greek culture, Lacan earmarks perversion as "sublimation" when it becomes "a product of culture."[4] Perversion as cultural sublimation in love returns us to the aforementioned *civil-ization* of perversion. The most consistent threads in Lacan's discussions of perversion are the imaginary order and fantasy. In *Seminar V*, he critiques the view that perversion is pre-Oedipal. For Lacan, perversion plays out in the Oedipal field. It is not a primordial pathological fixation because human desire has a perverse dimension. He calls perversion, an "invasion of the imaginary"[5] relating to the point where desires lead to fantasies.

Perversion is connected with fetishism where an object assumes a particular value for the subject's desire. The subject puts the phallus in the place of the mother in fetishism as it involves an imaginary identification with the desire of the mother.[6] The imaginary dimension of the mother's desire takes precedence over the symbolic operation of the Name-of-the-Father. This does not mean that the phallic signifier is missing in perversion. As Lacan reflects, at stake is an imaginary identification with the phallic signifier as a metonymic object of desire. It is not any ordinary identification with an object but a "radical" one that represents something "evasive" in the imaginary as the object takes "flight in the imaginary."[7] There is something in perversion that the subject does not want to recognize. They repress it.[8] The relation between perversion and the repressed re-affirms that it's not a pre-oedipal dynamic. In the same seminar, Lacan locates perversion in the "species of fantasy" as it offers an "imaginary satisfaction."[9] Discussing the imaginary order and fantasy scenarios, he reminds us that all this forms the signifying element of perversion where signifiers play a vital role. We are not talking about an imaginary, divested of the symbolic in perversion.

In *Seminar VI*, the line drawn between neurosis and perversion hinges on the two poles in the matheme of fantasy (*$<>a*). The emphasis in perversion is on the "imaginary correlative" of the object-cause of desire (*a*) while in neurosis, we stress the divided subject (*$*).[10] Lacan casts a critical glance on Glover's thesis of perversion as reality-testing that gives it a structure of repair. He does not negate this thesis but remains sceptical of the generalization that makes perversion into a phantasmatic cover up for a hole in reality.[11] In the same seminar, Lacan dwells on the distinction between perversion as structure and perverse fantasies and posits that the latter does not confirm the former as a psychic structure.[12] Masochism becomes a crucial element for perversion as Lacan goes into the pervert's dynamic of subjective division. Masochism is played out at the level of fantasy that fixes the subject's divided relation with their object of desire.[13] In *Seminar X*, he returns to this masochistic aspect of perversion. For Lacan, the masochist thinks, they are the Other's *jouissance* while what they truly seek is the Other's anxiety but without knowing it.[14] Masochism is called an enigma in the field of perversion, but it's not the only kind of perversion. The distinction Lacan makes is that the pervert "doesn't know who's enjoying"[15] while the masochist "believes" that the Other's *jouissance* is what they are after.

James Penney, in a study of perversion, glosses the pervert's manoeuvre with the Other:

> The pervert successfully avoids the consequences of castration only by castrating the Other, and it is precisely this aggression and violence which he jettisons from consciousness. [...] the pervert is anything but an agent: His ethically questionable activities are undertaken on behalf of the Other; [...], the pervert responds to an unconditional imperative to execute what for him is his victim/partner's sovereign will.[16]

Here the perverse subject inverts the fantasy from $(\$<>a)$ to $(a<>\$)$.[17] The pervert castrates the Other in order not to face the consequences of their own castration. The pervert operates from the pole of the object and not the barred subject though they do not have any real agency insofar as they are executing the Other's command. To quote from *Seminar XI*, "[i]t is the [perverse] subject who determines himself as object, in his encounter with the division of subjectivity."[18]

In *Seminar VI*, the writer André Gide becomes the site to situate the pervert's subjective splitting which in this case "presents itself in the form of an opposition between two identificatory sections, one of which is specifically linked to his narcissistic image of himself, *i(a)*, and the other to his mother."[19] We notice the pre-eminence of the mother's desire but also register an imaginary and phantasmatic self-identification of narcissism. In perverse structures, we encounter "the subject's identification with the phallus, inasmuch as the phallus emerges from his fantasizing about an object inside his mother."[20] While the neurotic can only have the phallic signifier by not having it, the pervert transcends this dialectic of castration by merging the "being" with the "having" of the phallus. The pervert is the phallus and has it. For perversion, this "has" turns towards the mother as the first object encountered. In Lacan's formulation, "[w]hat the subject is not, his ideal object is" or again "[t]he subject is the phallus qua object within the mother, and he has it in [or: possesses it via] the object of his desire."[21]

These articulations on the structure of perversion almost inevitably get placed in relation to homosexuality. Lacan considers homosexuality as a perversion of desire but this does not mean he collapses the two.[22] Perversion may exist without homosexuality as a psychic structure. The problem with this reading of Gide is that it often uses homosexuality and perversion interchangeably. In *Seminar VI*, he returns to perversion as a form of protest against social conformism with an implicit hint towards homosexuality. Lacan understands perversion "in its most general form as what in human beings resists all normalization."[23] The thesis that perversion is a form of sublimating desire comes here. It sublimates the desire of the subject by protesting social norms of desire or any other normative social practice. However, as Lacan reminds us in *Seminar X*, contrary to what appears, the pervert's subversion of law is supported by another law.

The pervert doesn't enjoy "unbounded satisfaction."[24] Something in perversion halts the subject's *jouissance*. What the "alienated" pervert follows is not their own *jouissance* but the *jouissance* of the Other. Talking about sadism in perversion, Sergio Benvenuto writes:

> [t]he perverse are not animals who get up to all sorts of things with no laws; on the contrary, they take pleasure in submitting to the law. [...] In a non-psychologistic perspective, the torturer enjoys pleasure because he interprets the law sadistically: to him the law is the Other's enjoyment.[25]

Sadistic perversion is not devoid of the law. It's an interpretation of law as the Other's enjoyment. The pervert submits themselves to this Other's *jouissance* as a matter of law.

Literature often lies in the context for Lacan's discussions on perversion in *Seminars V* and *VI*. In *V*, he talks through André Gide and Jean Genet, relating their homosexual object-choice with a perverse fantasy. In *VI*, Lacan explores perversion through Shakespeare's *Hamlet* and Vladimir Nabokov's 1955 novel *Lolita* that deals with an older man's sexual attraction for a 12-year old girl. Does the literary thread Lacan opens around perversion signify its symbolic dimension? The effect of the literary is bound up in the role of the signifier in perversion's signifying mechanism. If the symbolic governs the literary, the imaginary dimension of fantasy is not far behind. Literature acts as an archive of perverse fantasies with an overload of the imaginary. It is the double point of the symbolic and the imaginary that activates the literary around perversion.

Lacan mentions the famous sentence of whipping fantasy from Freud, "*Ein Kind wird geschlagen*" ("a child is being beaten") in discussing the ambiguity of perverse fantasy in *Seminars V* and *XIV*. What he highlights in this symbolic articulation of fantasy is that "it isn't the subject who beats, he is there as a spectator."[26] The ambivalence lies in the passive grammatical construction that occludes the *jouissance* of the Other. Who enjoys in this fantasy? The subject or the Other? For Lacan, if the subject is the spectator, it underlines the sado-masochistic nature of this perverse fantasy.[27] In his recounting of Freud's argument, the sentence enacts the Oedipal drama of the father who "withholds his love from the beaten child"[28] and arouses the little girl's desire to be beaten up by the father.[29]

This sadistic and masochistic aspect of perversion will become important for Lacan's characterization of sexuality as perverse.

In *Seminar XIV*, Lacan connects perversion with a first formulation of sexual non-rapport (sexuality as absence of relationality): "There is no sexual act" as a signifying practice.[30] For him, "perversion only takes on its value by being articulated with the sexual act."[31] As he reflects, the One of sexual union without partition makes way for the perverse subject's identification with the *object a* that holds onto their *jouissance*. The pervert becomes this *a object* through the fantasy of an undivided sexual union.[32] There is a "disjunction of the body and *jouissance*" in perversion. It leads the pervert to reconnect their *jouissance* with the body and hence the One of sexual union.[33] The signifying intervention of sexual act separates *jouissance* and body and the pervert wants to splice them back. This reconnecting act often assumes a sado-masochistic character. In the statement on sexual non-relation from *Seminar XX*, we often miss the signifier "perverse":

> There's no such thing as a sexual relationship because one's jouissance of the Other taken as a body is always inadequate—perverse, on the one hand, insofar as the Other is reduced to object a, and crazy and enigmatic, on the other[34]

To reduce the Other's *jouissance* to their corporeality is perverse and it is this perversion that makes sexual relation impossible. The splicing of body and *jouissance* fails when sexuality gets situated as an absence of relation. It is the perverse nature of sexuality that makes it fail as a relation.

Lacan's teachings on perversion work against characterizing it as a pre-Oedipal problem. How perversion is tied with the Other's *jouissance* clarifies its position in the Oedipal drama of the subject and the Other. But his thinking on perversion shifts within the Oedipal field from the focus on the mother's desire in the earlier seminars to the Name-of-the-Father in the late seminars. This happens when he delineates the patronymic as a *sinthome* that draws together the three orders of the unconscious: the real, the symbolic and the imaginary. Perversion is *père-version* in this Borromean clinic. For later-Lacan, the real, the symbolic and the imaginary are figured as a non-trivial form of Brunnian linking among three rings. None of the three has any one-on-one relation and yet they are topologically knotted by a twist that enables the third to go through the hole, half-shared by the other two. The rings are equivalent, lying on top of one another and can easily drift apart. From the end of *Seminar XXII*, continuing into *Seminar XXIII*, Lacan locates the fourth ring as a *sinthomatic* patronym that holds together the three drifty registers. The Name-of-the-Father is a binding symptom that creates a link among the three orders:

> It is not a break between the symbolic, the imaginary, and the real that defines perversion, it is that they already stand apart in such a way that a fourth term has to be supposed, which on this occasion is the sinthome. [...] what forms the Borromean link has to be supposed to be tetradic—that perversion merely means *version vers le pere*, a version towards the father—[...] the father is a symptom, or a sinthome, as you wish.[35]

In this important moment in Lacan's teaching, perversion becomes a version of the father as symptom through homophony. The Name-of-the-Father has always been a logical function of language: a quilting point. What is new is its symptomatic aspect. It is not just any other symptom. The father has a *sinthomatic* function for the pervert. In the pervert's unconscious, the three orders stand apart with nothing to link them except the patronym. This deepens the symbolic dimension in perversion. The paternal *sinthome* must be constructed on the symbolic order of language. It is a matter of invention. The pervert has to invent a *sinthomatic* father-function to relink their R-S-I. We could read into this emphasis on "constructing" or "inventing" the symptom, a creative logic of the literary. Literature is an invention and it's not far behind here in *Seminar XXIII*. The context for the discussion is the writings of James Joyce and Lacan wonders if Joyce wasn't a pervert (Fig. 3.1).[36]

In *Seminar XXII*, there is a pluralization of the "Name-of-the-Father" into "Names-of-the-Father."[37] Here we have Lacan's Biblical clarification that the real, the symbolic and the imaginary are three Names-of-the-Father insofar and together they form the father of the Holy Trinity.[38] The fundamental point is to take the three orders as naming something and producing "meaning" for the unconscious subject: "I reduce the

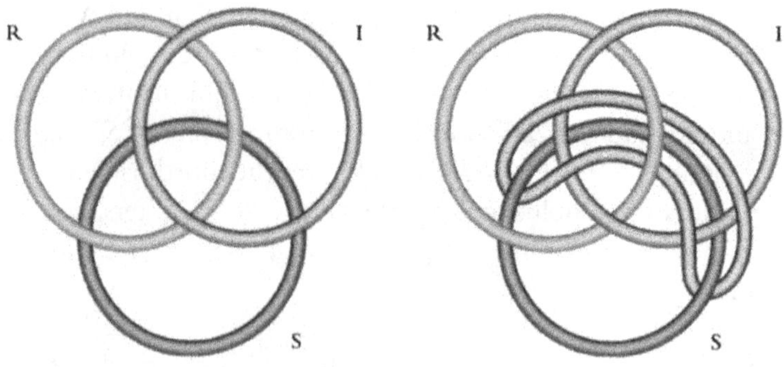

Fig. 3.1 Triple and Quadruple Borromean rings. The three separate rings (left); the rings linked by the fourth ring, the sinthome (right). (Source: Lacan, *Seminar XXIII*, 12)

Name-of-the-Father to its radical function which is to give a name to things."[39] The real, the symbolic and the imaginary name something for and in the unconscious. Beyond any biological network, Lacan is talking about paternity as a principle of naming in the quilting points of language. There are as many Names-of-the-Father in a signifying Borromean chain as a subject wants. Lacan specifies that this number could be "indefinite."[40] This prompts him to think about a fourth ring:

> In the three, one never knows which of the three is real and that indeed is why there must be four, because the four is what in this double buckle supports the Symbolic by what in effect it is made up of, namely, the Name-of-the-Father.[41]

The fourth ring as the Name-of-the-Father names the paternal knot by holding the three rings together. This is a support for the pervert's unconscious. This fourth ring is a "plus-one" that makes a "double-buckle" and helps keeping the R-S-I together (Fig. 3.2).

As both figures show, the *sinthome* is constructed on the symbolic order. It is an invention that operates on the fabric of language and gives birth to something new. Perversion as a constructed *sinthome* of the paternal signifier meets literature here as another inventive construction on the matrix of signifiers. This explains why literature exists in Lacan's

Fig. 3.2 Symbol-sinthome double-buckle. Symmetrical figuration of the four-component Borromean link. (Source: Lacan, *Seminar XXIII*, 13)

referential horizon, when he discusses perversion. The editors of *Perversion Now* ask, "Can one speak of a perverse sinthome?"[42] If one can, does that mean this perverse *sinthome* could be a sublimating literary construction on language? As Michael Newman observes, "[i]f perversion involves the construction of a relation to *jouissance*, this need not remain stuck at the Imaginary maternal phallus, but may also involve an intervention into the Symbolic."[43] Literature is an invention in perversion that creates a *sinthome*. I am arguing for this symbolic underlining of perversion that balances its imaginary overload. In the reading of the novel, I will signal this movement from the imaginary to the symbolic. The real in perversion is another topic and remains a touch beyond the scope of this chapter. But I will nevertheless indicate how the real is positioned in the novel's drama of perversion.

The psychoanalytic problem of cruelty is often invoked while discussing the perverse practices of sadism and masochism. Gilles Deleuze in his reading of Sacher-Masoch and Sade draws attention to "coldness" as the under-taste of cruelty. Cruelty implies and at the same time under-emphasizes the coldness, associated with it. For Deleuze, this coldness in the Sadist is an apathy, that is, a "negation of feeling" while in the masochist, it is about a "disavowal of sensuality."[44] The masochist's coldness has what Deleuze calls an underlying "sentimentality" with its own "wrath" and "cruelty."[45] Though Lacan does not explicitly theorize "cruelty," for him it's a matter of drive-aggressivity. In a piece on criminology and psychoanalysis, early-Lacan approaches cruelty as imaginary rivalry with a specular Other. The cruelty is seen at the level of the ego. If drives mark the "animal" aspect of the human subject, Lacan cites Gracián's *Criticón* to question this drive-animality link:

> what the moralist tradition means when it says that man's ferocity toward his semblable exceeds everything animals are capable of, and that carnivores themselves recoil in horror at the threat man poses to nature as a whole.[46]

Gracián's fable shows Lacan how human cruelty can far-surpass that of the non-human animal. Lacan treats cruelty as "ferocity" towards a semblable Other. On the one hand, he says that cruelty is not an animal act: "this very cruelty implies humanity."[47] But on the other, Lacan widens the scope of human cruelty to the human–non-human relation when he comments that the semblable Other of cruelty may be trans-species: "It targets a semblable, [...] a being from another species."[48]

Dog-Fantasy, Cruelty and a Version of the Father: Reading Sandipan

After developing the threads on perversion, I will now create a dialogue with Sandipan Chattopadhyay's (1933–2005) untranslated Bengali novel *Kukur Shamparke Du-Ekti Katha Ja Ami Jani* (*Kukur* hereafter) from 1991. The novel depicts incestual and perverse sexuality through the trope of the animal. In the authorial postface, Sandipan evokes Sophocles' treatment of the Oedipus myth and Freud to attend to animal sexuality, implicit in the Oedipus tale. Hemanga sees himself and all human beings as dogs. When he meets people, he wonders about their breed. The novel treats the human as animal and the sexual field is presented as an emanation of this basic animality of the human, metaphorized by the dog-species. Hemanga's canine sexual practices with wife Monica, their pet-dog "Beauty" and the climax where Monica's son from her previous marriage, Anirban, is "possessed" by a spirit and has sex with his mother, forcing Monica to commit suicide. I will underline the diverse approaches to perverse sexuality and cruelty in intimacy by dwelling on the implications of incest, animality, possession and the obsessional dog-fantasy. The aforementioned non-human question in cruelty becomes important for Chattopadhyay's dog-motif. Does Hemanga's dog-fantasy situate the non-human animal as an Other to project his imaginary rivalries?

A Bengali experimentalist who looked towards European thought with great intellectual curiosity, Chattopadhyay's interest in Freud is motivated by his obsessional accentuation of sexuality as a drive-force. In his works, the sexual reveals the animality of the human. For instance, his 1999 novel *Bharotborsho* (*India*) mentions the Freudian pleasure-principle as the driving force behind the Marxist theorization of human labour.[49] The Freudo-Marxism of Frankfurt school leaves a strong influence on him. It is evident in the epigraph of *Rikter Jatray Jago* (*Wake up to the Journey of the Oppressed*, 1993) where Chattopadhyay cites Herbert Marcuse: "So we can see, there has always been an analytic tradition that considers the thought of sexual liberation as an integral part of political protest."[50] The social repression of the sexual impedes the liberation of sexuality. As we have seen, perversion could act like a tool of protest against social normativization of desire. By virtue of the same logic, it could become a device to oppose social repression of sexuality. As we shall see, perversion enacts a subversive practice of incestual sexual liberation in *Kukur*.

Kukur is aware of its Oedipal overtones. The novel's postface is a paratext in which Chattopadhyay expresses his desire to craft a narrative to recast the Greek myth from a vantage of the non-human animal. It begins by invoking "psychology" to situate "the statue of the human" on the "foundation of animality."[51] Chattopadhyay's contention is that Sophocles and Freud dilute the sexual radicalism of the Oedipus tale by highlighting its tragic humanity. For Chattopadhyay, glorifying human tragedy in Oedipus takes our attention away from its animal-instinctual core. Therein lies its radical sexual edge. The dog becomes the chosen animal trope to allegorize the human subject's "foundational animality."[52]

The postface maintains that while Oedipus unwittingly became the father of his own mother's children by marrying Jocasta, in the novel, the son has conscious intercourse with his mother that makes her commit suicide.[53] The question remains though about how conscious this intercourse is. The novel deploys the occult motif of possession. Is Ani conscious when he sleeps with his mother Monica or is he possessed by the anonymous spirit? How is Hemanga's canine fantasy-scenario linked to what happens between his wife Monica and her son from the previous marriage? If Ani is not Hemanga's son, how is this family-complex, a variation on the Oedipal situation?

The novel's first part begins with Hemanga's fantasy of seeing dogs in humans. The narrator calls it an "obsession": "whenever anyone comes in front of him, he tries to understand, what dog, how much of a dog and what breed."[54] The fantasy is not dependent solely on gaze. When he thinks about a friend or his dead parents, his mind goes into a flight of thought that captures them as dogs. In gestures like scratching or rubbing the nose with the thumb, Hemanga finds dog-like echoes. His observations are behavioural. When someone behaves amicably, Hemanga can see their wagging tail. His fantasy reaches satisfaction when he diagnoses the dog-type in the human being. Hemanga follows this thinking consciously without telling anyone. The more he "broods," the more he becomes a part-dog from inside. The narrator calls it more of a "fruition" than a "becoming" as he always had a canine core hidden in him.[55] Hemanga participates in his fantasy as a dog himself. As Hemanga is on his way to the washroom after waking up at midnight, he also wakes up to the "dog-consciousness" which tells him that he can go through the wall if he wants to.[56] This consciousness is imposed on him by a mysteriously anonymous Other-function that reduces him to an object, producing perverse *jouissance* for the Other.

Hemanga and Monica have a pet female dog, Beauty who acts like a substitute-object after their daughter Poli leaves home in an elopement-turned-marriage. Beauty is a German Shepard in the class-divided society of dogs but the dog-instinct often flattens out the difference. In an important scene, we see Hemanga getting furious with Beauty when she disobeys him and runs to mate with the strays in the park. Though he enjoys Beauty's "total submission" to her paternal master, Hemanga is frustrated when the dog's sexual instinct takes over. He has to use a stone to defuse the strays. He can hear in Beauty's repentant look, the voice of his daughter, asking for her father's forgiveness. This is the reciprocity of Hemanga's fantasy. Just as he sees dogs in humans, he can see his daughter in the dog:

"this human presence in the dog, Poli in Beauty—this was Hemanga's flight through the wall! It was then that he got curious about the dog in the human."[57]

Hemanga's obsession stems from academic reading. He starts studying sexual behaviour and mating practices of dogs. The narrator cites the twentieth-century dog-breeder Thelma Gray.[58] Hemanga contrasts Beauty's return from the strays with Poli's marriage and departure from home. The dog, adopted six months after the daughter's marriage, hides the sexual non-rapport of the couple. As we have seen in the first part of this chapter, perversion has a function in the Lacanian thesis of sexual non-relation. There is something perverse about reducing the Other to the *object-a*. It is the object and not the subject that rules perversion. Hemanga's perverse fantasy attempts to reduce the Other to an enjoyable fetish-object though he unknowingly makes himself the object of the dog-Other's *jouissance* in his species-level fantasy. If intimate sexuality is cruel, dog-sexuality as a marker of conjugal relation becomes metaphorical of inter-species cruelty where the Other is non-human. It is not cruelty to the animal but a characterization of intimate sexual practices as acts of cruelty, represented by the animal-human doublet. The dog becomes the perverse fetish-object to supplement the "deception" in the conjugality of Hemanga and Monica. The narrator compares their vacuous relation with a shutter-clicking without photographs.[59] As Poli grew up, Monica started sleeping in her room and their sexual encounters became rare. After the daughter's marriage, they resumed sharing the bed but as the narrator reflects, twenty years of sleeping apart corroded the sexual drive and made them like brother and sister. The narrator marks their sexual non-rapport in a linguistic metaphor:

> As long as Poli was there like a hyphen in the joint words, Hemanga-Monica, the expression had some application and could be used in a sentence. When Poli left, it became apparent that the two words had no independent meaning. No language could come into being from it.[60]

The Lacanian echoes are too palpable here. The signifying practice of sexual non-relation brings in the child as the third. When Poli leaves, Monica and Hemanga need another third as replacement to hide the absence of their sexual relation. It is to address this solitude in coupledom that Hemanga brings home Beauty. Monica initially reacts against the labours of maintenance but soon grows maternal feelings for her. Hemanga's dog-ridden imagination recovers memories of canine maternal behaviour. He recalls how he had seen a grandmother-dog come to breastfeed her grandkids after her own puppies died. When Hemanga says, looking at Beauty for the first time reminded him of Poli, Monica remonstrates him for the perverse comparison. This analogy between Poli and Beauty is reinforced when we return to Poli's multiple romantic liaisons from her pubertal days and how she eloped eventually. Hemanga's friend Srikanto had compared Poli's wayward ways to that of "a bitch in heat."[61]

The last chapter of the first section offers an anthropological account of the human–animal relation. The narrator wonders why the dog was one of the first animals to be tamed by the human. Is the dog-species easy to control? There are reflections on the Egyptian mythology of dog-gods like Anubis, Mephistopheles in dog-avatar and the heavenly dog "Sarama" from whose name comes the Bengali word "saromeyo" for dog.[62] The chapter concludes with an inversion of power relations between the human and the animal by suggesting how dogs came to humans and submitted to them rather than human beings, establishing agency over them. The hunter-dogs in an ancient past submitted to the cave-dwellers for leftovers and it marked the beginning of the human–dog partnership.[63] Hemanga preserves the enigma of canine behaviour in their lament at the full moon or in the habit of covering their faeces with soil.

The novel's second part is narrated in Hemanga's first-person perspective. It goes into sub-plots as he continues to see dogs in people, most notably in his friend Lahiri when they drink together in pubs. The Oedipal motif of the perverse father is forefronted when Lahiri's adolescent daughter dies and he notices her pubic hair in the burning ghat during the cremation. Lahiri mentions this in a social conversation with friends and it puts them off. The narrator highlights the dog-metaphor while describing Lahiri's comment on his daughter's sexuality: "I saw with fear how his tail got stiff like a dagger about to strike, his fangs out and back legs, gathering force to jump."[64] The other men present there howl like dogs and ask him not to speak further on the matter: "We too have our daughters!"[65] Lahiri hits back by calling them "a bunch of daughter-fuckers."[66] The perverse father is thus connected with the metaphorical dog-image. It is the inverse of the son's attraction for the mother or the daughter's for the father. This is the father's erotic attachment with the daughter as a dog-fetish-object. This *père-version* fascinates Hemanga from the position of his significant Others like Lahiri. As a subject, he becomes an object-like receptacle for the Other's perverse sexual drives.

We come back to Beauty in the final chapter when her death is declared as "the death of the beautiful."[67] Before Hemanga and Monica could decide if they want her to breed, she develops photo-phobia and dies. When she is taken to the Anglo-Indian breeder Alfred Latif Das, he wonders if Beauty is actually a German Shepard or a stray in disguise. He passes on the information about the existence of incest among dogs: "it's an animal, sir. It can do its sister and even the mother."[68] The sexual practice of inbreeding connects the dog-metaphor with incest. Monica becomes an archetypal mother to Beauty in her final days as she takes care of her. In Hemanga's words, other than breast-feeding, she has done everything for her, including her death-care:

> The night before she left us, Monica would leave the bed numerously to have a look at Beauty. In the innate femininity of all the women in this world, she was not only helping her to live but also assisting her to die.[69]

She witnesses the instant of Beauty's death. She responds to Monica's call but cannot drink the holy water poured into her mouth. Monica's sobs as she narrates Beauty's death bespeak her maternal care as the obverse of Hemanga's Other-acquired *père-version*.

The third section "Karna-Kunti News" takes its title from Rabindranath Tagore's famous play on the estranged mother-son duo from the Hindu epic *Mahabharata*. As the narrator reflects, the sentimental and all-too human, mother–son relation of Karna and Kunti stands as a counterpoint to the animality of the Oedipus-Jocasta relation. The narrator adds that the incest happened unknowingly and there is no other way it could happen.[70] We come to know about Monica's first marriage that lasted less than a couple of years. Her husband Debitosh is dead (we do not know how) but she has a son from that marriage—Anirban who is still a minor.

After two decades, Debitosh's brother Mahitosh comes to visit Monica and requests her to go and see her son as he is sick. The void left by Beauty makes Hemanga suggest to Monica if they can have Ani in their house. This conversation happens as they are engaged in a sexual act. Monica says no, following the mutual decision during divorce that Ani would be the "possession" of his father's family.

Debitosh was a pedigree dog to Monica, but he was a stray for her. Monica did not consider him as partner until she left Debitosh. Hemanga is not sure why their marriage did not work out. His wishful explanation is that perhaps Debitosh was not much of a dog like him. Monica never shows her first husband's picture to her second husband. In the heyday of their romance and meetings on the river ghats, one evening in the middle of a wild storm, Hemanga and Monica get stuck in a boat. As fear of death starts looming on the dark riverscape, Hemanga recalls how he had forced himself on her. This strangely consentless and yet not completely non-consensual intercourse marks the beginning of their animal sexual practices. It is noteworthy that the text uses the strong signifier "rape" to mark this as an erotic enactment of intimate cruelty.[71] Before this abrupt situational moment of intercourse, their relation was entirely on the symbolic plane. They would talk on the ghats, often going into the boats. Their non-rapport is allegorized by the isomorphism of the two parallel rivers:

> We would listen intently to the wild sounds of water splashing on the oars. It had a language of its own. There was a gulf between us. As I said, we would talk but only about ourselves, never about each other. Perhaps that's what we have been doing for nineteen years! As if two rivers, moving on in their parallel pathways. There was always a strip of land between to divide us from one another.[72]

The passage is replete with a melancholic affect that stems from sexual non-rapport. Why does Hemanga force himself on Monica? They are in a relationship at the time and Monica's divorce is on the cards. Hemanga's insecure masculinity makes the violation, a triumphant testing ground of his gender. This is Chattopadhyay's problematization of sexual consent that acknowledges the fundamentally perverse character of human sexuality. It is this cruelty that makes us animal but as we saw with Lacan's comment in part one, it is this very cruelty that makes us intimately human. Monica decides to let go of her rights on son Anirban in order to marry Hemanga. The narrative description of this decision is juxtaposed by the narrator's invocation of a moment from the Oedipus tale in which the shepherd told Oedipus that the queen wanted to put him down when he was a kid. This was owing to the divine prophecy that he would have sexual intercourse with his mother.[73] Is Monica a cruel mother to have abandoned her son? This is cruelty as Deleuzean coldness, mapped by her indifference towards her son. Ani grows up without a mother. Is it this maternal abandonment that leads him towards incest as he hits puberty?

The last chapter of this section resorts to discursivity and theorizes questions of the human and the animal in love. It attacks the social repression of sexuality as dirty matter. This repression is likened with the dog's habit of covering its faeces with soil.[74] There is a lament over lovelessness as much as an attempt to establish human love on the foundation of animality. The social moralism that suppresses the erotic results in a deification of asexual love. Chattopadhyay's invective against this conformism is registered throughout the chapter. Hemanga's friend Lahiri in a drunken rage against social codes uses the dog-metaphor to point to the human act of self-hiding. The dog-trope is applied here in a statement on social de-humanization. What comes out in Hemanga's discursive commentary is the canine nature of human sexuality when it leaves the hypocritical cloaks of social conformity. He describes his sex life in terms of a violent masculinity that wants to rule the female body, reducing both to the species of the dog. The portrait of intimacy as cruelty becomes apparent in the following comment: "[a]fter the bedroom is bolted, the man who maintains his respectability is detestable."[75] This phallic eroticism can only be contained by the animal instincts of the human. This alpha-masculinity marks the sexual as a space of violence by objectifying the woman as much as it objectifies itself. The dog emerges as a metaphorical fetish-object that underwrites this perverse vision of human sexuality.

The final section named after Oedipus and Jocasta stages the climax of Ani's possession at the hands of a nameless spirit. It is seemingly under this possession by the Other that he sleeps with his mother Monica. Is Ani's incest a mirror of Hemanga's perverse masculinity? We see a move away from the father towards the mother in this last section that reverses Lacan's arc of changing emphasis from the mother to the father in perversion. While Lacan shifts from the mother's desire to the Name-of-the-Father in perversion, the novel goes in the other direction. After an initial diagnosis of atherosclerosis among other neurological symptoms, Ani starts to speak in another person's voice. His behavioural oddities confirm this to be a case of supernatural possession for his uncle Mahitosh, who is himself a practitioner of Tantra (an Indian indigenous spectrological system). When Hemanga sees the possessed Anirban, it reminds him of a puppy, looking for maternal nurturing.[76] The young boy uses abusive words and wants alcohol. In Hemanga's eyes, the possessed Ani is like a man-dog: "His red gumline and teeth lay bare now. Particularly notable was the long and bent canine."[77] The equivocal signifier "canine" bridges Ani's teeth with the dog-species. Hemanga calls him the "dog-king of ancient Ethiopia."[78] Ani's howls are called "canine cries of protest against the human who had shackled it in chain."[79] The spirit has laid down the condition that it will only leave Anirban if his mother Monica spends a night with him. Monica cannot be seen the following morning until her naked body is found in the neighbouring pond. She undressed herself before going into the water. Her clothes are worn by a wandering mad-woman who leads Hemanaga and Mahitosh to the spot. There is a heavy stone, tied to her head with a noose. Ani watches the bloated corpse from his wheelchair on the terrace. The last sentence of the novel makes the suggestion of incest all the more patent: "Nobody had the guts to turn her prone body on her back."[80]

The incest forms a perverse attempt to reclaim the mother's body on the part of the son. As we have seen in the first part, the pervert wants to get their body back to undo the disconnect between body and *jouissance*. To claim the mother's body is to claim one's own corporeal enjoyment of the Other. Hemanga's alienation from his own sexual life is marked by the dog-Other-fantasy. Ani is the Other, epitomizing Hemanga's forbidden incestual desire. The prohibited maternal body becomes the site for the intimate cruelty of his sado-masochistic act. In *Kukur*, the dog-fetish represents a perverse notion of sexuality that animalizes the human, anchoring the latter on the foundation of basal instincts. Apart from the linguistic troping of sexual non-relation and its connection with perversion, as glimpsed in Lacan, the novel also illuminates the problem of alterity in perversion. The dog is the animal-Other qua the human that enjoys at the subject's expense. The subjective dialectic is heavily skewed on the side of the object. Hemanga's perverse "dog-consciousness" makes him an object at the beck-and-call of the dog-Other's *jouissance*. As we have seen above, the pervert does not know who is enjoying! Hemanga feels he is enjoying himself but it is the dog that enjoys (through) him. This alterity is mirrored by the canine Others (like Lahiri as yet another perverse father) who pass on the dog-obsession to him. The final Other in this series is the nameless ghost who possesses Ani to make him into an *Ani-mal.*

The text softens up the radicality of the mother–son intercourse by using the supernatural trope of possession. We see a move from the father of *père-version* to the mother qua incest in the novel's climax. We cannot definitively say, despite Chattopadhyay's authorial claims, that Ani violates his mother knowingly. The possession underlines the conundrum of the Other in perversion. The supernatural possession doubles up and emphasizes that Ani has always been a "possessed" property, claimed by his paternal family and left unclaimed by his own mother. He is a "possession" objectified by his parents' failed marriage. Having said this, the trope of possession acts as a textual filter that reduces the socially revolting nature of the mother–son incest. Is Ani an extended incarnation of Hemanga's dog-fantasy? Does he do it simply because of the basal sexual drive or is it his vengeance against his absent mother? The incest that forces Monica to kill herself is another instance of intimate cruelty at the cusp of the human and the animal. Ani's incest mirrors Hemanga's own violation of Monica in the boat. Is it the dead Debitosh in the form of another spectral Other who comes back to enjoy his ex-wife through his son Ani? The cryptic climax does not answer these questions but keeps all the possibilities open in a tantalizing way.

As the novel shifts its preoccupation from Hemanga's *père-version* to zoom in on Monica's maternal self and Ani's intimate cruelty with her, we notice a rupture in the Oedipal triangle. The biological father is uncoupled from the scene of incest and made into a spectator. Just as in the perverse fantasy of "a child is being beaten," the subject was the spectator and not the abuser, in this scenario where "a mother is being violated",

Hemanga, the subject, is positioned as a spectator. The one who performs the incest is an Other who executes the perverse fantasy of yet an-Other (Debitosh) or himself (Hemanga). If Anirban has sex with his mother out of vindictiveness for Monica who had abandoned him as a child, this intimate cruelty becomes an illustration of Hemanga's vision of fetishistic dog-sexuality in human beings. Hemanga becomes the author of this perverse incest in a certain sense.

If Ani is possessed by his dead father, while violating his mother, it exposes another radical direction of intimate cruelty, bringing us back to a *père-version* of the father. Ani's perversion is his version of his father, a *père-version* that renders him at the service of the paternal *jouissance* over Monica. Ani thus becomes an object to deliver the paternal Other's *jouissance*. The spirit that possesses Ani is a nameless Other who echoes the novel's two patronyms: Debitosh and Hemanga. Monica as the *object-a* joins these two otherwise unrelated paternal names. If it is Debitosh's spirit, it places Ani and Hemanga in the same position of sexually enjoying Monica's body. This homology indicates the sharing of the incestual desire between Hemanga, the father and Ani, the son.

To conclude, *Kukur* unlocks a complex set of questions around sexual perversion and animality. It makes for a fruitful encounter with Lacanian paradigms of perversion. The literary text produces a new mythology of perversion here. It "invents" a particular aesthetic and cultural "sublimation" for the perverse, incestuous dog-fantasy that envisages human sexuality as perversion, if not *père-version*. Seen in this way, *Kukur* is a *sinthomatic* literary writing that invents a cultural narrative of sublimation for the problem of perversion by creating a new mythology. While the imaginary register of fantasy dominates the canine fetishism of sexuality, the symbolic order of language situates the non-rapport of sexes and in the process, glimpses the real of sexuality in incest. I have focused on the imaginary aspect of the dog-fantasy and the symbolic troping in the novel that draws attention to how language functions in the intersubjective domain of the Other. But, the novel's theme of sexual non-rapport that stumps language meets another level of impossibility in the sexual field, that is, incest. The novel comes to an end with an encounter with this real. Incest is encountered as the real of sex that stands with the absence of sexual relation as another real of sex.

The novel most radically underscores the problem of Otherness in perversion that we examined in the first part of the chapter. The dog becomes a crucial non-human instance of the Other that resonates with Lacan's rare reflection on cruelty. But the inter-subjective dialectic goes well beyond the specularity of the imaginary order. The novel consistently underpins the symbolic dimension by highlighting Hemanga or the narrator's phrasings—their metaphors and analogies. The fantasy of the dog is linguistically articulated, finding a strong lexical dimension in Hemanga. As we have analysed, the novel opens up a whole chain of Others in the pervert subject's self-alienated *jouissance*. The pervert unknowingly serves this inter-species Other that takes its cue from human Others in an allegorical axis. *Kukur* as a textual act of inscription invents a perverse mythology of sexuality as the bridge between humanity and animality. It is this *sinthome* of literary writing that splices the two of the animal–human double. Perverse sexuality is envisaged as an intimate cruelty that writes the interval between the human and the animal.

Notes

1. Dany Nobus does not consider perversion as a structure. See his "Perversion in the 21st Century: A Psychoanalytic Conundrum." In *Perversion Now* (Switzerland: Palgrave, 2017).
2. Lacan, Jacques. Seminar of Jacques Lacan *Book VII: The Ethics of Psychoanalysis* (London: Routledge, 1992), 194.
3. Lacan, *Seminar VII*, 194–5.
4. Lacan, *Seminar of Jacques Lacan Book VIII: Transference* (Cambridge: Polity, 2017), 31.
5. Lacan, Jacques. *Seminar of Jacques Lacan Book V: Formations of the Unconscious* (Cambridge: Polity, 2017), 148.
6. Ibid, 269.
7. Ibid, 214–5.
8. Ibid, 217.
9. Ibid, 235.
10. Lacan, *Seminar of Jacques Lacan* Jacques. *Book VI: Desire and Its Interpretation* (Cambridge: Polity, 2019), 314.
11. Ibid, 442.

12. Ibid.
13. Ibid, 456.
14. Ibid, 152.
15. Lacan, Jacques. *Seminar of Jacques Lacan Book X: Anxiety* (Cambridge: Polity, 2014), 151.
16. Penny, James. *The World of Perversion* (New York: State University of New York Press, 2006), 21.
17. Ibid.
18. Lacan, Jacques. *Seminar of Jacques Lacan Book XI: The Four Fundamental Concepts of Psychoanalysis* (New York: Norton, 1998), 185.
19. Lacan, Jacques. *Seminar of Jacques Lacan Book VI: Desire and Its Interpretation*, 462.
20. Ibid, 464.
21. Ibid, 465.
22. Ibid.
23. Ibid, 484.
24. Lacan, *Seminar X*, 150.
25. Benvenuto, Sergio. *What are Perversions?* (London: Karnac, 2016), 98.
26. Lacan, *Seminar V*, 219.
27. Ibid, 213.
28. Ibid, 220.
29. Ibid, 221.
30. Lacan, Jacques. *Seminar of Jacques Lacan Book XIV: The Logic of Fantasy*, session of 14.06.1967.
31. Ibid.
32. Ibid.
33. Ibid.
34. Lacan, Jacques. *Seminar of Jacques Lacan Book XX: On Feminine Sexuality: The Limits of Love and Knowledge* (London: Norton, 1999), 144.
35. Lacan, Jacques. *Seminar of Jacques Lacan Book XXIII: The Sinthome* (Cambridge: Polity, 2016), 11.
36. Lacan, *Seminar XXIII*, 131.
37. Lacan, Jacques. *Seminar of Jacques Lacan Book XXII: RSI*, session of 11.03.1975.
38. Ibid.
39. Ibid.
40. Ibid, session of 15.04.1975.
41. Ibid.

42. Caine, Diana and Colin Wright (eds.). *Perversion Now* (Switzerland: Palgrave, 2017), 16.
43. Ibid, 165.
44. Deleuze, Gilles. *Coldness and Cruelty* (New York: Zone Books, 1991), 52.
45. Ibid.
46. Lacan, Jacques. *Ecrits* (London: Norton, 2006), 120.
47. Ibid.
48. Ibid.
49. Chattopadhyay, Sandipan. "Bharotborsho (India)." In *Uponyash Shomogro-3* (Kolkata: Ajkal, 2006), 437.
50. Marcuse qtd in Chattopadhyay, Ibid, 143. All translations from Sandipan Chattopadhyay throughout the chapter are mine.
51. Chattopadhyay, Ibid, 244.
52. Chattopadhyay, Ibid, 244.
53. Ibid, 245.
54. Ibid, 187.
55. Ibid, 189.
56. Ibid.
57. Ibid, 191.
58. Ibid, 192.
59. Ibid, 193.
60. Ibid, 194.
61. Ibid, 203.
62. Ibid, 205.
63. Ibid, 206.
64. Ibid, 217.
65. Ibid.
66. Ibid, 218.
67. Ibid.
68. Ibid, 219.
69. Ibid, 220.
70. Ibid, 223.
71. Ibid, 228.
72. Ibid, 227.
73. Ibid, 229.
74. Ibid, 231.
75. Ibid, 233.
76. Ibid, 239.

77. Ibid.
78. Ibid.
79. Ibid, 240.
80. Ibid, 243.

Bibliography

Benvenuto, Sergio. *What are Perversions?: Sexuality, Ethics, Psychoanalysis*. London: Karnac, 2016.

Caine, Diana and Colin Wright (eds.). *Perversion Now*. Switzerland: Palgrave Macmillan, 2017.

Chattopadhyay, Sandipan. "Kukur." In *Uponyash Shomogro-3* (*Complete Novels-3*) Kolkata: Ajkal, 2006.

Deleuze, Gilles. *Coldness and Cruelty*. Translated by Jean McNeil. New York: Zone Books, 1991.

Lacan, Jacques. *Seminar of Jacques Lacan Book VII: Ethics of Psychoanalysis*. Edited by Jacques-Alain Miller. Translated by Dennis Porter. London: Routledge, 1992.

———. *Seminar of Jacques Lacan Book XI: The Four Fundamental Concepts of Psychoanalysis*. Edited by Jacques-Alain Miller. Translated by Alan Sheridan. New York: Norton, 1998.

———. *Seminar of Jacques Lacan Book XX: On Feminine Sexuality: The Limits of Love and Knowledge*. Edited by Jacques-Alain Miller. Translated by Russell Grigg. London: Norton, 1999.

———. *Ecrits*. Translated by Bruce Fink, London: Norton, 2006.

———. *Seminar of Jacques Lacan Book X: Anxiety*. Edited by Jacques-Alain Miller. Translated by A.R. Price. Cambridge: Polity, 2014.

———. *Seminar of Jacques Lacan Book XXIII: The Sinthome*. Edited by Jacques-Alain Miller. Translated by A.R. Price. Cambridge: Polity, 2016.

———. *Seminar of Jacques Lacan Book V (Keep the Same Way for All the Rest of Lacan Seminars): Formations of the Unconscious*. Edited by Jacques-Alain Miller. Translated by Russell Grigg. Cambridge: Polity, 2017a.

———. *Seminar of Jacques Lacan Book VIII: Transference*. Edited by Jacques-Alain Miller. Translated by Bruce Fink. Cambridge: Polity, 2017b.

———. *Seminar of Jacques Lacan Book VI: Desire and Its Interpretation*. Edited by Jacques-Alain Miller. Translated by Bruce Fink. Cambridge: Polity, 2019.

———. *Seminar of Jacques Lacan Book XIV: The Logic of Fantasy*. Translated by Cormac Gallagher. http://www.lacaninireland.com/web/wp-content/uploads/2010/06/14-Logic-of-Phantasy-Complete.pdf. Accessed March 1, 2021.

———. *Seminar of Jacques Lacan Book XXII*: RSI. Translated by Cormac Gallagher. http://www.lacaninireland.com/web/wp-content/uploads/2010/06/RSI-Complete-With-Diagrams.pdf. Accessed March 1, 2021.

Newman, Michael. "The Ball-Joint and the Anagram: Perversion and Jouissance in Hans Bellmer." In *Perversion Now*. Edited by Diana Caine and Colin Wright, 157–168. Switzerland: Palgrave Macmillan, 2017.

Nobus, Dany. "Perversion in the 21st Century: A Psychoanalytic Conundrum." In *Perversion Now*. Edited by Diana Caine and Colin Wright, 93–108. Switzerland: Palgrave Macmillan, 2017.

Penny, James. *The World of Perversion: Psychoanalysis and the Impossible Absolute of Desire*. New York: State University of New York Press, 2006.

4

On the Right to Jouissance

Gregg Lambert

In this chapter, I will return to a commonplace topic of Lacanian commentary in order, once again, to interrogate the proposition that Sade represents the truth of Kant's moral law. This truth-claim has been written in several ways, but usually takes the form of the following proposition, established by Slavoj Žižek, that "Sade is to be taken as the truth of Kant."[1] It will be my contention that we still have little understanding of what this might mean for us today, a fact which has been frustrated by reducing the complexity of Lacan's original statement to a simple proposition. Here is the original proposition in question in French to avoid any question on this point: "*Si, apres avoir vu qu'elle s'y accorde, nous demontrons qu'elle la complete, nous dirons qu'elle donne la verité de la Critique.*"[2] The statement is translated by Fink in its full context as follows: "The *Philosophy of the Bedroom* came eight years after *The Critique of Practical Reason*. If, after showing that the former is consistent with the latter, I shall be able to claim that it yields the truth of the Critique."[3] Although

G. Lambert (✉)
Syracuse University, Syracuse, NY, USA
e-mail: glambert@syr.edu

M. Lee (ed.), *Lacan's Cruelty*, The Palgrave Lacan Series,
https://doi.org/10.1007/978-3-031-06238-4_4

at first it might appear that both formulations of the proposition are the same, the difference lies in what logicians would call "the time of conclusion." In other words, whereas Žižek's statement appears self-evident, Lacan's is offered as a premise of a demonstration, the conclusion of which is more like a legal judgment that will occur at the end of the trial. It is only at that point that we can legitimately say that "it [i.e., *Philosophy in the Bedroom*] gives the truth," not of Kant, but rather of the *Critique of Practical Reason* concerning the a priori condition of the moral law.

For some, the difference I have underscored may seem like splitting hairs; however, I am simply pointing out the absence of the conditional tense that is present in Lacan's original phrasing of 1963, the trace of an original historical context in the immediate wake of post-war France and can also be found in several other revolutionary tracts published during this same period. Commensurate with the mantra of the Existentialist philosophy (i.e., "everything is permitted") that was popularized by Sartre for a younger generation of French intelligentsia, these writings were especially occasioned by the actual trial of Sade's French publisher sixteen years earlier, which instigated a flurry of depositions concerning moral worth of the Sadean experience. For example, I refer to a few of the texts and writers who are cross-referenced through Sade: Klossowski, *Sade mon prochain* (1947); Paulhan, *"Le marquis de Sade et sa complice"* (1947), Blanchot, *Lautreamont et Sade* (1949), Caillois, *L'Homme et le Sacre* (1950), Bataille, *L'Eroticism* (1957), De Beauvoir, *Marquis de Sade* (1961). Of course, one discovers that this context is completely absent from Žižek's rephrasing of the truth of Sade, and perhaps this is what allows him to reduce this truth to a simple allegory of reading. I hope I am not making too much of this context; however, I would argue that the true value of the Sadean experience remains somewhat remote for us today, and that it is no longer our historical distance from this experience—*in fact, it is our proximity!*—that today prevents us from perceiving the originality of Lacan's gesture of reading "Kant with Sade."

In the context of the moral and legal controversy surrounding the publication of Sade's writings sixteen years earlier, Lacan's own presentation of "Kant with Sade" can be read as a brilliant legal defense before the moral tribunal, the major argument of which can be phrased as follows: "You put Sade on trial, but you've got the wrong man! In fact, the true subject of this proceeding should have been Kant all along!" The major argument for the defense is that Sade can be charged as being nothing more than a willing accomplice, since his "calumny" was completely authorized by the Kantian categorical imperative—that is, Sade who merely *institutes* the Kantian moral law, since the maxim of the Sadean experience obeys the criteria that Kant prescribed concerning the complete deduction of pure practical reason. Lacan transcribes the Sadean maxim from the second chapter, "On the Concept of an Object of Pure Practical Reason": "'I have the right to enjoy your body,' anyone can say to me, 'and I will exercise this right without any limit to the capriciousness of the exactions I may wish to satiate your body.'"[4] At first, it could appear that the argument for the defense is purely circumstantial and speculative, based on the fact that *The Philosophy in the Bedroom* appeared eight years after the *Critique of Practical Reason*, which was published in 1788. Here, there is an implicit hypothesis that while he was in the Bastille, a year before he was transferred to the asylum at Charenton, he had been afforded ample time for reading and writing, and as a wealthy nobleman he bribed the guards to smuggle in the latest works of philosophy, especially the most recent cutting-edge works in moral philosophy coming out of Germany. According to this intrigue, a copy of Kant's latest treatise suddenly fell into his willing hands. In reading through Kant's meticulous argument concerning the a priori determination of the object of the Highest Good, Sade suddenly had an "Eureka effect," which might be compared with the discovery of an Archemedean point. Sade realized that the Kantian formula of the Categorical Imperative could be employed as the primary vehicle for his revolutionary anti-clerical program: a demonstration of the maxim concerning the supreme principle of *Jouissance* (i.e., the form of sexual enjoyment that assumes as its object the Highest Good) *is nothing less than a fundamental human right!*

At this point, of course, we might expect that the prosecution might object—as many Kantians have—that what Sade merely accomplishes is to "instrumentalize" the Categorical Imperative in the manner of what Kant had already named as the "hypothetical imperative"; thereby demoting the object of the moral will to an impure and pathological determination of the highest good. This is the first meaning of "perversion," which is the inversion or reversal (*Verkerht*) in the sense of substituting the lower for the higher value, but in the Nietzschean sense of overturning of all previous higher Christian values (piety, charity, devotion, respect, etc.) by placing the passions that were originally degraded and excluded in their former position. At first blush (here, the prosecution continues), the perversion of the source of all higher values can easily be dismissed out of hand since it violates the Kantian dictum that the a priori determination of the moral good cannot be based on the feelings of pleasure or displeasure (i.e., by a passive receptivity belonging to inner sense). Therefore, the concept of ultimate "well-being" (*Das Gute*) cannot be based upon any sensation of gratification, no matter how supreme, that can be experienced by the empirical subject.

In his reply to this objection, Lacan points out an instance in the deduction of the source of the moral good where Kant himself must admit that the negative effect of the moral law on the subject's desire is, in fact, a sensible *feeling* (*Gefühl*). "Consequently," he concludes:

> we can now see a priori that the moral law as the determining basis of the will, by infringing all our inclinations, must bring about a feeling that can be called pain; and here we have, then, the first and perhaps the only case where we have been able to determine from a priori concepts the relation of a cognition (here a cognition of pure practical reason) to the feeling of pleasure or displeasure.[5]

However, the "sense of feeling" that is the basis of Kant's use of *Gefühl* in this instance is not the same as the reflexive perception of the sense organs, which is the source of *Empfindung* that determines the object of sensation. Although it belongs to the sensibility according to the requirement of reason's presentation of the subjective affects of inclination or inhibition, this feeling is directly attached to the intention of the subject's will and is not contingent upon any object of sensation (i.e., the sense organs, the body, etc.). Thus, Lacan underlines the passages in the original argument that show how the negative effects of the moral law actually function as a "counterweight" to the pathologically determined feelings of selfishness (*solipsismus*), self-conceit (*arogantia*), and even "self-love" or "self-benevolence" (*Wohlwollen*). In each case, it is crucial to see that the negative feeling introjected by the moral law inhibits the subject from taking its own image of "well-being" as the object-cause of desire, or in Lacanian terms, effects a permanent war against the imaginary edifice of the Ego.

For example, as Kant says, while the moral law simply "impairs" (*Abbruch*) the pathological feelings of love for oneself, it "strikes dead" (*erschlagen*) all the egotistic virtues of arrogance, pride, and self-conceit altogether.[6] It is according to this sense that the power of the will itself is felt either as a kind of pleasure or pain the cause of which is the joyful or debilitating effects of "the desire of the Other" on the "self-love" of the Ego. It is here we can see the precise meaning of what Lacan refers to as Kant's "Copernican revolution," the "truth" of which is confirmed by Sade: whereas ancient moral philosophies of the Stoics and the Cynics located the primary conflict between reason and the sensibility in the inhibition of one's own body's pleasures and displeasures (primarily concerned the "care" for one's own bodily drives and passions, as Foucault has shown us), modern morality directs this conflict toward a feeling (*Gefühl*) that can only be located in another body, which must be subjugated by the pure will. In Book II of the *Critique of Practical Reason* ("On a Dialectic of Pure Reason in Determining the Concept of the Highest Good"), only the feeling of pure reason provides the subject with "the sole source of an unchangeable satisfaction that can be called rational."[7] Lacan traces the evolution of this moral feeling from the Stoic attitude of "indifference" (*adiaphora*) to the bourgeois invention of scientific rationality, and finally, to the subject of the Sadean executioner. (Of course, this genealogy is not originally Lacan's own construction, but rather one he had actually pilfered from the third chapter of Horkheimer and Adorno's *Dialectic of Enlightenment*, a mimeographed copy of which had been circulating around Paris during this period.)[8] Nevertheless, it is the supreme indifference on the part of the moral law to the sensible determination of pleasure or displeasure of the body, a feeling that can only be understood by the pathologically determined Ego as extreme apathy (i.e., not merely indifference, but the desire for cruelty). Kant defines this feeling as a "negative liking for one's existence," which, just as in Stoic *autarkeia*, is also directed toward the pleasures and pains of the body; except in the case of modern morality, this feeling must now be directed toward the bodies of others.

It is precisely this expansion of the subject's power to affect itself through the instrument of the moral law that its truth now takes a dialectical path through the body of another, which demands that its principle be communicated directly to the locus of the subject's freedom to desire. Kant demands that the power of desire be communicated and thus shared between a maximum number of subjects, and Sade demands that feeling of desire must become generalizable as the universal right that is affected through the Sadean experience of the moral law. Therefore, what Lacan chooses to call *jouissance* can be now defined as a "moral feeling" of the most supreme Good that attaches directly to the extreme or quantitative limit of the subjective experience of desire. I have already shown this subjective determination was already present in Kant, who argued that this supreme feeling "cannot be classed either with gratification or with pain, and yet it produces an interest in compliance with the law, which can be called *moral* interest."[9] In other words, while pleasure or displeasure can be felt by the subject alone (*solipsismus*), given that its locus is the body's own sensibility, desire requires a maximal extension of the will that assumes the form of a community of intelligent beings, just as the corresponding moral feeling necessarily requires the multiplication of bodies to convert this feeling into the form of a "general will" (i.e., law). In other words, one can no longer privately enjoy one's own "well-being" (*bien-être*), as was the case with the Stoic conception of happiness as "self-sufficiency" (*Selbstfriedenheit*), which could be translated into Freudian terminology as "secondary narcissism."

At this point, we can now return to the maxim that "Sade is to be taken as the truth of Kant" and revise our understanding of the concept of truth as properly dialectical, following the Lacanian demonstration. As Lacan said concerning this dialectical path, it is only halftime, "even though we are still ahead."[10] I will now conclude my own demonstration by completing this dialectic; however, I will read it forward from *Sade to Kant*, and not backward, from *Kant to Sade*, as Lacan did. In one of those examples of famous missed encounters, instead of reading *The Critique of Practical Reason*, if Lacan had found a copy of *The Science of Right* (*Rechtlehre*), which was published just a year after *Philosophy in the Bedroom* in 1796, he would have discovered a deduction of the juridical law in the form of a jurisprudence that in many ways takes the Sadean moral universe as its very point of departure (although, as I will show, Kant's original aim was to restrict the Sadean right to *jouissance* so that it would be compatible with Bourgeois post-revolutionary society). Here, I will not bother speculating whether Kant kept up on the revolutionary literature that was circulating throughout Europe during the "reign of terror," which was a bit like pornography for German philosophers of this period, and suddenly discovered Sade's "modest proposal" slipped in between the sheets of *Philosophy in the Bedroom*. If we were to entertain such a delicious fiction, certainly the revolutionary moral treatise would naturally be of great interest, not only because he might accept the plagiarism as a secret act of homage to his own moral philosophy, but because concerns nothing less than the sublime destination of the Republican constitution, which was a favorite topic for the late Kant!

What Lacan would have immediately discovered in the later document, which is different from the purely speculative critique of practical reason, is what he referred to as the conclusion of the dialectic when all the maxims that comprise the categorical imperatives are realized into a concrete system of rights, or positive laws. To begin, Kant argues that the distinction between natural law and legal right is temporal; therefore, the adage that *might makes right* is merely provisional, and it is only legal right that guarantees that you can keep what you have already stolen in the first place. (Of course, this will become the principal interpretation of Marx as well.) Therefore, "anything External is acquired by a certain free Exercise of Will that is either unilateral, as the act of a single Will (*de facto*), or bilateral, as the act of two Wills (*pacto*), or omnilateral, as the act of all the Wills of a Community together (*lege*)."[11] Second, after establishing the legal basis for the division between "mine and thine" as the founding principle of private property ("ownership of the soil"), Kant establishes the legal right to own another's sexual organs, if not their entire personhood (*Persönlichtkeit*), but only under the condition of the reciprocity of the action:

> For, this natural '*Commercium*'—as a '*usus membrorum sexualium alterius*'—is an enjoyment for which the one person is given up to the other. In this relation the human individual makes himself a '*res*,' which is contrary to the Right of Humanity in his own Person. This, however, is only

> possible under the one condition, that as the one Person is acquired by the other as a *res*, that same Person also equally acquires the other reciprocally, and thus regains and re-establishes the rational Personality.[12]

In other words, to possess the part also "signifies" the possession of the entire person, and here the signifying relation is a synecdoche. For example, when I claim to possess the sail or rudder of a ship (*de facto*), am I not also claiming that I own the entire ship? According to the same principle of reason, however, the subject would enjoy the right to possess another's sexual organs, or to occupy their body as external *res* (a thing).

Concerning the act of mutual possession, the first observation to be made, of course, is the presupposition of the equality of the sexes as the condition of the reciprocity of the act, but the second is the requirement that the act be both unconditional and permanent in order to rectify the major contradiction that is introduced in the categorical imperative that the "Humanity in the person" not be used as a means but is an end in itself, which is the second sense of the "thing" (*Das Ding*). Thus, it is only for this reason that Kant insists on monogamy and the permanent nature of the civil contract of marriage as the only legal exception to the exclusion of the ownership of another person, *pars pro toto*, but immediately excludes what could be called purely "service contracts"—for example, prostitution (*pactum fornicationis*), concubinage or pornography (*pactum turpe*), "left handed marriages" contracted to turn the social in equality into an advantage for one or both parties, and finally, Kant even excludes the biological determination of marriage for the reproduction of children.[13] Thus, as he concludes, the only guarantee of the permanence of the contract is law (*leges*), that is,

> the juridical consequence of the obligation that is formed by two Persons entering into a sexual Union solely on the basis of a reciprocal Possession of each other, which Possession at the same time is only effected in reality by the reciprocal '*usus facultatum sexualium* alterius' (the special use of the sexual faculty).[14]

I will return in a moment to address the first observation through Lacan's criticism of this appearance of "reciprocity in structures, especially subjective ones, that are strictly incompatible with reciprocity," but first we must ask what is a contract and how does it determine the reciprocal relation between a law (*leges*) and a Right (*jus*)? In the analysis of the contract, Kant stipulates four moments or acts that must be fulfilled for the right to be legitimate, particularly in the case of the right to possess or to occupy an external thing (*res*) such as the body of another person:

> In every CONTRACT there are four Juridical Acts of Will involved; two of them being preparatory Acts, and two of them constitutive Acts. The two Preparatory Acts, as forms of treating in the Transaction, are OFFER (*oblatio*) and APPROVAL (*approbatio*); the two Constitutive Acts, as the forms of concluding the transaction, are PROMISE (*promissum*) and ACCEPTANCE (*acceptatio*).[15]

The term of each separate act must be fulfilled and forms a condition of the others, since an *offer* must be *approved* as agreeable to the other party before a *promise* of delivery or transfer can take place and is accepted by the same party. Moreover, Kant argues, the constitutive acts of promising and accepting do not follow one another in time, but rather occur "simultaneously" as it were, conferring upon the contract both its permanent signifying character and its objective status as a "fact." What is interesting in all this is the acts of offering, approving, promising, and accepting are all performative by expressing in language what is not yet the actual possession of thing in question. For real possession to take place, two further acts must occur which are outside the speech-act of the legal contract, but which every contract refers to in a performative manner, which are "transfer" and "acquisition." It is here we see the entire problematic that Kant is attempting to address, which is the delayed temporality between promise (which is symbolic) and acquisition (which is real); "hence, the Right arising from a contract is only a Personal [subjective] Right, and it only becomes a Real [objective] Right by delivery."[16] This is nothing other than what Lacan enunciates as the signifying dimension of the law, which refers to an object of a statement rather than to the thing itself.

To illustrate this temporal problem, I will take up the same example that Kant employs to discuss a "possessory act" (*actum possessorium*) concerning the sale of a certain horse, especially when possession is not immediate. In such a case, the contract can only take as its object the statement by the seller "I will deliver the horse to you on Tuesday," which might also be comparable to the statement of the marriage vow in consigning the delivery of the goods in question to some indefinite point in the future (e.g., "until death do you part"). Of course, the right over one's own sexual organs are not comparable to the sale of a horse, since they remain permanently corralled in the original owner's barn, so to speak, and under the personal will of the previous owner. In other words, the problem is that the legal contract of marriage creates a formal right to possess the person an object of the law but leaves the personal right over the body and its sexual organs intact. In other words, because the nature of the contract (*pacto*) between two wills is merely subjective, there must be an objective side to the agreement in order to guarantee that the "harmony between the two wills" is "real in kind" and has the characteristic of an objective fact. The maintenance of objective harmony between two wills is the necessary principle of the will to maintain unity with its own concept, especially when it is divided up between two subjects (or, according to Lacanian algebra, when the subject's own will has to be "pinned together into a single body" by the barred *S*).[17] On the other hand, if the contract was only bilateral or an act of two wills, the voluntary breaking of the contract would destroy the necessary fiction of the legal personality (*Persönlichtkeit*), and it solely for this reason the contract must also be compelled by force of Law in order to guarantee the permanence of its Subject.

The second problem and more serious problem is that the sexual right is no longer based on pleasure or happiness, but rather on something that resembles moral respect for the other's entire person. Therefore, pleasure is indeed repressed by the law (albeit not prohibited, but rather according to the psychoanalytic understanding as "deferred" or "delayed") but only by taking the Humanity in the person of the other as its object, *which cannot be an object of pleasure*, but only the object of pure practical reason (i.e., will, desire). Although this might also be felt by the subject of pleasure as a form of pain or inhibition, it defers the moment of gratification to a higher form of desire and to a moral feeling of "respect" for the entire person. Thus, Kant compares this elevation of the pathological object of pleasure to an object that is placed in elliptical orbit by the law whereby the highest point may be regarded as at the same time both rising and falling, or according to the analogy, the point where the body as object of "mine and thine" is shared equally by both subjects without suffering the loss of personal right over their own bodies. "This continuity, however, implies that it is not a particular will of either the promisor or the acceptor, but their united Will in common, that transfers what is mine to another."[18] However, the point is that the subject would never have access to a higher form of desire without the law taking the supersensible idea of the unified personhood (*Persönlichtkeit*) as its sole object. In other words, here we might find a modern version of Stoicism that Lacan often ascribes to Kantian moral philosophy, except that instead of a feeling of complete indifference to the body as an "external thing," which Plato had earlier condemned to the tomb, Kant chooses instead to leave in place the pleasures of the body under the categorical requirement of pure practical reason that the moral law *must* maintain a relationship with the pleasure and pain that determines the object of sensibility.

At this point, let us now turn to Sade's concept of right that is delivered a year earlier in the manifesto "Yet Another Effort, Frenchmen, If You Would Become Republicans."

After having made it clear in the preamble that any remaining superstitions of Theism should be rooted out of the post-revolutionary Republican constitution, in the "philosophy of manners" that follows and comprises the entire second part of the manifesto, a major point of contrast with Kant would be the complete rejection of any further legal claim of the institution of Monogamy, which is only the final form of slavery invented by religious custom and maintained by Bourgeois civil society:

> The act of possession can only be exercised upon a chattel or an animal, never upon an individual who resembles us, and all the ties which can bind a woman to a man are quite as unjust as illusory. […] Never may an act of possession be exercised upon a free being; the exclusive possession of a woman is no less unjust than the possession of slaves; all men are born free, all have equal rights: never should we lose sight of those principles; according to which never may there be granted to one sex the legitimate right to

> lay monopolizing hands upon the other, and never may one of these sexes, or classes, arbitrarily possess the other.[19]

However, instead of ascribing the legal right of possession of the body and its sexual organs to one sex, or even to both sexes in the case of monogamy, Sade consigns the possession of the body of all women to the entire community. It is on this basis that Sade declares as a maxim that no woman can refuse a sexual possession of her *res* based on the exclusion of private property, since all men may possess the body of all women as the embodiment of the "humanity in her person." Hence,

> [A] woman existing in the purity of Nature's laws cannot allege, as justification for refusing herself to someone who desires her, the love she bears another, because such a response is based upon exclusion, and no man may be excluded from the having of a woman as of the moment it is clear she definitely belongs to all men, then it becomes incontestable that we have received from Nature the right indiscriminately to express our wishes to all women, it likewise becomes incontestable that we have the right to compel their submission, not exclusively, for I should then be contradicting myself, but temporarily. It cannot be denied that we have the right to decree laws that compel woman to yield to the flames of him who would have her; violence itself being one of that right's effects, we can employ it lawfully. Indeed! has Nature not proven that we have that right, by bestowing upon us the strength needed to bend women to our will?[20]

According to the Sadean maxim of the universal right to jouissance, therefore, a woman existing in the purity of Nature's laws cannot allege, as justification for refusing herself to someone who desires her, the love she bears another, because such a response is based upon private exclusion of personal property, and no man may be excluded from the having of a woman as of the moment it is clear she definitely belongs to all men. In other words, in keeping with the effect of perversion as inversion between part and whole, Sade declares that because the community already possesses the whole person that I have right to use its parts (it's sexual organs) as common property. Here, one can see a revolutionary principle of the "common possession" of property is applied to the body as the primary *res* of property in the division of mine and thine. Thus, in the constitution of a Republic that abolishes the very principle of private property, then all private contracts and pacts between individuals or classes that were the very basis of the claim to the body as private property—and especially the pleasure of a woman's body that was fashioned by the Christian virtue of chastity—are also null and void. At this point, the right to the other's body that Kant had wanted to restrict to a very special civil contract (*pacto*) between the sexes is thereby fashioned into a maxim of universal right that can only be guaranteed by objective law (*leges*).

It is clear from this outcome that the Sadean moral universe is no less moral than the Kantian one, since both are conditioned by the concept of freedom and equality of all reasonable beings, given that sexual satisfaction is no longer determined as a private end of the individual, but rather as the necessary and universal good of the community. In the end, the only difference between the Kantian maxim of the moral law of monogamy and the Sadean maxim of universal *jouissance* is the principle of law that guarantees the right over another's individual's body as the will of the community. As Lacan says, however, while the former deduces the moral law from an existing right, the latter depends on the existence of a society that might one day exist that would forcibly implement this maxim as the legal basis of personhood, so that everyone's jouissance will be submitted to all the wills of the community.[21] In other words, a simple error of jurisprudence has occurred in the history of modern commentary on Sade in formulating what remains only a speculative maxim of universal right as if it were a real objective law (*leges*). In this regard, the Sadean maxim has suffered the same ambiguity as other maxims concerning universal human rights; in addition to encountering multiple empirical and practical obstacles, it has never achieved a complete agreement on the part of the entire human community and is still restricted for the most part to legal sexual minorities. In other words, by translating the Sadean maxim of the right to *jouissance* into a universal human right that must be enjoyed by everyone, it has actually turned it into just another impractical idea like world peace, and this becomes a constant source of frustration and pain for the real practical subjects of sadism and masochism today. (Here, I would simply point to the history of the legal battles engaged by the BDSM community.)

On the other hand, let us not imagine for one moment that if the right to *jouissance* were one day to be legislated in the constitution of the new Republic, it would be any less repressive or overtly coercive (i.e., compelled by force of law), especially since the act of coming would now become a "moral duty" that the subject must perform on command, rather than a pathologically determined pleasure that often seems to occur by happy accident, as if according to will of some unknown prime mover who might be comparable to God. We could formulate the Sadean categorical imperative as "you have the duty to enjoy!" which can also be heard by the addressor (*sujet d'enunciation*) as "you have the duty to take advantage" (*vous avez le devoir de profiter*). The only difference is that the "feeling" (*Gefühl*) of pain effected by the Kantian moral law, and the consequent feeling of disempowerment and humiliation suffered by the ego, would be reduced to the punctiform command—"Enjoy!" (*jouir!*). Thus, under the Sadean injunction, the object of the will is the pure act of jouissance, which is why any continuation of the subject's impure and pathological demand for pleasure is either met with a Stoic indifference or "scorn," as Lacan also observed, often accompanied by insults directed against the Ego's bodily image (*Körper-Ich*), reinforced by punishments inflicted on the body itself.

At the same time, Lacan himself can be constantly heard to complain about the tedium of the Sadean scenes of jouissance that function more like geometrical diagrams than pornographic illustrations, as if they were also designed to drain the last once of pleasure from the bodies of victims and executioners alike. Here, it is significant that Sade often measures the quantity of semen according to the universal table of weights and measures, as in the example of the lugubrious final exchange between La Chevelier, Dolmance, and Eugenie, who exclaims: "Alas! dear master… you see how your disciples have accommodated me! I have a mouthful of fuck and half a pint in my ass, 'tis all I am disgorging on both ends."[22] If the Sadean maxim of jouissance is designed to enfranchise all the limits of Christian morality, these demonstrations have a comparable function as the schema of the imagination in the *Critique of Pure Reason*, which serve to provide sensuous representations of the concepts of the Understanding in accordance with the speculative interest of pure reason. Just as in the case of the first critique, all these demonstrations only manage to prove the absolute poverty of the imagination to present the pure idea of free moral will. Contrary to the idea that there are no limits to Sadean excesses, however, the conclusion of the manifesto contains a revelation that there is still what could be called a limit to jouissance; although, this limit does not strike against what is doable, anything that can be imagined must be permitted, but instead against what is "sayable," as if Sade was already prefiguring Wittgenstein's maxim concerning silence as a violation of the Kantian maxim of universal communication. Consequently, there are some acts that cannot be publicly demonstrated even though they can certainly be imagined; thus they are relegated to the silent and solipsistic space where the subject of desire can enjoy an almost limitless right to *jouissance*:

> MADAME DE SAINT-ANGE—Is there, do you think, any conceivable infamy we are not worthy to hear of and execute? LE CHEVALIER—Wait, sister. I'll tell you. (He whispers to the two women.) EUGENIE, with a look of revulsion—You are right, 'tis hideous. MADAME DE SAINT-ANGE—Why, I suspected as much. DOLMANCE—You see very well I had to be silent upon this caprice; and you grasp now that one must be alone and in the deepest shadow in order to give oneself over to such turpitudes.[23]

To now conclude our dialectic path leading up to the contemporary moment, we should acknowledge that while the vision of Sadean excess might have scandalized the original eighteenth-century readers, today it represents the most run of the mill and common scenes of pornography that are universally accessible by everyone on the web. Nevertheless, the same principles of tedium and incessant repetition are situated *beyond the pleasure principle*; although, the contemporary imagination is stripped of any intellectual or Stoic ethical dimension, and the moral feeling of pain has been replaced by an intense feeling of nausea! Therefore, returning to the temporal basis of the dialectic that "Sade can be taken as the truth of Kant," I would suggest that it is only after the Sadean truth of the moral law has been established as "real," that the truth of what Kant called pure practical reason is longer be possible for us today. In other words, neither the Sadean truth of Kant, nor the Kantian truth of Sade, determines the truth of the sexual relation today, especially given the dominantly held belief that the sexual relation exists in a manner that we can fashion it in just about any way we like, along with our bodies. And yet, while we can make endless new arrangements with the objects of our fantasy—in this regard, it is technology and not politics that has served us in our efforts to enfranchise every limit established by Bourgeois liberal society—nevertheless, we are still confronted by what Lacan called "the radical freedom of the Other" as a higher power of desire that neither Kant nor Sade would ever have dreamed of! For example, Kant would never have imagined that "the starry skies above us" would one day be claimed by billionaires flying in their own personal rocket ships, just as Sade would never have dreamed that "the moral law within us" would belong to the most common citizen, or that one day the law could be written down in porno books.

Notes

1. Slavoj Žižek, *For They Know Not What They Do: Enjoyment as a Political Factor* (London: Verso Publishing, 1991), 229.
2. Jacques Lacan, *Écrits* (Paris: Éditions du Seuil, 1966), 765–6.
3. Jacques Lacan, *Écrits*. Translated by Bruce Fink (New York: W.W. Norton, 1996), 646.
4. Ibid., 648.
5. Immanuel Kant, *Critique of Practical Reason*. Translated by Werner S. Pluhar (Indianapolis: Hackett Publishing Co, 2002), 96.
6. Ibid.
7. Ibid., 149.
8. See "Juliette or Enlightenment Morality," in Adorno-Horkheimer, *The Dialectic of Enlightenment*, trans. John Cumming (London: Verso, 1997), 80–119.
9. Kant, *Critique of Practical Reason*, 104.
10. Lacan, *Écrits* (1996), 660.
11. Kant, *The Philosophy of Law*, 85ff.
12. Kant, *The Philosophy of Law*, 111–2.
13. Kant, *The Philosophy of Law*, 110–2.
14. Kant, *The Philosophy of Law*, 113.

15. Kant, *The Philosophy of Law*, 101.
16. Ibid., 106.
17. Lacan, *Écrits* (1996), 654.
18. Kant, *Philosophy of Law*, 105.
19. Sade, *Philosophy in the Boudoir*, 146.
20. Ibid., 146.
21. Lacan, *Écrits* (1996), 648.
22. Sade, *Philosophy in the Boudoir*, 175.
23. Ibid., 175.

Bibliography

Horkheimer, Max and Adorno, Theodor. *The Dialectic of Enlightenment*. Translated by John Cumming. London: Verso, 1997.

Kant, Immanuel. *Critique of Practical Reason*. Translated by Werner S. Pluhar. Indianapolis: Hackett Publishing Co, 2002.

———. *The Philosophy of Law: An Exposition of the Fundamental Principles of Jurisprudence as the Science of Right*. Translated by W. Hastie, B.D. Edinburgh: T & T Clark, 2010.

Lacan, Jacques. *Écrits*. Paris: Éditions du Seuil, 1966.

———. *Écrits*. Translated by Bruce Fink. New York: W.W. Norton, 1996.

Sade, Marquis de. *Philosophy in the Boudoir*. Locus Elm Press (Kindle Ed.), n.d.

Zizek, Slavoj. *For They Know Not What They Do: Enjoyment as a Political Factor*. London: Verso Publishing, 1991.

5

A Perverse Fascination for Death and Jouissance: Bataille, Lacan and the Anti-social Turn in Queer Theory

Frédéric Baitinger

To the question "Is sex worth dying for?" Kant's answer is categoric. No rational man, applying to his action the moral maxim of his pure practical reason, would be willing to die for his lustful inclination.[1] However, according to Lacan, it would suffice to substitute for the idea of pleasure the one of jouissance for the whole example to be ruined.[2] Because jouissance, contrary to what one may think, should not be confused with the idea of pleasure, since it is always tie to an unconscious imperative to "enjoy," even when to "enjoy" means to suffer! Such is the cruel paradox that lies at the very heart of the notion of jouissance, and what makes of Kant's famous example of the Gallows man, an example that simply ignores the sinful nature of jouissance, which is to say the secret link that unites the notion of jouissance to the one of the death drive.

Lacan, in his famous text "Kant with Sade," went even further and argued that the structure of the moral subject, as defined by Kant in *The Critique of Practical Reason*, was similar to the structure of the subject

F. Baitinger (✉)
The Research Chair in Philosophy at the Hospital, GHU Psychiatry and Neuroscience, Paris, France

M. Lee (ed.), *Lacan's Cruelty*, The Palgrave Lacan Series,
https://doi.org/10.1007/978-3-031-06238-4_5

implied by the maxim defended by the marquis de Sade, both of them implying a subject gaining its agency out of a form of cruelty powered by the death drive.[3] Expanding on this idea in a text called "The Unconscious and the Speaking Body," Jacques-Alain Miller ventured for his part that the paradigm of our time was no longer the one of repression, so well analyzed by Freud in *Civilization and its Discontent* (1930), but the one of perversion, inasmuch as perversion implies the same structure, which is to say the same injunction coming from the super-ego, although this time it orders us to enjoy, to unleash our fantasies, to act upon them, even when theses fantasies keep disappointing us.[4]

And finally, it is as a reaction to this shift of paradigm (from repression to perversion) that some recent queer scholars belonging to what Jack Halberstam has called, "the Anti-Social Thesis in Queer Theory,"[5] made a return to Lacan's insight about jouissance and its relation to the death drive to support their right to opt out, which is to say to oppose the Imaginary injunction of the neoliberal super-ego to enjoy, to be happy, to keep working and consuming in agreement with the discourse of the master.[6]

If we look, indeed, at the work of one of its best representative, Lee Edelman, and pay particular attention to the way in which, in *No Future: Queer Theory and the Death Drive*, Edelman mobilizes Lacan's teaching, one can see that he does so to make visible the fact that the word queer does not refer only to the LGBTIQ++ movement and its political quest for recognition, but also to what incarnates the presence within society of the death drive. To substantiate his claim, Edelman uses one of Lacan's late inventions, the sinthome, to create a new term, sinthomosexuality, to which he assigns the task of conveying the idea that within queerness lies the sinthome, which "as a stupid enjoyment, as the node of senseless compulsion on which the subject's singularity depends—connects us to something Real beyond the 'discourse' of the symptom, connects us to the unsymbolyzable Thing over which we constantly stumble, and so, in turn, to the death drive, about which Lacan declares in his seminar devoted to the sinthome: 'The death drive, it is the Real in so far as it can only be thought as Impossible, which is to say that each time it shows the tip of its nose it is unthinkable.'"[7] By forging the word sinthomosexuality, Edelman makes apparent at the level of the letter the proximity between what remains meaningless in queerness[8] and the meaninglessness of one's own opaque mode of jouissance,[9] which, in turn, leads Edelman to advocate in favor of a queer politics that would not be framed by the meaningful framework of "reproductive futurism," but by what could be called, after Georges Bataille and its rereading by Derrida, an "expenditure without reserve."[10]

However, is this articulation put forth by Edelman and other anti-relational queer scholars between the death drive, the sinthome, the Real and the Bataillant notion of "expenditure without reserve," the only one capable of subverting the cruel optimism that lies at the core of "reproductive futurism"? Or is such articulation hiding a potential misunderstanding of the Lacanian notion of the sinthome and its articulation with the meaninglessness of jouissance and the death drive? To explore these questions, this chapter will show first how Georges Bataille's thinking, which was redescribed by Shannon Winnubst as pre-queer scholarship, foreshadowed through his definition of inner experience, the notion of queerness defended by Edelman and other anti-social thinkers.[11] Second, it will explain why Bataille's definition of inner experience, which was characterized by Allan Stoekl[12] as an urtext for Derrida's deconstruction, also furnished the basis upon which Lacan developed his notion of the Real,[13] and conceived his late approach to jouissance, which is at once an approach that takes into account, as Bataille and anti-social thinkers do, what unites the notion of jouissance to the one of the death drive,[14] but that is also working at "limiting" the cruelty and the morbidity contained in jouissance through one of Lacan's late clinical inventions: the "know how" [savoir faire].

Bataille's Queerness and the Death Drive

When Bataille wrote his book *Inner Experience* (1943) during the Second World War, he had the ambition to elaborate, very much like Edelman, a subjective experience that would not be subordinated to any form of salvation, and thus to any form of socially acceptable fantasies about what is good and what is evil. Because fantasies, according to Bataille, are always, in one way or another, what assigns to our jouissance its limits, which is why *inner experience*, as *queerness* for Edelman, opposes the power of fantasies when fantasies pretend to rule over jouissance. The crux of the matter being to recognize the limits that the Imaginary is imposing on jouissance in so far as it is linked to the negativity of the death drive. Which is also why, concludes Bataille, "no inner experience is possible for those who allow themselves to be dominated by pleasure and pain."[15] For to be dominated by pleasure and pain is to be dominated by the *pleasure principle*, and thus by the commonly accepted fantasies that work in agreement with this principle.[16] Unbound from such fantasies, Bataille's *inner experience*, like Edelman's anti-social sinthomosexuality, aspire to "naturally exceed the subordination of human life to the search from pleasure, to the flight from pain. It postulates a positive value beyond pleasure."[17]

Of course, to give a "positive value" to what stands beyond the pleasure principle is the "true" difficulty that weighs down the notion of inner experience, as well as what makes problematic the anti-social turn defended by Edelman and other queer scholars.[18] Well aware of this conundrum, Bataille admits that "the essential difficulty begins here. The search for a beyond in relation to immediate interests appears from the beginning as a principle of contestation."[19] Normally, what rules over human experience is what Bataille calls the possible and Edelman the Child.[20] The possible is equated by Bataille to the realm of organic life and its development in a favorable setting. The impossible, or queerness for Edelman, on the contrary, is equated to the presence of death in life. This is why we generally associate the possible with what is good, and the impossible with evil. As such, one could say that there exists a profound agreement between human experience and the possible, and that this agreement is what fuels human belief in God, or in authoritative figures thanks to whom the realm of the impossible is turned into an illusion, into a test imposed on men before eternal life. Bataille writes, "there is not an impossible if God exists, or at least the impossible is illusory: it is a test imposed on man while the triumph of the possible is given in advance."[21] As soon as the idea of God is given existence, its existence casts away the very possibility of the impossible as the expression of contingency, and substitutes for it something that has to do with man's guilt and misbehavior first, and then with the idea of salvation. Salvation being, for Bataille, the element in every religious system that indicates the will to escape the confrontation with the impossible. Likewise, for Edelman, the Child is the element in every political system that indicates the will to escape the confrontation with queerness, which is to say with "the place of the social order death drive."[22]

This is why Bataille's *inner experience*, just like Edelman's definition of queerness, by "asserting itself against futurity,"[23] is an experience that implies renouncing any desire for salvation or political recognition, as well as an experience that implies renouncing the most laudable illusion—happiness. For happiness, just like salvation or political recognition, reduces life to the realm of the possible and, consequently, rejects outside politics the presence of the death drive. Consequently, to affirm the possibility of *inner experience*, or *queerness* is to affirm that such presence cannot be completely overthrown. Even if we imagine, like Hegel or Fukuyama, the end of history as a moment of complete victory of the possible over the impossible, a certain remainder will persist. As Bataille states in "Nietzsche's Laughter,"

> an impossible exists in man that nothing will reduce, the same, in a fundamental way, for the happiest and for the most disinherited. The difference is in the illusion; happiness is no doubt a desirable form of illusion, but happiness can only defer the deadline. As we cannot limit ourselves to postponing the deadline, in the end, we can only face the impossible.[24]

The deadline that happiness (as an illusion) is postponing is the one of becoming fully conscious of the fact that at the very core of life does not stand the Good and the possible but, as the Marquis de Sade's works show, the impossible.

However, what is important to notice is that the impossible can be recognized only if the possible, or the fantasy of "reproductive futurism" for Edelman, has been also recognized as such. For if the possible is not recognized first, it will tend to deny the very existence of the impossible through the concept of salvation, or through the concept of the Good, or through the concept of the Child. And, reciprocally, the impossible, if not recognized as such, would be reduced to the domain of evil (from a religious point of view), instead of marking the place of the Real and the death drive. Bataille writes: "The impossible needs the possible from which to be disengaged. Salvation is the possible required by the mind for a confrontation with the impossible. But in salvation, the possible is the end of the impossible: it is therefore the evasion of the impossible."[25] The impossible or queerness is thus something that is inconceivable without the possible that constantly strives to reduce it to its own domain. And, reciprocally, the possible is what produces logically the impossible each time it fails to embrace what goes beyond it, or each time it discovers elements that cannot be reintegrated in its larger "positive" and thus meaningful narrative.

In "The Use-Value of D.A.F de Sade (An Open Letter to My Current Comrades)"[26] Bataille connects his reflection on the impossible to Sade's vision of morals, and gives to it a *use-value* that is not easy to grasp. For Sade's teaching is not addressed to the "normal man," nor is Edelman's teaching on queerness, in so far as the "normal man," submitted to "fear," and more broadly to the castration complex or the fantasy of "reproductive futurism," can only feel but disgust toward Sade's vision of the world. "The figure of Sade," writes Bataille, "is certainly unsympathetic to people moved by need and by fear. The sympathies and the dreads—the cowardice too, one must add—which determine man's usual behavior are diametrically opposed to the passion responsible for the sovereignty of the voluptuary."[27] Which is why, if one wants to discover the use-value of Sade, one has to learn how to think *with Sade*, which means that one has to learn how to think the human condition by putting at its very core the impossible, or queerness as Edelman defines it. Bataille writes:

> Without a profound complicity with natural forces such as violent death, gushing blood, sudden catastrophes and the horrible cries of pain that accompany them, terrifying ruptures of what had seemed to be immutable, the fall into stinking filth of what had been elevated–without a sadistic understanding of an incontestably thundering and torrential nature, there could be no revolutionaries, there could only be a revolting utopian sentimentality.[28]

But to come to terms with this sadistic understanding, it is first necessary to acknowledge that Sade's experience is grounded on a paradox. Put in a syllogism, this paradox goes as follows. If life is the pursuit of pleasure, and if the intensity of pleasure is a direct ratio of the destruction of life, then life can only reach its highest intensity through a monstrous denial of its own principle. To make the paradox more vivid, it is important to connect its first part—the pursuit of pleasure—to the fact that Sade's heroes have to destroy in themselves all the limits that society has tried to impose on their pursuit of pleasure. And second, that they have to come to terms with the "odd" fact that they have to apply to themselves the very principle that they use to subject others to their quest of pleasure. In other words, to make room for the impossible in their life, Sade's heroes have not only to deny the existence of others, but they have also to be able to fully deny their own existence. For it is only on that condition—which defines the condition of perversion for Lacan—that Sade's world becomes not only a world divided into victims and torturers, but a world where each torturer accepts, in the name of the impossible, to be the victim of someone else's pursuit of pleasure. Which is why Sade's world is a world in which the possible and the impossible are not only connected to one another, but one in which they ceaselessly pass into one another. In this regard, Sade's apathy should not be confused, as it is often the case, with a purely selfish quest for unlimited pleasure, but praised as a "moral" experience that requires a form of inner cruelty that is at the service of what Bataille calls "communication."

To illustrate his concept of communication, Bataille proposes, in "Discussion on Sin," a re-reading of the sacrifice of Christ on the Cross as a form of Sadean apathy.[29] From a Christian's point of view, this sacrifice represents the summit of evilness. Men, by accomplishing this act, not only killed an innocent man, but they also killed the Son of God himself. Nonetheless, it is also through this crime that the being of God was wounded by men for the first time, and that the being of men, in return, got wounded by God. Through the culpability that His murder generated in them (Felix Culpa!), men and God broke their isolation and started to "communicate" with one another. Which leads Bataille to conclude that "it thus becomes visible from here that the 'communication' between separate being is rendered possible by evil. Human beings, without the presence of evil, would be encapsulated within themselves, locked up in their independent sphere."[30] But if it is true, it also means that human beings are facing an "impossible" moral situation. They can either persevere in their own being at the price of maintaining their fundamental isolation from one another, or they can try to "communicate" with one another by taking the risk of violating their integrity as well as the integrity of others. In both cases, however, what is at stake is the way in which the death drive can be taken into account, and used to create a community of beings that are either the victims of their own cruelty, or the agent of a cruel and potentially perverse quest for communication and selflessness.

Bataille with Lacan: The Paradox of Jouissance

To understand how Bataille's thinking about the impossible, as well as his reading of Sade, had an influence on Lacan's own approach to ethics and jouissance, one has to understand, first, how Lacan considered the work of Sade, and the kind of misunderstanding that it could potentially engender, and especially in the thinking of "pioneers or militants embracing a radical position" like Bataille and Edelman.

Lacan, right at the opening of a lesson devoted to the question of "Jouissance and transgression," during his seminar year on *The Ethics of psychoanalysis*, says:

> I would like at least during this lecture to clear up the misunderstanding that might occur because we are dealing with Sade, and it might be thought that that constitutes a wholly external way of looking upon ourselves as pioneers or militants embracing a radical position. Such a view implies that, as a result of our function or profession, we are destined to embrace extremes, so to speak, and that Sade in this respect is our progenitor or precursor, who supposedly opened up some impasse, aberration or aporia, in that domain of ethics we have chosen to explore this year, and that we would be well-advised to follow him. It is very important to clear up that misunderstanding, which is related to a number of others I am struggling against in order to make some progress here before you.[31]

It is, I suppose, a fair guess to identify, under the periphrasis "militants embracing a radical position," not only the surrealists who praised Sade after Breton, but Bataille himself who was one of the few who took Sade's aberration very seriously. However, in order to be able to explain in more detail what Lacan is reproaching Bataille for and, indirectly, what Lacan would have perhaps reproached the "anti-social turn" in queer theory for, it is necessary to articulate better the relationship between the work of Kant, Sade and Freud.

In his text "Kant with Sade," Lacan introduced three thesis regarding the works of Kant, Sade and Freud.[32] In the first one, Lacan stated that "Sade did indeed begin the groundwork that was to progress for a hundred years in the depth of the taste in order for Freud's path to be passable,"[33] which is to say for Freud to be able to enunciate his pleasure principle without having to indicate what distinguishes it from the function of pleasure in traditional ethics. In his second thesis, Lacan put forward the idea that Sade's works were also representing, in this regard, the first step of an ethical subversion of which Kant marks the turning point. And finally, in his third thesis, Lacan ventured the idea that Sade's *Philosophy in the Bedroom* (1795) was not only consistent with Kant's *Critique of Practical Reason* (1788), but "it yields the truth of the Critique."[34] To justify his first thesis, Lacan argued that it was thanks to Sade's work that the Good lost its natural attraction and that Freud, freed from this bias, was finally able to approach scientifically the question of pleasure. To justify his second thesis about Kant's relation to Sade, Lacan underlined that Kant was in fact the first one to contest the natural attractiveness of the Good, which is to say the old link between the Supreme Good and the Supreme Truth on which the tradition of antiquity (of discriminating taste for various kinds of objects) was grounded. And by contesting this natural connection, Kant not only generated a kind of Terror in the field of ethics, but he also created a void; "The void of all that is 'pathological' in the subject. Pathological meaning, here, pathos, emotion, all the subject's sensory interests, everything that gives pleasure" as Miller puts it in "A discussion on Lacan's Kant with Sade,"[35] as well as a void that he filled with an inner "voice"—the voice of the super-ego—which he made appear at the very moment of the disappearance of the object. The Voice formulates an imperative. And the subject obeys it.

Which brings us to Lacan's third thesis about Sade's relation to Kant, which Lacan justified by saying that while the Voice, in Kant's work, presents itself as an auto-affection of the subject, in Sade's work, it reveals its true nature in so far as Sade's paradox, as Bataille described it, exhibits the inner division of the subject, while making the sadistic component of the super-ego visible, and not hidden in the depth of the moral subject. In the formulation, "I have the right to enjoy any parts of your body," the "I" is not the one of the one speaking, but the "I" of the one who will abuse. This is why the subject is split in two parts. Thus, the subject is no longer S, but $ as it is split between the Other and itself. In Sade's characters, the law reveals itself as being the inverse of desire and vice versa since what we call duty (moral duty) is connected to the drives and libidinal enjoyment. Miller writes:

> Hence, my client is much more honest than Kant. Kant leads us to believe that the subject is speaking to himself, enunciating a law that terrorizes him. Whereas Sade presents us with a formulation in which the distinction between subject and other is explicit. He reveals the division of the subject, whereas Kant makes us think it is an auto-affectation.[36]

From there, one can conclude that Bataille's reading of Sade prefigured, in a way, the one of Lacan in the sense that it also emphasized what was related, in Sade's apathy, to Kant's rejection of the old link between the supreme Good and the supreme Truth. But Lacan's reading of Sade differs from the one of Bataille in as much as Lacan does not make of Sade's experience of apathy the product of a transgression of the moral law, but rather what reveals the division of the subject, and the impact of the sadistic super-ego on the subject's mode of jouissance.[37] More importantly, Lacan's reading of Sade leads also to questioning the potentially perverse nature of Bataille's effort to think with Sade, and especially when it comes to articulating between the notion of jouissance and the notion of knowledge, since Bataille's inner experience, like Edelman's experience of queerness, is not only opposed to knowledge when knowledge claims to rule over experience, but it also culminates, as we will see, in a form of non-knowledge.

For Lacan, however, Bataille's notion of non-knowledge is not only obscure, if not mystical, but also, a notion that can potentially introduce a definitive confusion about "the sensible frontier between truth and knowledge." Lacan said during his conference *Talking to Brick Walls*,

> Those who have heard me quite well—or at least as best as they could—when I talked about knowledge as being the correlate of ignorance, and this idea tormented them a little. And there are some among them that have been poked by God knows which fly, a literary fly of course, things that can be found in Georges Bataille's writings, because, otherwise, I don't think they would have thought about it. I am talking about non-knowledge.
>
> Georges Bataille gave a conference on non-knowledge one day, it might be found in two or three different places in his writings. God knows that he did not make a fuss of it. And especially the day he gave his conference in the Salle de Géographie de Saint-Germain-des-Prés, which you must know because it is a renowned place of culture, he did not utter a word, which was not a bad way to show his own non-knowledge. People laughed, but they were wrong because now, it is very fancy, the non-knowledge. It can be found all over the place in the mystics, it is even from them that the notion comes from, it is with them that the notion has a meaning. And also, people know that I have insisted on the difference between knowledge and truth. Thus, if truth is not knowledge, it must then be non-knowledge. Aristotelian logic: everything that is not black is the non-black. (...) It is a discovery this non-knowledge. One could not find a better way to introduce a definitive confusion on a delicate subject matter, the point in question in psychoanalysis being what I called the sensible frontier between truth and knowledge.[38]

But how does Lacan define this "sensible frontier between truth and knowledge," and how should this sensible frontier be linked to Bataille's notion of non-knowledge, and to Edelman's definition of queerness?

To understand what the notion of non-knowledge means for Lacan, one has to interrogate, as Miller suggests in his Seminar *The Banquet of the Analysts*, the nature of the negation that is affecting the term "knowledge" in the signifier "non-knowledge."[39] What is the status and the function that determines the prefix *non*, in the notion of "non-knowledge"?

Lacan, in his teaching, constructed a table of three binary oppositions to order them. The first opposition is the one that opposes ignorance to naivety. While ignorance is a lack of knowledge at a place where a specific knowledge could be present, naivety marks a kind of lack of knowledge that opens onto the possible acquisition of new knowledge. In other words, if ignorance is the failed experience of acquiring knowledge, naivety is the subjective position that is required to be taught by experience, and thus to be able to acquire new knowledge. From this opposition, it then becomes possible to understand the two statuses that Lacan gives to the notion of zero in mathematics.

On the side of ignorance, zero is the mark of an incompetency, the mark of a privation, of an absence. Zero in this case indicates that the element that should have been marked into a certain set cannot be granted its entry into it for lack of conformity to the norms that defines that set. On the side of naivety, the zero indicates a form of positivity. It is the mark of what is to come. Another way to distinguish these two kinds of zero is to say that zero, on the side of naivety, is a zero that is a *relative*. It is a zero that is initial and arbitrary, and also a zero from which it becomes possible to introduce a difference between the Real as what is completely unmarked, and the Real as what can be marked. In this sense, the zero is like a point of orientation. It is a zero that opens up the rest of the process of developing knowledge. On the contrary, on the side of ignorance, the zero is a neutral element, just like the zero in mathematical addition. One can add as many zeros to any number and no changes will happen to the original number. The zero is simply a neutral element, something that does not count, that has, strictly speaking, no impact whatsoever.

It is from there that Lacan makes a new distinction between the void and nothingness. The void is what can contain the empty locus that can receive something, while nothingness is the content of the primordial void. Nothingness is thus the equivalent of the neutral zero, while the void is the equivalent of the relative zero upon which everything else can be constructed. When the void is reified, when one refers to it as a something, it becomes nothingness. And in order for it to become nothingness, it has to be localized. In other words, one has to be able to name it in order to make nothingness appear. Nothingness is the name of a localized lack, the name of a place that can be filled with a presence, or hollowed out. Such an articulation of the two notions, nonetheless, does not fully satisfy the definitions of the two terms, for it leaves outside of its scope the possibility that the void could be limitless. The void, indeed, in the previous articulation, is always already posited as a limited void that can be instantly converted into a container, that is, into a locus.

But the void can also be equated to the infinite, and the limitless. This ambiguity in the definition of the void is at the root of the *différend* between Bataille and Lacan. If one gives to the void the sense of the limitless, it then becomes the support of a limitless non-knowledge *à la Bataille*, while if one gives to the limitless void the meaning of the zero, it then becomes possible to posit the relative zero, which is to say the void as the primitive set, the very framework that will shelter the future development of the natural number, and by extension the future development of knowledge. But in order for the void to become the support of knowledge, and not the justification of an ultimate and definitive non-knowledge, one has to reduce the limitless void to a limited void that can be equated to a concept reduced to its very core, that is, to the dimension of a mathematical set. The void becomes then the relative zero as it acquires the qualities of a locus, and through this quality, the mathematical properties of a set. This is why Miller can write, taking a stand against a possible confusion between Lacan's notion of non-knowledge and Bataille definition of non-knowledge:

> Even if it is a short cut, one can say already, from the point that we have reached, that psychoanalysis is not a mystique of non-knowledge, and that in this disposition one makes room for non-knowledge of the analyst at the beginning, but one does not consider that for the reason non-knowledge is the *culmen* of experience.[40]

While, for Bataille, the movement goes from knowledge to non-knowledge, it goes from non-knowledge to knowledge in Lacan. This also means that where Bataille posits the limitless void as the truth of inner experience, Lacan posits the infinite void as the truth of the analytic experience. On the side of Bataille, it is the eternal contestation of the infinite void in the name of the limitless, while on the side of Lacan, it is the infinite quest for knowledge in the name of the contestation of the limitless void.

The Sinthome and the Meaninglessness of Jouissance

However, if the opposition between Bataille and Lacan is true when it comes to Lacan's early teaching, it is less certain that the same opposition could be made between knowledge and non-knowledge in Lacan's late teaching, and especially when it comes to the notion of the sinthome. In which way could we say that Bataille's notion of non-knowledge and Edelman's notion of queerness as *sinthomo*sexuality are in agreement with what Lacan tried to convey under the banner of the sinthome in his late and last teaching, or in which way this apparent agreement should be contested or nuanced?

The term sinthome, written with "th," is an old French term for symptom that Lacan used for the first time in a presentation on James Joyce, in June 1975, which became "Joyce the Symptom I," and "Joyce the Symptom & II," and then the title of his *Seminar XXIII*.[41] In the term sinthome, one can hear, in French, the word "Saint Homme," which means the "Holy man," and also, as Edelman emphasizes in his own definition of *sinthomo*sexuality, the word "sin." As such the word "sinthome" is a word that is marked, at the level of the letter, with a profound equivocity. And this equivocity is already an indication about the nature of the notion. The sinthome is not univocal. And it is not univocal because it is agitated by a kind of dance that makes its meaning incessantly go from the potentially unholy side of the drives, always ready to sin, to the potentially holy side of the Saint, always calling for new forms of sublimation.

More importantly, it is a term, as Miller suggests in his text "Pure Psychoanalysis, Applied Psychoanalysis," that represents the great future of Lacan's teaching inasmuch as it sketches a dance between the drives and the fantasy to the point of making it a concept, the sinthome.[42] What is at stake with the notion of sinthome is the possibility of understanding the symptom as a point of fixation of jouissance (body event), and not as a meaningful formation of the unconscious (fantasy).[43] The sinthome is not a formation of the unconscious that is interpretable within the framework of the transferential unconscious, but a body event to which is attached a certain opaque jouissance, resistant to meaning.[44]

While, in the perspective of Freud and the early Lacan, the fantasy was considered to be what was true as well as what was the most Real in one's symptom (what was occupying the position of a fixed and unmodifiable principle) it becomes, for the late Lacan, what occupies the status of an ever changing *lying truth*.[45] For the early Lacan, the process of an analysis was based on the idea that it was possible to intervene on the symptom as the metaphor of the subject through the progressive *construction* of the *fundamental fantasy*, which was supposed to rule over the symptom. The end of analysis, within this perspective, coincided with the traversal of the fundamental fantasy, which was supposed to provoke the disappearance of the symptoms that had brought the analysand into therapy in the first place. It is what Lacan explained in his Seminar XII, *La Logique du fantasme*, and what Miller summarizes by saying that within the perspective of the *transferential unconscious*, there is a primacy of meaning over jouissance, and thus a primacy of the Symbolic over the Real.[46]

But in the perspective of the late Lacan, it is the very notion of truth, as well as its connection to the fantasy that is questioned. The fantasy is no longer considered to be the unconscious truth of the symptom but, on the contrary, what potentially prevents an analysand from getting in touch with the Real of his symptom, that is, with what is meaningless in his symptom. If the sinthome differs from the symptom, it is in the sense that the sinthome is resistant to the unconscious, and thus to the setting of the transferential unconscious that defines the early teaching of Lacan. And this leads Miller to conclude that "neurotics expect to be liberated from their symptom, precisely because they do not manage to turn it into a sinthome."[47] But how is it possible to turn a symptom into a sinthome?

To turn a symptom into a sinthome, one has to learn how to deal with what is meaningless in one's symptom, and thus stop hoping, unlike the neurotics or the early Lacan, to cure the symptom by getting rid of it. On the contrary, one has to be prepared to make of the unreadable part of the symptom the very core onto which one can build his identity—as well as his *escabeau (a stepstool)*—which means one's own singular ability to understand and develop an *oeuvre* out of the meaninglessness of one's own symptom.[48] This makes of the sinthome not only a clinical question but also an ethical quandary that places at the core of Lacan's late teaching the question of the possible usefulness of the meaningless singularity of one's mode of jouissance.[49]

By making of the notion of the symptom not only something abnormal, nor something that needs to be cured, but also something that is absolutely unavoidable for all speaking beings, Lacan gave reason to Bataille's claim on the impossible, and agreed in advance with Edelman's point about queerness and *sinthomosexuality* as representing the reverse of "reproductive futurism." However, the problem with this enlarged definition of the symptom is that it leaves unresolved the question of how to deal with the excessive amount of opaque jouissance that is also attached to a symptom and that leads to the possibility of interpreting the sinthome, as Edelman did, I would say, in a Bataillean manner, which is to say as a form "an expenditure without reserve."

To explore the way in which a sinthome can be manipulated, and thus limited in its excess, Lacan did not follow Freud and his theory of the unconscious, nor Bataille and his definition of inner experience and non-knowledge, but he chose to follow James Joyce, and more specifically the way in which Joyce practiced his art of *cruelfiction*.[50] Joyce, to put it in a Kantian manner, awoke Lacan from his "dogmatic slumber," inasmuch as he showed to him what it means to "incarnate the symptom."

To incarnate the symptom is the opposite of giving a meaning to it, of reducing it to a form of the universal. Joyce, in his last book, *Finnegan's Wake*, managed to abstract his symptom (probably some imposed speech) from the system of interpretation through which he was previously understood.[51] Or rather, Joyce forced his readers to ponder in front of the text's enigma, which is to say, not on its lack of meaning, but on its excess. Through this effect of enigma, what is at stake, for Lacan, is Joyce's attack on the dream of literature, as Lacan puts it, which means as an attack on all the elements that were still subordinating literature to the realm of fiction. By doing so, Joyce did nothing less, for Lacan than "unhooking himself from the unconscious," as well as proving that a subject can do without the Name-of-the-father on the condition that one *knows how* to makes use of the function for oneself.

Conclusion: The Sinthome, a Heresy of the Good Kind

It is thus this singular *know how*, I would conclude, this singular use of the function of the Name-of-the-Father, which Lacan renamed *RSI* [Real, Symbolic, Imaginary], an acronym that can also be pronounced, in French, he-re-sy.[52] But while some heresies are conceptually or artistically weak and destined to be soon forgotten by the orthodoxy, some other are said by Lacan to be of the good kind, which means heresies that are not ruled over by their opaque jouissance, but ones that contain a certain "know-how," which means a certain capacity to manipulate and to valorize one's own mode of meaningless jouissance. Joyce, for example, who knew how to develop out of his meaningless jouissance his excruciating art of *cruelfictions*. In this sense, one could say that when it comes to the sinthome, the only relevant question is: how can one turn something completely contingent, traumatic and meaningless (e.g., the beating that Joyce received) into an *escabeau*, which is to say into a platform onto which one can present to others, at its most singular, his own meaninglessness.[53]

Such is the ultimate orientation of Lacan's late teaching. And this orientation, I would argue, makes of the late Lacan a good companion to Bataille's inner experience, and a good ally of Edelman's queerness, since it is a Lacan that makes room for the meaninglessness of one's own singular mode of jouissance. But it is also a Lacan that promotes a queerness of the good kind, I would add, since it is a queerness that is not strictly onto death, but one that permits redescribing the bar that Lacan puts on the S of the subject—the bar of its division—as a trait of "noble bastardy."

Notes

1. "Suppose someone alleges that his lustful inclination is quite irresistible to him when he encounters the favored object and the opportunity. [Ask him] whether, if in front of the house where he finds this opportunity a gallows were erected on which he would be strung up immediately after gratifying his lust, he would not then conquer his inclination. One does

not have to guess long what he would reply." See Emmanuel Kant, *Critique of Practical Reason,* trans. Mary Gregor (Cambridge: Cambridge University Press, 2015), Part I, paragraph 6.

2. "For the sake of spending a night with a woman, no one would be mad enough to accept an outcome that would be fatal to him, since it isn't a question of combat but of death by hanging. For Kant, the answer to this question is in no doubt. (…) But it is important to note that one only has to make a conceptual shift and move the night spent with the lady from the category of pleasure to that of jouissance, given that jouissance implies precisely to accept death—and there's no need of sublimation—for the example to be ruined. In other words, it is enough for jouissance to be a form of evil, for the whole thing to change its character completely, and for the meaning of the moral law itself to be completely changed. Anyone can see that if the moral law is, in effect, capable of playing some role here, it is precisely as a support for the jouissance involved; it is so that the sin becomes what Saint Paul calls inordinately sinful. That's what Kant on this occasion simply ignores." See Jacques Lacan, *The Seminar of Jacques Lacan, Book VII: The Ethics of Psychoanalysis, 1959–1960*, ed. Jacques-Alain Miller, trans. Dennis Porter (New York: W. W. Norton, 1992), 189.
3. Dany Nous, *The Law of Desire: On Lacan's "Kant with Sade"* (Cham: Palgrave Macmillan, 2017).
4. "From Victoria to porno, we have not only passed from prohibition to permission, but to incitation, intrusion, provocation, and forcing. What is pornography but a fantasy that has been filmed with enough variety to satisfy perverse appetites in all their diversity?" See Jacques-Alain Miller, "The Unconscious and the Speaking Body," trans. Adrian Price, *Hurly Burly* (no. 12, 2015), 119–32.
5. The antisocial turn consists of prominent Lacanian scholars who, beyond their differences, valorize negativity in order to oppose what they consider to be the "fake" optimism of the LGBTIQ++ movement. See for more details Leo Bersani, *Is the Rectum a Grave? And Other Essays* (Chicago: University of Chicago Press, 2010); Lee Edelman, *No Future: Queer Theory and the Death Drive* (Durham SP: Duke University Press, 2007); Lynne Huffer, *Mad for Foucault: Rethinking the Foundations of Queer Theory* (New York, NY: Columbia Univeristy Press, 2010); Lynne Huffer, *Are the Lips a Grave? Queer Feminist Reflections on the Ethics of Sex* (New York: Columbia University Press, 2013); Michael Warner, *The*

Trouble with Normal: Sex, Politics, and the Ethics of Queer Life (Cambridge: Harvard University Press, 2003).

6. See Robert L. Caserio, Lee Edelman, Judith Halberstam, José Esteban Muñoz, and Tim Dean. "The Antisocial Thesis in Queer Theory," (*PMLA* 121, no. 3, 2006), 819–28.
7. Lee Edelman, *No Future: Queer Theory and the Death Drive* (Durham SP: Duke University Press, 2007), 38.
8. "Queerness is never a matter of being or becoming but, rather, of embodying the remainder of the Real internal to the Symbolic order. One name for this unnamable remainder, as Lacan describes it, is jouissance," Ibid., 25.
9. "I am calling *sinthono*sexuality the site where the fantasy of futurism confronts the insistence of a jouissance that rends it precisely by rendering it in relation to the [death] drive. *Sinthomo*sexuality also speaks, as neologistic signifier, to the 'sin' that continues to attach itself to "homosexuality (…) and materializes the threat to the subject's faith that its proper home is in meaning, a threat made Real by the homosexual link to a less reassuring 'home': the sinthome as a site of jouissance around and against which the subject takes shape and in which it finds its consistency." Ibid., 38–9.
10. "[Heterosexuality] must recognize the extraneous in sex that is never extraneous to sex, and that marks it as a "useless function," as a meaningless and irrecuperable." Or even, as Jacques Derrida has written with regard to *différance*, as "an expenditure without reserve" (64). See also, for Derrida's definition of the notion of *expenditure without reserve* in relation to Bataille's thinking, Jacques Derrida, "From Restricted to General Economy, a Hegelianism without Reserve," in *Writing and Difference*, trans. Alan Bass (Chicago: University of Chicago Press. 1978), 251–77. See also Carolyn J. Dean, *The Self and Its Pleasures: Bataille, Lacan, and the History of the Decentered Subject* (Ithaca and London: Cornell University Press, 2017).
11. "If queer acts of pleasure are to dislodge the totalizing restricted economies of desire-prohibition-teleology, it may be through the valorization of their very lack of purpose: this particular kind of lack may usher in a general economy of excessive pleasures that are gloriously useless." See, for more details, "Bataille's Queer Pleasures: The Universe as Spider or Spit" in *Reading Bataille Now*, ed. Shannon Winnubst (Bloomington: Indiana University Press, 200), 75–93.

12. See Allan Stoekl, "Derrida, Foucault and their Precursors," in *Politics, Writing, Mutilation: The Case of Bataille, Blanchot, Roussel, Leiris, and Ponge* (Minneapolis: University of Minnesota Press, 1985).
13. Even though one has to acknowledge that Lacan was careful enough, in his *Ecrits*, "On a question prior to the treatment of psychosis," to position himself against Bataille by identifying Schreber's psychotic episode with Bataille's *inner experience*. Lacan said in the last footnote of his text: "The last word with which our century's 'inner experience' has yielded us its computation was thus articulated fifty years ahead of its time by the theodicy to which Schreber was exposed: 'God is a whore.' This is the term in which the process by which the signifier was 'unleashed' in the Real culminates, after the Name-of-the-Father began to collapse—the latter being the signifier which, in the other, qua locus of the signifier, is the signifier of the Other qua locus of the law." And to make sure that his critique of "inner-experience" could not be associated with the wrong person, Lacan added, right after: "The inner experience I am speaking here is a reference to Georges Bataille's work. In *Madame Edwarda*, he describes the odd extremity of this experience." See, Jacques Lacan, *Ecrits*, trans. B. Fink (New York: Norton & Company, 2002), 583–4.
14. See, for example, Panu Minkkinen, "Lacan avec Bataille avec Nietzsche: A politics of the impossible?" in *Jacques Lacan Between Psychoanalysis and Politics*, ed. Samo Tomšič and Andreja Zevnik (New York: Routledge, 2016).
15. Georges Bataille, "Socratic College," in *The unfinished System of Non-Knowledge*, ed. Stuart Kendall, trans. Michelle Kendall & Stuart Kendall (Minneapolis, University of Minnesota Press, 2001), 14.
16. For a very interesting reading of Freud's death drive and its link to Bataille and Lacan's work, see Richard Boothby, *Death and Desire* (New York: Routledge, 1991).
17. Ibid.
18. See, for a very stimulating reading of this debate over negativity, the death drive and its relation to Lacan's teaching, Mari Ruti, *Ethics of Opting Out* (New York: Columbia University Press, 2017).
19. Ibid.
20. "That figural Child alone embodies the citizen as an ideal, entitled to claim full rights to its future share in the nation's good, through always at the cost of limiting the rights 'real' citizens are allowed. For the social order exists to preserve for this universalized subject, this fantastic Child,

a notional freedom more highly valued than the actuality of freedom itself, which might, after all, put at risk the Child to whom such a freedom falls due. Hence, whatever refuses this mandate by which our political institutions compel the collective reproduction of the Child must appear as a threat not only to the organization of a given social order but also, and far more ominously, to social order as such, insofar as it threatens the logic of futurism on which meaning depends," Ibid., 11.

21. Georges Bataille, "Nietzsche's Laughter," in *The Unfinished system of Non-Knowledge*, 18.
22. Edelman, *Not Future*, 3.
23. Ibid., 33.
24. Bataille, "Nietzsche's Laughter," 18–27.
25. Ibid., 21.
26. See Georges Bataille, "The Use-Value of D.A.F de Sade (An Open Letter to My Current Comrades)" in *The Bataille Reader*, Part II, "Heterology," ed. and trans. F. Botting and S. Wilson (New York: Blackwell Publishing, 1997), 147–60.
27. Ibid., 149.
28. Ibid., 157.
29. Georges Bataille, "Discussion on Sin," in *The Unfinished System of Non-knowledge*, 26–74. For a full analysis of Bataille's reading of the sacrifice of Christ on the Cross, see Frédéric Baitinger, "De l'innocence de la victime aux délices angoissées du sacrificateur: Georges Bataille, René Girard et la question du sacrifice," in *Les Représentations du Sacrifice et du Don*, ed. I. Chassaing, J. Valcke and Z. Yang (Moncton: Perce-Neige, 2017), 97–111.
30. Ibid., 56.
31. Lacan, *The Seminar of Jacques Lacan, Book VII: The Ethics of Psychoanalysis*, 191.
32. Lacan, "Kant with Sade," in *Ecrits*, 645–70.
33. Ibid., 765.
34. Ibid., 766.
35. See Jacques-Alain Miller, "A Discussion on Lacan's Kant with Sade," in *Reading Seminar I and II, Lacan's Return to Freud*, ed. R. Feldstein, B. Fink and M.Jaanus (Albany: State University of New York, 1996), 212–40.
36. Ibid., 234.
37. See, on this point, Silvia Lippi, "Grandeur et décadence de la transgression," in *Transgressions, Bataille, Lacan* (Paris, Edition Erès, 2008).

38. Jacques Lacan, *Talking to Brick Walls*, trans. Adrian Price (Cambridge: Polity Press, 2017), 16–7.
39. Jacques-Alain Miller, "Logics of Non-Knowledge," trans. A. Alvarez, *Lacanian Ink* (#37, Spring 2011), 6–27.
40. Ibid., 25.
41. See, Jacques Lacan, Seminar XXIII, *The Sinthome,* ed. Jacques-Alain Miller and trans. Adrian Price, (Cambridge, Polity Press, 2016). See also Jacques Lacan, "Joyce le symptôme I" in *Autres Écrits* (Paris: Edition du Seuil, 2001). And see also for an excellent reading of the late Lacan, Jacques-Alain Miller, "The Sinthome, A Mixture of Symptom and Fantasy," in *Psychoanalytical Notebooks,* (#5, 2001), 9–31; "The Presentation of the *Sinthome,*" trans. S. Seth, *Lacanian Ink* (#49, Spring 2017), 98–137; "The Unconscious and the *Sinthome,*" trans. A. Price, in *Hurly Burly,* (#5, 2011), 39–49; and finally, for a very good reading of *Seminar XXIII, The Sinthome,* see Eric Laurent, *L'envers de la biopolitique. Une écriture pour la jouissance* (Paris: Navarin, Le champ freudien, 2016).
42. See Jacques-Alain Miller, "Pure Psychoanalysis, Applied Psychoanalysis and Psychotherapy" trans. B. P. Fulks, in *Lacanian Ink* (20, Spring 2002), 4–43.
43. See Jacques-Alain Miller, "Lacanian Biology and the Body Event," trans. B. P. Fulks and J. Jauregui, in *Lacanian Ink* (#18, Spring 2001), 6–29.
44. See Jacques-Alain Miller, "The Real Unconscious," trans. F. Baitinger & A. Kahn, in *Lacanian Ink* (#50, Spring 2017), 22–41.
45. See Jacques-Alain Miller, "The Lying Truth," trans. F. Baitinger and R. Raber, in *The Lacanian Review* (#7, Spring 2019), 149–55.
46. See Jacques-Alain Miller, "Fantasy and the Desire of the Other," trans. E. Ragland, *(Re)-turn: A Journal of Lacanian Studies* (vol. 3 & 4, Spring 2008), 9–32.
47. Miller, "Pure Psychoanalysis, Applied Psychoanalysis and Psychotherapy," 117.
48. See Colette Soler, "L'escabeau,"in *Lacan, lecteur de Joyce* (Paris: PUF, 2015), 163–94.
49. See Jacques-Alain Miller, "A New Alliance with Jouissance," trans. J. Snowden and R. Litten, in *The Lacanian Review*, Issue 2 (Autumn 2016), 105–16.
50. "O, you were excruciated, in honor bound to the cross of your own cruelfiction!" See James Joyce, *Finnegans Wake* (London: Penguins Classics, 1999).

51. See Colette Soler, "L'art-dieure," Ibid., 179–95.
52. See Jacques-Alain Miller, "Heretics." trans. B. Wolf. *Psychoanalytical Notebooks* (no. 32, 2018), 11–21.
53. See Miller, Jacques-Alain. "Speaking Through One's Body." trans. A. Price. *Hurly Burly* (no. 11, 2014), 131–7.

Bibliography

Bataille, Georges. *The Unfinished System of Non-knowledge*. Edited by Stuart Kendall and Translated by Michelle and Stuart Kendall. Minneapolis: University of Minnesota Press, 2001.

———. *Bataille Reader*. Edited and Translated by Fred Botting and Scott Wilson. New York: Blackwell Publishing, 1997: 147–160.

———. *Inner Experience: L'experience Intérieure*. Translated by Stuart Kendall. Albany: State University of New York Press, 2014.

———. *Eroticism, Death and Sensuality*. Translated by Mary Dalwood. San Francisco: City Lights Books, 1986.

Berlant, Lauren. *Cruel Optimism*. Durham: Duke University Press, 2011.

Bersani, Leo. *Is the Rectum a Grave? And Other Essays*. Chicago: University of Chicago Press, 2010.

Boothby, Richard. *Death and Desire*. New York: Routledge, 1991.

Dean, Carolyn J. *The Self and Its Pleasures: Bataille, Lacan, and the History of the Decentered Subject*. Ithaca and London: Cornell University Press, 2017.

Derrida, Jacques. *Writing and Difference*. Translated by Alan Bass. Chicago: University of Chicago Press, 1978: 251–277.

Edelman, Lee. *No Future: Queer Theory and the Death Drive*. Durham: Duke University Press, 2004.

Freud, Sigmund. *Beyond the Pleasure Principle*. Edited and translated by James Strachey. New York: Norton & Company, 1961.

Kant, Emmanuel. *Critique of Practical Reason*. Translated by Mary Gregor. Cambridge: Cambridge University Press, 2015.

Lacan, Jacques. *Ecrits, The First Complete Edition in English*. Translated by Bruce Fink. New York: Norton & Company, 2006a.

———. "Kant with Sade." In *Ecrits: The First Complete Edition in English*. Translated by Bruce Fink, 645–668. New York: W. W. Norton, 2006b.

———. *The Seminar of Jacques Lacan, Book VII: The Ethics of Psychoanalysis, 1959–1960*. Edited by Jacques-Alain Miller. Translated by Dennis Porter. New York: W. W. Norton, 1992.

———. *The Sinthome: The Seminar of Jacques Lacan Book Xxiii*. Translated by A. R. Price, Malden: Polity, 2016.

———. *Autres Écrits*. Paris: Edition du Seuil, 2001.

Miller, Jacques-Alain. "Speaking Through One's Body." Translated by A. Price. *Hurly Burly* no. 11, 2014: 131–137.

———. "Heretics." Translated by B. Wolf. *Psychoanalytical Notebooks*, no. 32, 2018: 11–21.

———. "Pure Psychoanalysis, Applied Psychoanalysis and Psychotherapy." Translated by B. P. Fulks. *Lacanian Ink 20*, Spring 2002: 4–43.

———. "A Discussion on Lacan's 'Kant with Sade.' In *Reading Seminar I and II, Lacan's Return to Freud*. Edited by Richard Feldstein, Bruce Fink and Maire Jaanus. Albany: State University of New York, 1996: 212–240.

———. "Duty and the Drives," *NFF* 6.1 & 2 Spring/Fall 1992: 5–15.

Nobus, Dany. *The Law of Desire: On Lacan's "Kant with Sade."* Cham: Palgrave Macmillan, 2017.

Ruti, Mari. *The Ethics of Opting Out: Queer Theory's Defiant Subject*. New York: Columbia University Press, 2017.

Sade (de). *Philosophy in the Boudoir*. Translated by Joachim Neugroschel. New York: Pinguine Classics Edition, 2006.

Sasso, Robert. *Georges Bataille: Le système du non-savoir, Une ontologie du jeu*. Paris: Les Editions de Minuit, Col. "Arguments," 1978.

Soler, Colette. *Lacan Reading Joyce*. Translated by Devra Simiu. New York: Routledge, 2018.

Stoeckl, Alan. *Politics, Writing, Mutilation: The Case of Bataille, Blanchot, Roussel, Leiris, and Ponge*. Minneapolis: University of Minnesota Press, 1985.

Winnubst, Shannon (Ed.) *Reading Bataille Now*. Bloomington: Indiana University Press, 2007.

6

Perversion After Freud: From the Cruel Father to the Joycean Clinic

Meera Lee

Concerning Sigmund Freud's idea of perversion, in his late *Seminar XXIII*, Jacques Lacan states:

> [A]ll human sexuality is perverse if we carefully follow what Freud says. He never managed to conceive of sexuality except as something perverse, and this is precisely why I question the fruitfulness of psychoanalysis. You've often heard me state that psychoanalysis hasn't even been bloody capable of inventing *a new perversion*. It's sad. If perversion is the essence of man, what a fruitless practice this is. Well, I think that, thanks to Joyce, we touch upon something [real] I hadn't thought of.[1]

In this seminar, where he introduces his concept of *sinthome* (Lacan's neologism for symptom), derived from James Joyce's writing and furthermore opposed to Freud's universalist view of perversion as an inherent

M. Lee (✉)
Asian American Studies Program, Hunter College, CUNY,
New York, NY, USA
e-mail: ml6732@hunter.cuny.edu

M. Lee (ed.), *Lacan's Cruelty*, The Palgrave Lacan Series,
https://doi.org/10.1007/978-3-031-06238-4_6

and fundamental part of human sexuality, Lacan designates perversion as *père-version* referring to "a version (or versions) toward the father." Formalizing the Borromean "knot" (or rather "link," as he insists) as a graphemic logic of sinthome, he posits that there is a fourth link that holds together the three registers of the symbolic, the imaginary and the real, a modification of his earlier view of the three registers as separate. This additional link, in Lacan's term, is the Name-of-the-Father. For the purposes of this essay, it is important to note that Lacan's the Name-of-the-Father goes back to the master signifier S, extracted from Freud's conception of the cruel father as "the bearer of castration."[2]

In Lacan's formalized Borromean knot, the symbolic has a particular status as foreclosed, subsequently reappearing *in* or *as* the real, and, as a result, there is another dimensionality in the knot, which can be called the symbolized real. The primary outcome of this foreclosure (*Verwerfung*) is a creation of the hole or the void in the signifying chain in which no univocity emerges between the signifier and signified as the promised meaning always fails—a psychical process that circumscribes the structure of psychosis—through which we can interpret Joyce's disowning of his biological father and his "schizophrenic" writing. For Lacan Joyce's writing—a writing that does not produce a discourse—is the symbolized real; hence the sinthome. Joyce's impossible stopping of the cruelty of castration, despite his repudiating of his father, *re*-turns as another version of the father in the art form writing. For Joyce writing then becomes the fourth link, namely, the Name-of-the-Father, that holds together the three linked registers. At this time of Lacan's development of psychanalytic theory, writing is thus conceived as both a symptom and the Name-of-the-Father, which also amounts to suggesting these two entities cannot be isolated or separated from one another. Considered in this way, perversion, in the Lacanian sense, "merely means *version vers le père*,"[3] a version or versions toward the father as a product of the metonymic chain of signifiers—namely, *père-version*—whereby writing is a *perverse* symptom, which describes what can be called "the Joycean clinic."

That Lacan returned to the question of perversion in his very late teaching on the sinthome as such indicates his sustained concern with a psychoanalytic thinking of perversion. He, however, during his career, never delivered a stand-alone seminar specifically on perversion even though he cared to bring the concept to our attention, albeit sporadically, throughout his teachings. Discussion of perversion is primarily found in his *Seminars VII* and *XXIII* and his written text "Kant with Sade." On this point, in this essay, I attempt to revisit Lacan's formulation of perversion within the following framework: perversion after Freud. This is, in other words, to ask: what is *perverse* in or about perversion? With these questions in mind, I intend to investigate perversion from the vantage point of the Joycean clinic described above to illuminate linguistic pervertability. More specifically, I attempt to examine, beyond the Freudian catalogue, the structure of perversion from the perspective of the symbolic function of the father as the master signifier in relation to the Oedipus complex. In so doing, the essay's ultimate aim is to propose a *new version of perversion*—one that is prescribed at the level of language (e.g., signifier, speech, and writing) rather than at the level of sexuality. That is to say, a new version I propose is a desexualized perversion, namely, *père-version*, which is indexed to psychic cruelty, as opposed to physical cruelty ascribed to a psychiatric differential diagnosis of perversion as a perverted sexual tendency or deviated sexual practice.

The *Voice* of the Superego: Desexualization of the Oedipal Desire

Lacan's formulation of perversion as a version or versions toward the father is predicated on a specific kind of desire, that is, the desire for the father. There is an apparent paradox, however, between *père-version* and the Oedipal father that the subject wants to kill in the Freudian perspective. The latter father threatens to castrate and thereby desexualize the Oedipal wishes that are inherently sexualized on the side of the son. This paradox implicates a certain perversity in the Name-of-the-Father. To further investigate this contradiction, let us turn to Freud, the first to theorize perversion psychoanalytically, in order to trace a trajectory of perversion in relation to the father.

In "The Ego and the Id" (1923), Freud formulates perversion in the economy of the two vicissitudes, *active* cruelty and *passive* cruelty, formalizing his topology of the ego, the id, and the superego. Influenced by the authority of the superego, he writes, the ego abandons the sexual aims derived from the id by way of introjecting the sexual object into itself. The aim of the ego's narcissistic object-identification is to repress the incestual Oedipal wishes and thus successfully overcome the Oedipus complex. Through this process of identification, which demands that the ego submit its Oedipal wishes to the superego by destroying its life, the ego ultimately preserves itself. Freud thus posits that "the superego is the heir of the Oedipus complex,"[4] that is, the representative of the id in the external world. The ego's "dependent relations" to the superego is prescribed on the latter's commanding of the id supported by the death drive. At this point, life is retained in the form of Thanatos, whereby Eros is transformed into a non-eroticized ego-libido—a process that Freud calls "desexualization." Here, his earlier conception of perversion as an originally polymorphous autoeroticism becomes desexualized, from which the sexual aim was directly diverted. "The superego–the conscience at work in the ego—may then become harsh, cruel and inexorable against the ego which is in its charge."[5] Put differently, the superego is a sadist and the ego a masochist.

To translate the cruelty of the superego into Lacanian terms, while the ego preserves life through a paternal image in the imaginary (*ought to*), the symbolic also enters to prohibit the Oedipal wish to sleep with the mother (*ought not to*). In the Lacanian sense, the *voice* of the superego thus echoes Freud's maxims that not only *You ought to be like your father*[6] (masculine or non-homosexual) but also *You ought not to be like your father*[7] (not to sleep with the mother). It is the father from whom the *voice* of the superego comes, signifying the law of "Yes" and "No," or "permission and "prohibition," concerning the subject's desire, a law that functions at the level of signifier, that is, at the Name-of-the-Father, and not according to judicial imperatives. This father is both the imaginary father who permits and the symbolic father who deprives the son of his desire. In this logic, Lacan claims that castration is a symbolic act whose agent is the real father in the imaginary.[8] If the superego is a sadist and the ego a masochist in Freud's terms, for Lacan, "[s]adism is for the father, masochism for the son."[9]

Lacan's intention to make this division of sadism and masochism in terms of the father–son relation is not the same, however, as Freud's. Contrary to the reversibility of these two sexual perversions in Freud, in Lacan's formulation, sadism and masochism do not readily intersect with one another. Lacan's separating each out as singular mode of perversion is precisely to reverse Freud's claim that sadism and masochism are two sides of the same coin. In effect, he argues that the two sexual perversions bear no relation to one another. In so doing, he extracts from this reversibility the master signifier of the symbolic father who generates relentless cruelty and perpetual seduction. To put it in the Freudian formula of opposition, the son is merely the inheritor of the *active* cruelty of the father as a representative of *passive* cruelty, giving rise to, following Lacan's term, a transmission of castration that effectively makes it so that the son continues to want the cruel and seductive father. It is "the transmission of the phallus from father to son," necessitating "something that cancels out the father's phallus before the son has right to bear it."[10] For Lacan, castration is therefore purely symbolic—it is the father's symbolic act of transmitting the phallus—whereas the privation father, who threatens the son with castration and thus deprives him of his Oedipal wishes for the mother, is real in the imaginary. In light of this dual logic of permission and prohibition, we can grasp Lacan's idea that the Name-of-the-Father is a symptom, more specifically, a symptom of the transmission of the phallus, whereby the real and the symbolic encounter each another through the support of the consistency of the imaginary. This consequently explains why in Freud's theory of persecutory paranoia the person whom one loves the most is often a persecutor, the seductive authority of the superego (as in the case of homosexuality).[11]

Psychic Cruelty and Seduction: The Prehistoric Father

There seems to be, however, another contradiction in the supposition that the Name-of-the-Father signifies the cruelty and seduction of the father. In Lacan's formalism of the Borromean knot, the

Name-of-the-Father has a pacifying effect that organizes life by holding together the three knots of the real, the symbolic and the imaginary. It seems also paradoxical when we consider Lacan's axiom that the Name-of-the-Father is a pure signifier—a signifier that signifies nothing. To explicate this unsettling relation of the symbolic signification of the Name-of-the-Father and the seduction and cruelty of the father, let us thus trace the "originary" father. In "The Ego and the Id," Freud states that the origin of the ego-ideal (or the superego) is "prehistoric"—while there seems to be a vague distinction between the ego-ideal and the superego, Freud uses the terms interchangeably throughout his writings. Since, however, he does not fully illustrate this concept of prehistoric identification in relation to the Oedipus complex in this specific essay, the most recognizable way to trace the historic father in Freud's theory is to reexamine his reconstruction of myths (e.g., Greek mythology, religion, or totem). If we interpret Freud's concept of prehistory within the context of mythic paternal figures, we then have, as Lacan formulates it, two different kinds of prehistoric father: the "normative" Oedipal father and the "pathogenic" Oedipal father.[12]

In *Seminar XVII*, in his demystifying of Freud's mytheme of the Oedipus complex, Lacan reorganizes the contours of the Oedipus myth: the son has no awareness of his killing of the father or his having the mother enjoy him, or the fact that he enjoys her.[13] The Oedipal wishes can never be satisfied directly but only indirectly by virtue of "the murder of the father and jouissance of the mother,"[14] says Lacan, as a result of which the phallus is transmitted from the father to the son, attributed to the function of the unconscious. What Lacan extracts from the Freudian field of the Oedipus myth is less the content of the Oedipal drama (a daddy–mummy–me triangle) than the relation of truth and jouissance derived from the murder of the father. This is where we can see Lacan's move from Freud's developmental organization of the Oedipus complex to the structure of desire. The mother's jouissance is possible only through the son's brute killing of the father (though unwittingly). In Lacan's demethologized version of the Oedipus complex, the son is endowed with the privilege to kill the father and provide the mother with the status of the object of incestuous desire, namely, the Other, in which her jouissance is guaranteed. Hence, "[i]f God is dead, then everything is permitted" as Lacan puts it in a twist on the Nietzsche's famous axiom "God is dead."[15] To secure the mother's jouissance, the death of the father is a necessary condition.

There is, however, "the other side" or "the hidden side" of this normative Oedipal father. Since the Oedipal wishes are an incestual taboo and therefore must be repressed, the truth of the Oedipus complex lies in the opposite of what actually happened in the narrative of the myth. Retroactively, the death of the father signifies precisely the prohibition, not the permission, of the jouissance of the Mother. In other words, now that God is dead, nothing is permitted. This un-permitting or prohibiting father can be found more concretely in Freud's *Totem and Taboo* (1913), where the result of the Oedipal process stands in contrast to the normative Oedipal father, who is subject to the law, as portrayed in the Greek tragedy *Oedipus Rex*. The father in this totemic myth remains "an exception"[16] to this law, or in other words, the father is outside the law: the pathogenic Oedipal father. In *Totem and Taboo*, Freud states that the sons' primordial act of killing the father of the primal horde—for whom they simultaneously have admiration and horror—is an act that also murders the prohibiting father, which Freud considers the "real." The sons want to kill the father so as to fulfill their incestuous wishes and also to preserve the pack. Moreover, they want to get rid of him because he remains a severe father who does not allow the transmission of the phallus.

What is striking in this mythic version of the father is that even after the sons' successful murder of the *père sévère*, their direct sexual satisfactions or incestuous wishes are never achieved, and furthermore, there is still only the persistent threat of castration by the father that intensifies the son's ambivalent mixture of love and hate. In the end, they do not take their mother or sisters, as Lacan notes. On the other hand, while they remain austere from their direct sexual satisfaction, the sons' identification with the father continues and returns as their desire to preserve the horde increases—it is at this moment that Freud suggests the incest and taboo arose in human society. The father is dead insofar as he is also eternal, depriving the sons of their instinctual desires. Even after his death, this private father continues to occupy the position of the symbolic outside the normative law of the Oedipus complex, and hence there is no transmission of the phallus in the sons' imaginary. In this myth, the sons are therefore not inheritors of the phallus but rather of castration. Even though this dead father resides in the imaginary of the sons, he is still present as real in the *voice* of the symbolic, saying "You shall not," eternally depriving the sons of their direct sexual satisfaction. In Lacan's reading of Freud's pre-historic father in *Totem and Taboo*, jouissance is for the dead father, not for the mother of the Other. It is in this sense that for Lacan, there can be no equivalence between the father and the son, in contrast to the reversibility of sadism and masochism in Freud's theory, because the dead father is from where the prohibition of jouissance originated, and this is the "truth" of jouissance and, after all, the myths. The phallus is, as Lorenzo Chiesa puts it, "the signifier of an impossible absolute *jouissance*… yet *also* concomitantly of the phallic *jouissance* that replaces it."[17] The phallus here is then a purely symbolic phallus or, better, the "Phallus" that is "the Father qua exceptional existence that does *not* abide by the phallic function."[18] This impossibility of the transmission of the phallus consequently suggests the impossibility of the real, which might explain why Lacan says that Freud's mytheme is "the field of bullshitting."[19] Thus, for Lacan castration, which can be classified as the master signifier, maintains the symbolic function through the articulation of signifiers, while frustration is in the imaginary and privation is in the real.[20]

At the outset, these two fathers seem different. They are, indeed. They stand in opposition to one another in relation to the law (the *inside* law and the *outside* law) and therefore occupy different registers (the symbolic and the imaginary) in relation to the subject. However, if we look at them more closely, these two fathers share something in common. They do not sever the emotional tie with the son(s) originally established in the primary identification on both occasions of the transmission of the phallus and privation. In the case of the symbolic father, who resides inside the law, the son is "permitted" to *have* the mother—"Go ahead and enjoy the mother"—insofar as he is in need of the father in order to be the supposed successor of the phallus. Here, the father frees the son's desire with permission. Nevertheless, the son never fulfills his direct satisfaction precisely because the father's everlasting *voice* of "Yes" produces what Freud calls unconscious guilt. In the case of the imaginary father, who resides outside the law, the sons are still banned from *having* the mother—"You must not enjoy the mother." On the other hand, the father remains the sons' eternal object of the horror, the object of love that invokes the voice of "Yes" to their original incestuous desire for him. Functioning in this seemingly contradictory manner, the father in Freud's mytheme, in whatever form he might be or whatever law he might follow, is *cruel*. He is cruel not simply because he controls the son's desire or deprives the son of his desire but because, quite the contrary, he frees the son's desire within the law—either inside or outside. In other words, the father "seduces" the son with the *voice* of "Yes" in the apparent disguise of "No," making the child continue to need him. It is precisely this paternal seduction that constitutes the cruelty of the father, with the result that the son is dependent on the father eternally—"Yes, you *shall* or *ought to* continue to desire me," without "your sexual satisfaction" ever being gratified. The father's *perverse* voice of "Yes" or "You shall"—it is perverse because he de-eroticizes the son's Oedipal wishes by way of eroticization—persistently haunts the children in the Name-of-the-Father. Described in this way, the father's desexualized seduction, I argue, comes from precisely this symbolic function of the language he enunciates, and this linguistic pervertability gives rise to psychic cruelty in the subject.

In reverse, the cruelty of the father (or the superego) is necessary for the son's (or the ego's) love for the father. It is a love that is eternal, with Lacan remarking that "[t]he sons love the father to the very extent that they are deprived of women,"[21] and this aspect of love shows "how far *père-version* can extend."[22] Love in the Lacanian sense therefore appears by way of the father's threat of castration as a symbolic function—it is in this sense that Lacan's Name-of-the-Father echoes Freud's prehistoric father. While love and cruelty at this point become blurred, the severity of the father paradoxically serves as a quilting point in which the subject's desire is organized. From this vantage point, we can grasp Lacan's concept of the Name-of-the-Father as a pure signifier that transcends its representation by anything and signifies nothing but a "version" of the (im)possibility that serves to arrange the subject's desire in relation to the law to produce jouissance.

The Law and Jouissance: Kant as the Truth of Sade

In the relation of the law and desire in the context of perversion, both Freud and Lacan note resonances with Kant's categorical imperative from *Critique of Practical Reason*. Kant's categorical imperative serves to formulate Freud's theory of "enjoyment" beyond the pleasure principle and Lacan's construction of the Sadean fantasy. Freud writes, "Kant's categorical imperative is a direct heir of the Oedipus complex"[23] in which the ego's relation to the object of the id becomes desexualized. While suggesting that the cruelty of the superego is *like* Kant's categorical imperative in its command of desire, he never quite cares to explain the link between the two entities clearly. It is Lacan who provides us with the way in which the law of desire is similar to Kant's moral law in his reading of Sade in "Kant with Sade," written following Alexandre Kojève's lectures on Hegel—a task that Freud left behind. Lacan's reading of Sade's writing via Kant's *voice* as implied in his phrase "[*Philosophy in the Bedroom*] yields the truth of the *Critique*" is radical to the extent that it gives rise to "the great revolutionary crisis of morality."[24] What exactly is this morality to which Lacan refers? In what law does the Name-of-the-Father allow desire in perversion? Accordingly, in what law does perversion satisfy its aim of jouissance?

In *Critique of Practical Reason*, Kant establishes the maxim, "So act that the maxim of your will could always hold at the same time as a principle in a giving of universal law."[25] In this maxim, Kant claims that the subject's ethical action must come from the will to do the "good," but this will should be driven by pure reason, which should not involve the subject's interest. It is not the will for the sake of duty but the "thing-in-itself" in Kant's terms. Kant claims that "[i]f a rational being is to think of his maxims as practical universal laws, he can think of them only as principles that contain the determining ground of the will not by their matter but only by their *form*."[26] This unconditional will is the a priori that determines not *what* the will involves but the very *form* of giving itself a moral law, which Kant calls the categorical imperative. Therefore, the foundation of the a priori is fundamentally objective, no matter how subjective it was originally, void of any kind of personal feelings or intuition but only with moral feelings with regard to the empirical object. According to Kant, "[p]ure reason is, [therefore], practical of itself alone and gives [to the human being] a universal law which we call the *moral law*."[27] Kant's moral law mirrors the way in which the voice of the cruel superego commands the law and thereby withholds direct sexual satisfaction, giving rise to the enjoyment of suffering in excess, according to which we can make sense of Freud's reference to Kant's categorical imperative in his delineation of the authority of the superego. What Sade reveals in Lacan's synthetic analysis of Kant is, as Jacques-Alain Miller puts it, that "this voice is not nobody's. It is the very same voice as *the voice of the drives*. That is, it is *the voice of the sadistic superego*. It is the voice of the devilish characters."[28]

If we can grasp Kant's moral law and its connection with the severity of the superego in this way, what then does Kant have to do with Sade? What is Lacan's intention in pairing these two seemingly unrelated figures in the post-Kojèvian era with regard to the law of desire? The name Sade is already associated with a certain kind of pervertedness in sexual practice—sadism derives from his very name. Slavoj Žižek argues that Lacan's *odd* coupling of Kant and Sade has produced the classical statement "Kant is Sade." This construction is made on the assumption that there is an equal relation between the two apparent opposites, positing that the Kantian formalist law is as obscene as the cold, bloody sadistic sexual acts or cruel torture of the gas chambers in Auschwitz.[29] In Žižek's version, the conjunction "with" in the title, "Kant with Sade," can be read as an expression of the Sadean obscenity, which is a parody of the perversity of Kant's system of the (stoic) moral law, and which deprives the subject of any feelings (e.g., love, compassion, sympathy and the like) categorized as "pathological"; hence, Kant is a Sadean philosopher. In contrast, a reading that Žižek suggests, and to which Lacan himself alluded, is that the Sadean fantasy is constructed in the same way that Kant's universal moral law is legislated. In reverse, this is to suggest that there is *eroticism* rather than obscenity in Kant's formalism in "[t]he way in which the object of the moral law keeps returning as an empirical force behind Kant's carefully crafted philosophical veils... in the shape of the 'voice of reason' that sends out to the rational human being its unassailable command to obey,"[30] as Dany Nobus remarks. Therefore, the actual focus of Lacan in his essay is Sade not Kant—that is, Sade as the truth of Kant—which gives rise to the new formulation, "Kant *in* Sade": "it is not Kant who was a closet sadist, it is Sade who is a closet Kantian."[31] Now, we have a reversal of the classical reading of the Kant-Sade relation, that is to say, Sade as a Kantian writer is perhaps more Kantian than Kant himself. Lacan locates the Sadean fantasy, the most lewd and sinful erotic acts, in the utterly banal and pure form of the Kantian moral law (the Law) or the cruel command of the superego. To put this in a Lacanian formulation, the Sadean fantasy is structured *like* the Kantian universal ethic.[32] Simply put, perversion is the universal moral law.

Lacan's paradoxical construction of Kant as the truth of Sade is to argue that desire itself can no longer be grounded in any "pathological" motivations, and in this logic, the Sadean fantasy meets the criteria of the Kantian moral feeling. Therefore, to act on one's desire is to do one's duty. For Lacan, in the context of "Kant with Sade," to follow one's desire is, furthermore, to negate the law (the positive or the legal law) insofar as this negation institutes the universal maxim outside the right to good feelings. Insofar as the subject's reason for acting "good" follows the pure form of practical reason, his or her "good feelings" fall into the universally valid moral law, even if that reason involves sleeping with one's own mother. This Law demands, as such, that the law to be lawless to produce a *pure* form. This *form* of form is "a pure waste," since it is extra, that beckons the real, which can be called "surplus jouissance," as Lacan terms it in *Seminar XVII*, and from which we can also see Lacan's formulation of the lawlessness of the real. In Lacan's logic of desire, this "pure waste" appears in the letter *a* in the object, *object a*, which Lacan separates out from the object of desire, in the drive; the *pure* form is thus the object cause of desire in relation to signifier. Surplus jouissance is a residue of *pure* form, Lacan implies, very much like the remainder of Kant's practical reason which provides the foundation for universal ethics not as utilitarian agency but as a product of form. Insofar as jouissance remains the aim of perversion, the Sadean "bedroom" is arranged according to this strictly Kantian universal moral law without any subjective involvement. In perversion, there is no subjection or subjectivization while there is excess *jouissance* to be wasted. What can be extracted in this lawless legislation is that perversion, inscribed in the Law within which the law erases or destroys itself beyond the pleasure principle, is indexed to the real that is sustained by the symbolic cause of form and the imaginary fulfillment of fantasy toward the right to jouissance. "The pervert," in this sense, Lacan remarks, "is he who, in short circuit, more directly than any other, succeeds in his aim [the jouissance]."[33] This illustrates how Lacan's barred S of jouissance is born out of practical reason subtracted from the S originary subject of pleasure in relation to the Other. According to this logic of the law of desire, we can reformulate perversion in the Sadean "bedroom"—that is a shift from the Sadean fantasy with the right to pleasure to the Sadean ethics with the right to jouissance. Lacan's "affinity" between Sadean ethics and psychoanalysis therefore "does not indicate a complicity but rather a common knowledge that has to do with perversion and jouissance insofar as they are both determined by the Other."[34] For Lacan the "task of psychoanalysis" is therefore not to "[t]ame perverse *jouissance*"[35] or to reinforce "moralism" (especially Christian morality) and mutual communication, so much as it is to encounter the real at the site of jouissance. When Lacan alluded to the necessity of the revolutionary crises of morality in pleasure in relation to the law, he intended to make a critique precisely toward this moralized and democratized notion of pleasure.

Sadean ethics ultimately illustrates the *impossibility* of the real insofar as the lawless legislation engenders jouissance in excess. The real emerges precisely from the impossibility of the actualization of the Sadean fantasy, which is to say, it is not that the real itself is impossible, but it comes from the *impossible*. On this point, to articulate the impossibility of the Sadean fantasy, it is important to note Lacan's mention of the limits of Kant's moral law in the latter part of "Kant with Sade." In the minute the truth of Kant is said, implies Lacan, there appears an error toward Sade, as if he was trying to prove his definition of the signifier as a representative of the subject for another signifier, which echoes his concept of *half said* or *lying truth* further developed by Miller. This is what he demonstrates as the impossible real of Kant's categorical imperative, which arrives not as a duty for the sake of duty but as practical reason without any attachment to the social link—that is, as pure waste. In a short circuit, Lacan's analysis of Kant as the truth of Sade can be paradoxically said to be an analogy of analytic discourse in non-rapport rather than a negation of the pathological.

Universal Delusion and Non-sexual Rapport: "Ordinary" Perversion

Echoing the discrepancy between the form and the meaning of the content in Kant's universal ethics, in his lecture, "Ironic Clinic" Miller introduces us to what he calls "the universal clinic of delusion," positing that "there is no discourse that is not of *semblant*," and hence "everyone is mad."[36] According to Miller, that all discourses are *semblant* suggests that there is no acknowledgment of the subject supposed to know but only the subject itself, much in the same way that irony works. He thus conjectures that the *semblance* of discourse implicates a delusion on the side of the real to the extent that the man speaks. In other words, insofar as human beings speak, there is a guaranty of delusion. From this logic, he extracts the axiom, "Everyone is mad," namely that the universal clinic of delusion derives from the element of schizophrenia in psychosis. In accordance with foreclosure, where the symbolic encounters the real—a fundamental psychic phenomenon of psychosis—the quintessential feature of the universal clinic of delusion is the negation of the Other. What is foreclosed is the possibility of the signifier's metonymic movement in the subject for another signifier within discourse. As Miller says, madness therefore frees man from any discourse in any social link. The clinic of ordinary madness in this logic illustrates Lacan's famous maxim of non-rapport constituted by a lapse between signifier and signified, and furthermore, a gap between language and the real in analytic situations. This hole signifies the impossibility of a human relation, more specifically, and the impossibility of a sexual relation. Thus, we have another famous phrase of Lacan's: "no such thing as sexual relation." The Sadean fantasy delineated in "Kant with Sade" illustrates a non-rapport as well, as we will see in the following pages, allowing us to reconsider perversion in light of Miller's notion of everyday delusion.

Let us turn our attention to Lacan's maxim from "Kant with Sade," presumably reconstructed from Sade's novel *Juliette*, though the exact statement cannot be found in any of Sade's writings. This injunction might perhaps be the most humorous and *ironic* among all Lacan's maxims in the *voice* of Kant, and which might best delineate the fantasy of sadism: "'I have the right to enjoy your body,' anyone can say to me, 'and I will exercise this right without any limit to the capriciousness of the exactions I may wish to satiate with your body.'"[37] Here, Lacan stresses the "right to enjoyment," that the "I" has the full privilege to enjoy the other's body limitlessly and without restriction. This first phrase, "I have the right to enjoy your body," uttered by the "I," renders him the aggressor who takes pleasure in tormenting the other's body, namely, the body of the victim. If we also refer to the maxim from Lacan's *Seminar VII*, a presumably earlier version of *Écrits*, the subject's right to enjoyment can be better understood in light of Kant's moral law: "Let us take as the *universal maxim* of our conduct the right to enjoy any other person whatever as the instrument of our pleasure."[38] Similar to the "I" in the first phrase, the "I" in the second is the subject that enunciates his right to *jouissance* to the other, and this right to use the other as an instrument is attributed to the universal maxim. Read in this way, in Lacan's version Sade demonstrates in the "play" of sadism the actualized version of Kant's universal ethics, divorced from any affective feelings such as love or compassion, and from any social link. On the other hand, the phrase in the middle from the first axiom, "anyone can say to me," catches our attention, complicating, if not outright reversing, the relation of the "I" and the "me" in Lacan's Sadean dialectics. "Anyone" is the sadist-pervert, the one who has the right to enjoy the other's body and is NOT the one who utters the entire maxim. In the *actual* experience of sadism, while the "I," the pervert, torments the other, the victim, in Lacan's Sadean ethics, the "I" is the subject who enunciates (the subject of enunciation), and the "me," the instrument, is the subject who is stated (subject of the statement). The strangeness of this maxim lies in the fact that the victim enunciates the tormentor's right to enjoy her body on his behalf, and the fact that the utterance of this right came from the victim makes the tormentor's will to pleasure even more ethical. In terms of subject-position, this reading contradicts the first reading of the maxim in the sense that the speaking-subject ("me") is not identical to the utterer of the statement ("I").

The seemingly absurd logic in Lacan's Sadean maxim suggests the subversion of the subject, more specifically, a *subject disparity* manifesting in the function of the letter chasing the Other's desire. What is implied here is that in Lacan's construction of perversion, sadism and masochism do not remain in polarity as "the pair of the opposite," as Freud posits, and furthermore the subject positions of the sadist and the masochist are not marked by reciprocity as if "[it were] a relation that is reversible… [and] unites the two subjects… in the sense of 'my turn next time.'"[39] Rather, perversion is constructed on a non-reciprocal relation, that is to say, the *relation* outside discourse, in which the subject's desire is transmitted to the Other while at the same time there is a *semblance* of discourse therein. On the contrary, there is a gap between these two subjects: "[T]here is someone else who enunciates the duty, and he who enunciates the duty is not dutiful. He who enunciates the duty is not subject to the duty he enunciates."[40] Lacan explains this discrepancy in light of equivocation in speech, echoed again in his late career in *Seminar XXIII*, the absurdity of the way in which language operates in Joyce's writing. Since there is no equivalence between signifier and signified as demonstrated in Joyce's writing, the enunciation and the statement in Sadean dialectics have no relation to one another, and hence no sexual relation. The non-sexual relation of the human beings can only be known to us through a non-rapport between the speaking subjects in the guise of symptom. Viewed in reverse, sexual relation exists only at the level of *parlêtre*, "speaking-being."[41] What Lacan's reading of Sade through Kant tells us is that perversion is less about the content of sexual acts or the sadist's treatment of the victim than about the formalism of the speech act itself. In other words, the very fact of saying of "I have the right to enjoy your body" as the truth, whether or not the other agrees to it, is what reveals the perversion, and not the actual perverse sexual acts on the other's body. "The contractual sexual relations" that Sacher-Masoch practiced and "the sexual education" that Sade instituted are cases in point: what made these writers a masochist and a sadist was their writing, a form of speech act, and not their sexual perversity in the real world.

Ironically, what enables the subject to be a *parlêtre*—a speaking being—and to exist in non-rapport and non-sexual relation in the Sadean fantasy, is certainty. It is the certainty of the real derived from the drive. But in perversion, certainty works only insofar as there is disavowal (*Verleugnun*). For example, according to Lacan' scopic drive, what the pervert sees is not the object but precisely the absence of the *object a*. What he attains is never there. The voyeur fantasizes the most beautiful woman behind the curtain, "any magic presence,"[42] even though there is only a furry man. In reverse, he is looking for the non-object, "the absence of phallus."[43] It is in this sense that the pervert is constituted by disavowal, a disavowal of the phallus. This certainty of not seeing, the disavowal of the object, presumes some degree of delusion because the fact is that there is, after all, an object to see in reality.

Although Miller does not explain his concept of the universal clinic of delusion in terms of Lacan's formula of the drives, one can postulate that ordinary madness is assumed to disavow what is present. Grasped in this way, the Sadean bedroom is composed of a delusion that entails the certainty of the existence of the absence. The Sadean fantasy is specific to the invocatory drive, which from the perspective of the clinic of psychosis might echo a verbal hallucination. Lacan's Sadean maxim, especially the second version, incites the voice of the symbolic in reference to the "universal maxim of our conduct." But it has an empty reference (no signified meaning); it has only the real of impossibility (jouissance), supported by the consistency of the imaginary (fantasy). The way in which the real appears in the Sadean bedroom is through a speech act, in specific, the scheme of *making the voice heard* designated as a kind of invocatory hallucination. The sufferer anticipates the voice that commands her subjection by articulating the law herself as if she heard it when, in fact, there is no "real" Other. "Anyone" is an invention of the speaking "I" in the imaginary that does not occupy any symbolic place in relation to the subject. It is the Other but one outside truth and any social link. One can see that the Other in the Sadean universe is not the same as the Other in neurosis. What the enunciating "I" *hears* in the form of "anyone can say to me" is the voice of the universal maxim, the form itself, not the voice of the other. She just wants her *voice of conscience* to be heard (by whom?) much like the Kantian *voice*. The Sadean maxim in this way is thus an invocatory delusion with the certainty of the absence of the thing. The objective of the Sadean victim's uttering the law of the play is less to anticipate sadistic treatment than to *make herself heard* without any concern of a signified meaning to her speech; hence the non-sexual rapport. In other words, Lacan's construction of perversion in his reading of Sade is predicated on the voice with an empty reference outside the signifying chain whereby the symbolic is foreclosed, a thesis he did not articulate in his essay in "Kant with Sade" until much later in his late conceptualization of the Name-of-the-Father in the sinthome. In this sense, perversion, I maintain, is structured at the level of the equivocation of speaking and not at the level of the obscenity of sexuality. Simply put, perversion is in the Joycean clinic, appearing as a symptom.

The Joycean Clinic: Writing as a Perverse Symptom

In the very beginning of *Seminar XXIII*, Lacan says that the term sinthome is an old way of spelling the French term *symptōme*. Introjecting Greek into French intends to invoke Joyce's recreating his mother tongue English (or Gaelic) in the foreign tongue of the Hellenic to claim that "[the] tongue was already one that bore little consistency,"[44] which appears in *lalangue*, another peculiar neologism of Lacan's. Lacan's alteration of the spelling of symptom encompasses another dimension of punning in the French. This particular way of spelling the term designates the "sin of the man" (sinthome or sin de homme).[45] "The sin of the man" refers to the original sin of having the "tongue," a signifier of the phallus. Lacan reveals that this sin can stop only when castration is possible: "[The] *possible* is *what stops, being written*." But Lacan immediately reformulates the phrase as "The *possible* is *what stops*, comma, *being written*."[46] In these "virtually" same sentences, Lacan highlights the sign or word "comma" placed between the two phrases. In his brief explanation of this phrase, he seems to suggest that castration refers to *what stops* as a *possibility*, and this possibility is possible only when it is *being written*. Put differently, castration is the stop of the sin, and this stop is possible only in the form of writing, more precisely, writing in lalangue. Lacan considers Joyce's writing as an ideal illustration of this concept of the *stop* of castration as *possible* in which discourse becomes "a discourse" that is "not semblance."[47]

This conceptualization of "stop" further explains the signification of Joyce's writing. As Lacan notes, Joyce struggled for "having" the father, which once again eventually led him to disown him. The weight of the phallus of the father that signifies castration was too much for Joyce, and the reason he spent his entire life in writing. His writing is, in other words, a reflection of his agony against the symbolic to the extent that he foreclosed any symbolic function of the father or any symbolic meaning of language. His foreclosure of the symbolic is contradictory to his passion for writing to stop castration. It is this strange tension that gave rise to "the Joycean writing," implies Lacan, a writing that is without a semblance or a resemblance to the "mother tongue." Writing served Joyce as a mechanism that enabled him to accept the original sin and, as a result, avoid transgressing the law of the Father while he resisted the cruelty of the father, the threat of castration. Despite this ambivalence, however, for Joyce writing had a pacifying effect for maintaining the substance of life. In other words, writing was his *maddening* search for *père-version*, a version toward the father (the Name-of-the-Father), or the father who has a name or names the law (The Father-of-the-Name).

In a radical turn, through this Joycean clinic, we come to see that perversion is ultimately a search for the social link, contradictory to my claim made earlier that perversion is a detachment from the social relation. But it is not contradictory, after all, considering that this search for the social bond is possible only through the system of the non-sense, non-relation or lalangue outside discourse as shown in Joyce. "[T]hrough imposing or introducing this strange literature that is outside of discourse, [Joyce] manages to restore the social link that his writing abolishes and to promote himself to the place of the exception,"[48] as Russell Grigg puts it. Grasped in this way, Joycean writing is a demonstration of the truth of the real as impossibility, revealing that in the Joycean clinic, writing is a perverse symptom. The Joycean clinic thus cannot be reduced to Joyce's writing and symptom alone. In fact, it may not be surprising to see that writing was a quilting point for the "ordinary madness" of Sade and Sacher-Masoch, as well as the "extraordinary delusion" of Schreber even though the form of their jouissance appeared differently. Rather than understanding it in a literal sense, the Joycean clinic can thus serve as a conceptual frame that allows us to rethink the psychoanalytically proper idea of perversion after Freud and beyond the register of sexual libido. The Joycean clinic exemplifies this newly proposed psychoanalytic concept of desexualized perversion that searches for the Name-of-the-Father whereby the cruelty of the father itself persists as a necessary condition for the social link in our everyday life.

Notes

1. Jacques Lacan, *The Seminar of Jacques Lacan, Book XVII: The Other Side of Psychoanalysis, 1959–1960*, ed. Jacques-Allain Miller, trans. Russell Grigg (New York: W.W. Norton, 2007), 132. Emphasis added.
2. Ibid., 130.
3. Ibid., 11.
4. Sigmund Freud, "The Ego and the Id," In *The Standard Edition Volume XIV* (1923), trans. James Strachey (London: The Hogarth Press, 2001), 36.
5. Ibid., 167.
6. Ibid., 34.
7. Ibid.
8. Jacques Lacan, *The Seminar of Jacques Lacan, Book V: Formations of the Unconscious*, ed. Jacques-Allain Miller, trans. Russell Grigg (Cambridge: Polity, 2017), 156.
9. Lacan, *Seminar XVII*, 69.
10. Ibid.
11. Placing perversion in the psychotic structure was, in fact, already alluded to in Freud's theory of homosexuality—whose features first appear in the Oedipal—as it was characterized as an aberrant perverse sexuality.
12. Jacques Lacan, "The Neurotic's Individual Myth," *Psychoanalytic Quarterly* 48 (1979), 405–25.
13. Lacan, *Seminar XVII*, 114.
14. Ibid.
15. Ibid., 119.

16. Russell Grigg, *Lacan, Language, and Philosophy* (Albany: SUNY Press, 2009), 31. Emphasis added.
17. Lorenzo Chiesa, *The Not-Two: Logic and God In Lacan* (Cambridge: MIT Press, 2016), 119.
18. Ibid.
19. Lacan, *Seminar XVII*, 124.
20. Ibid. For the function of the father in the triangle configuration that was previously discussed in Lacan's *Seminar V*, see Chapter IX.
21. Lacan, *Seminar XVII*, 130.
22. Ibid.
23. Sigmund Freud, "The Ego and the Id," 167.
24. Lacan, *Seminar XVII*, 70.
25. Immanuel Kant, *Critique of Practical Reason*, trans. Mary Gregor (Cambridge: Cambridge University Press, 2015), 28.
26. Ibid., 24. Emphasis added.
27. Ibid., 29.
28. Jacques-Allain Miller, "A Discussion of Lacan's 'Kant with Sade.'" In *Reading Seminars I and II: Lacan's Return to Freud*, eds. Richard Feldstein, Bruce Fink and Maire Jaanus (Albany: SUNY Press, 1996), 222.
29. Slavoj Žižek, "Kant and Sade: The Ideal Couple," *Lacanian Ink* 12 (1998), 1–2. https://www.lacan.com/zizlacan4.htm. Accessed March 12, 2021.
30. Nobus, *The Law of Desire*, 16.
31. Žižek, "Kant and Sade: The Ideal Couple," 2.
32. That the Kantian universal maxim provides the kernel for the function of sadism sounds, from the outset, however, paradoxical for it is absurd to think that causing pain in the other by committing sinful violence is a universally ethical eroticism. Here, one must distinguish the explicit sexual content of Sade's writing from the system of his text just as his writing must be separated from the individual Sade—let us keep in mind that it was primarily his writing and not his sexual practice that put Sade into a jail. This is not to say that the content and the text are antithetical to one another. Rather they are complementary in the sense that the distinction between content and method in Sade echoes Kant's formalism in law-making, which subsequently explains why in his earlier teachings Lacan turns to Kant to establish the logic of psychoanalysis through the effects, and not meanings, of language. This footnote repeats note 33—which one do you want to keep?

33. Jacques Lacan, *The Four Fundamental Concepts of Psycho-Analysis*, ed. Jacques-Alain Miller, trans. Alan Sheridan (New York: Penguin Books, 1979), 206.
34. Jean-Michel Rabaté, *Jacques Lacan: Psychoanalysis and the Subject of Literature* (New York: Palgrave, 2001), 87.
35. Lacan, *Seminar XVII*, 7.
36. Jacques-Allain Miller, "Ironic Clinic." The Vth International Encounter of the Freudian Field, Buenos Aires (1988), 10. Unpublished translation by Véronique Voruz and Bogdan Wolf.
37. Lacan, *Écrits*, 648.
38. Lacan, *Seminar VII*, 79. Emphasis added.
39. Lacan, *Écrits*, 649.
40. Miller, "A Discussion of Lacan's 'Kant with Sade,'" 222.
41. Lacan, *Seminar XXIII*, 84.
42. Lacan, *Seminar XI*, 182.
43. Ibid.
44. Lacan, *Seminar XXIII*, 3.
45. Ibid., 5.
46. Ibid.
47. Ibid.
48. Grigg, *Lacan, Language, and Philosophy*, 22–3.

Bibliography

Chiesa, Lorenzo. *The Not-Two: Logic and God in Lacan*. Cambridge: The MIT Press, 2016.

Freud, Sigmund. "Instincts and Their Vicissitudes." In *Standard Edition Volume XIV: On the History of the Psycho-Analytic Movement, Papers on Metapsychology and Other Works* (1915). Translated by James Strachey. London: The Hogarth Pres, 2001a.

———. "The Ego and the Id." In *The Standard Edition Volume XVIIII: The Ego and the Id and Other Works* (1923). Translated by James Strachey. London: The Hogarth Press, 2001b.

———. "Economic Problem of Masochism." In *The Standard Edition Volume XIX: The Ego and the Id and Other Works* (1924). Translated by James Strachey. London: The Hogarth Pres, 2001c.

———. "Civilization and Its Discontents." In *The Standard Edition Volume XXI: The Future of an Illusion, Civilization and its Discontents, and Other Works* (1930). Translated by James Strachey. London: The Hogarth Press, 2001d.

———. "Totem and Taboo." In *The Standard Edition Volume XIII: Totem and Taboo and Other Works* (1939). Translated by James Strachey. London: The Hogarth Pres, 2001e.

Grigg, Russell. *Lacan, Language, and Philosophy*. Albany: SUNY Press, 2009.

Kant, Immanuel. *Critique of Practical Reason*. Translated by Mary Gregor. Cambridge: Cambridge University Press, 2015.

Lacan, Jacques. *The Four Fundamental Concepts of Psycho-Analysis*. Edited by Jacques-Allain Miller. Translated by Alan Sheridan. New York: Penguin Books, 1979a.

———. "The Neurotic's Individual Myth." *Psychoanalytic Quarterly*, 48 (1979b): 405–25.

———. "Kant with Sade." In *Écrits: The First Complete Edition in English*. Translated by Bruce Fink. New York: W.W. Norton, 2006.

———. *The Seminar of Jacques Lacan Book V: Formations of the Unconscious*. Edited by Jacques-Allain Miller. Translated by Russell Grigg. Cambridge: Polity, 2017.

———. *The Seminar of Jacques Lacan Book XVII: The Other Side of Psychoanalysis, 1959–1960*. Edited by Jacques-Allain Miller. Translated by Russell Grigg. New York: W.W. Norton, 2007.

———. *The Seminar of Jacques Lacan Book XXIII: The Sinthome*. Edited by Jacques-Allain Miller. Translated by Adrian Price. Cambridge: Polity, 2016.

Miller, Jacques-Allain. Ironic Clinic." The Vth International Encounter of the Freudian Field, Buenos Aires (1988). Unpublished translation by Véronique Voruz and Bogdan Wolf.

———. "A Discussion of Lacan's 'Kant with Sade.'" In *Reading Seminars I and II: Lacan's Return to Freud*. Edited by Richard Feldstein, Bruce Fink and Maire Jaanus. Albany: SUNY Press, 1996.

Nobus, Dany. *The Law of Desire: On Lacan's 'Kant with Sade.'* London: Palgrave Macmillan, 2017.

Rabaté, Jean-Michel. *Jacques Lacan: Psychoanalysis and the Subject of Literature*. New York: Palgrave, 2001.

Žižek, Slavoj. "Kant and Sade: The Ideal Couple." *Lacanian Ink* 12 (1998): https://www.lacan.com/zizlacan4.htm. Accessed March 12, 2021.

7

The Anxiety at the Heart of Perverse Experience: A Clinical Perspective

Tracy McNulty

Our conception of the perversions is often based on a caricature, in which the sensational archetypes of the sexual predator, the sociopath, and the serial killer loom large. No doubt this is due in large measure to how the works of history's most famous pervert, the Marquis de Sade, have been received, evaluated, and reappropriated since their first clandestine publication. Their reception is often marked by a fundamental misapprehension, which consists in confusing the position of Sade himself with the libertine characters who populate his imaginative works.

For Lacan, Sadean "apathy" is about much more than indifference to pain and suffering. It signs instead the subordination or even evacuation of the pervert's own subjective desire with regard to the Mother's enjoyment, to which he is bound like a slave to a master. Even the libertine protagonists of Sade's major works constantly remind us that it is not for

T. McNulty (✉)
Cornell University, Ithaca, NY, USA
e-mail: tkm9@cornell.edu

M. Lee (ed.), *Lacan's Cruelty*, The Palgrave Lacan Series,
https://doi.org/10.1007/978-3-031-06238-4_7

their *own* pleasure that they torture or rape, but because Mother Nature commands it. In *Philosophy in the Bedroom*, Dolmancé proclaims that:

> Destruction being one of the chief laws of Nature, nothing that destroys can be criminal; how might an action which so well serves Nature ever be outrageous to her? …Murder is no destruction; he who commits it does but alter forms, he gives back to Nature the elements whereof the hand of this skilled artisan instantly re-creates other beings: …the murderer thus prepares for Nature a pleasure most agreeable, he furnishes her materials, she employs them without delay, and the act fools have had the madness to blame is nothing but meritorious in the universal agent's eye. 'Tis our pride prompts us to elevate murder into crime. Esteeming ourselves the foremost of the universe's creatures, …we have believed Nature would perish should our marvelous species chance to be blotted out of existence, while the whole extirpation of the breed would, by returning to Nature the creative faculty she has entrusted to us, reinvigorate her, she would have again that energy we deprive her of by propagating our own selves.[1]

In the gloss of Serge André, "the Sadean henchman [*bourreau*] sacrifices his own subjectivity to this bloodthirsty and constraining Other. He reduces himself to being nothing more than a voice that enunciates the natural commandment of jouissance, and an instrument that executes it in the manner of a zealous functionary."[2]

Hence, Lacan's fundamental insight that Sade was not a sadist, but a *masochist*.[3] Perversion for him was not about the pleasure taken in cruelty, but about a submission to the law of the Mother's desire that gives rise to what André describes as a "morality of strict obedience": "we must enjoy, it's an obligation."[4] Sade's Last Will and Testament stipulated that his body should be buried in a clearing in the woods in an unmarked grave, whose site would then be strewn with acorns: these would then reforest the site of the breach, ensuring that "the traces of my grave may disappear from the face of the earth as I trust the memory of me shall fade out of the minds of all men."[5] In vanishing from the earth without leaving a trace, Sade upholds the completeness of Mother Nature by ceding his symbolic place to her, healing the cut introduced into her great body by the laws of speech and language.

In the clinical setting, the analysand with a perverse structure generally experiences this captive position with respect to the mother's desire—and corresponding effacement of his own subjective position—both with less clarity and with less zeal. Indeed, the lived experience of perversion is often one of acute, even debilitating anxiety, frequently aggravated by the serious difficulties many perverts encounter in their attempts to create and maintain an independent life or find an outlet for their own desires. One analysand dreamt that he saw his lifeless body hanging in the vestibule of the family home; the noose that was looped around his neck was not a rope, an umbilical cord binding him to his mother. Another dreamt as a child of being sealed in a vessel and buried in the ground by a woman who even then he understood to represent his mother. He spent his life reenacting this burial in different ways, including by sabotaging all of his attempts to make an independent life for himself.

I would argue that the best way to approach the logic of the perversions is not through cruelty, instrumentalization, or even apathy—however significant these may be in some cases—but through the interrogation of what perverse practices respond to and defend against: namely, a fundamental anxiety resulting from the pervert's captive position with respect to the mother's dissatisfaction, which he feels uniquely called upon to address.

Most readers know that the perversions, for Freud, are defined by the "disavowal [*Verleugnung*] of castration."[6] But while this may be depicted in imaginative works by or about perverse subjects in the fantasmatic form of an unlimited sex drive, the castration at stake in disavowal is not concerned solely or even primarily with sexual potency, the organic integrity of the body, or even to the narcissism that attaches to the male penis in Freud's account of childhood sexuality. Instead, castration as Lacan in particular allows us to understand it is about the limit imposed on the subject's quest for satisfaction by the fact of having to pass through language, the field of the Other.

Human sexuality is mediated by signifiers, by language and the address, and not by the genital organs. Unlike other animals, we have no direct, instinctual access to the other members of our species. This is why sexual difference, for the human being, must be distinguished from sexual compatibility or complementarity. Difference is a logic of the signifier, which supposes a discontinuity or gap between terms that is itself the condition of signification. Compatibility, on the other hand, is a logic of nature, an instinctual logic: there is no sexual difference in nature, no unbridgeable gap between the male and the female of the species. Human beings, however, are never really compatible in this way: there is always some gap between us, some distance, some fundamental unknowability. No two human beings have the same fantasy, and our fantasies are not complementary or compatible. The "castration" the pervert at once acknowledges and repudiates is concerned with something very different than the absence of the penile organ, therefore. Castration could be defined most simply as the loss of full being to language, or the fact that for the human being, it is not possible to return to a purely instinctual existence (defined by the successful fulfillment of specific instinctual aims or by the infallible ability to locate and obtain certain objects within a given natural environment).

The axiom that the pervert disavows castration potentially give rise to a misunderstanding, however, according to which the refusal of castration and its consequences is unique to the perversions and not present in other psychic structures. But the neurotic and the psychotic also refuse castration in their own way. What then is the specificity of perverse disavowal, and how does it differ from these other responses?

The neurotic appeals to interpersonal relationships, and more broadly the cultural construction of sexuality, to repress unconscious desire and to avoid taking responsibility for the subject's solitude with respect to the disorganizing effects of the free drive on the body and on mental life. In the logic traced by Lacan in his early essay on the Mirror Stage, the ego is constructed as an object offered up to the gaze of an imaginary Other who is called on to unify the fragmented body of the drives.[7] The aim of seduction is to maintain this Other in place, and so repress the fact that for the human being, for whom language deviates the quest for satisfaction, there is no object that would satisfy desire: and, at the same time, that one cannot be the object of desire for another person. The neurotic, and especially the hysteric, appeals to the Other to manage the free drive or accuses the Other of being responsible for its effects.

In perversion, something very different is at stake. The pervert is caught up in the mother's complaint concerning her dissatisfaction, or the obstacle that her quest for jouissance encounters in the desire of the Other. The pervert's mother, that is, is almost certainly a neurotic: most likely a hysteric who still waits in vain for an identificatory signifier that would constitute her as the object of the Other's desire.[8] The perverse child is acutely aware that the father is unable to give the mother what she seeks, or to support and uphold the feminine jouissance at work in her body. Unlike the neurotic child, that is, the pervert has no illusions about the fact that there is no sexual relation, that as human beings we are unable either to find a partner who would fulfill our desires or to be that object for someone else. But he also feels called upon to provide a solution, another way of addressing his mother's complaints. The pervert rejects the fact that jouissance is mediated by language, by the address, by the assent or refusal of the Other. More specifically, he wants to demonstrate to the Mother that it is not necessary to deal with the desire of the father: there is another way, which will be formulated and staged by the perverse demonstration and the scenario it proposes as a way to control and master the manifestation of jouissance.

The castration that is disavowed in this way is first and foremost the castration of the *Mother*, therefore. To demonstrate to the mother that she is not castrated is to demonstrate that her jouissance need not be limited by or dependent upon the desire of another person. In the perversions, then, the disavowal of castration really means the disavowal of desire: the desire of the father, the desire of the pervert's eventual partner, but also his *own* desire (a point I will explore in more detail in what follows). The pervert does not want to confront the irreducible obstacle that the Other's desire represents, to address the Other as someone who has a power of refusal over our demands or who can present an obstacle to enjoyment.

This insight is central to Freud's 1927 essay "Fetishism," where he observes that the choice of the fetish as a sexual object obviates the need to encounter the obstacle that the other's desire represents. "In later life," Freud writes,

> the fetishist sees other advantages in his substitute for the genital. The significance of fetishes is not known to the world at large and therefore not prohibited; they are easily obtainable and sexual gratification by their

> means is thus very convenient. The fetishist has no trouble in getting what other men have to woo and exert themselves to obtain.[9]

One does not have to address a fetish in language, to seduce it, convince it, or obtain its consent.

A second singular feature of the perverse repudiation of castration is expressed very neatly by the English "disavowal," which translates the German term *Verleugnung*. Freud already emphasizes that the dis-avowal of castration is a two-part operation, which involves both affirmation *and* denial: castration is first avowed, recognized, and then repudiated or denied.[10] Psychoanalyst Lucie Cantin, whose pathbreaking clinical work on perversion will be a recurring point of reference in this chapter, captures very well the stakes of this two-part operation when she writes that:

> the subject's way of handling the drives reveals the pervert's will to obscure the logic of the drive's functioning by…[attempting] to veil—or maintain the veil on—the necessary submission and articulation of the subject to the Law of the Other's desire. This denial, which Freud considered central to the perverse position, implies a twofold movement—a simultaneous affirmation and denial. Indeed the affirmation is essential to making the denial possible. This fact is confirmed in many ways in clinical practice, where the pervert's attempt to deny any articulation of the subject's desire to the Other's desire demonstrates in fact a constant reaffirmation of the pervert's position precisely as a captive object of the law of the Mother's desire, where the pervert remains.[11]

In more schematic terms, the twofold character of disavowal as Cantin describes it here can be broken down as follows:

1. There is an implicit avowal or recognition of words, of the signifiers of the Other's desire as the source of the drive, and therefore of the mental representation around which the fantasy turns.
2. This origin is then disavowed or repudiated by means of a demonstration which aims to show that we don't need words, we don't need the desire of the Other, to provoke in her a jouissance.

The demonstration has the same function for the pervert as interpersonal relationships for the neurotic, or the delusion for the psychotic: namely, to avoid the realization that there is nothing the subject can do against the work of the free drive. More specifically, the demonstration aims to calm the pervert's own anxiety by pretending to control and manage the manifestation of the free drive—in the body of the partner, but more importantly in *him*.

In what follows, I will explore the structure of the perverse demonstration and the anxiety it seeks to manage through some clinical examples, as well as through the work of Cantin and of Willy Apollon—two contemporary psychoanalysts of Lacanian orientation who have significantly advanced our understanding both of the logic and of the perversions and the clinical challenges they present. In the interest of confidentiality, I will share only a few isolated examples from my own clinical practice, but will draw at length on an already published case by the late Belgian psychoanalyst Serge André to explore in more detail the logic of a specific fantasy. This brief case history, titled "Dany, or the Choice of Masochism," appears at the end of the introductory chapter to André's 1993 book *L'imposture perverse*—an important contribution to the Lacanian clinic of the perversions that unfortunately has yet to appear in English translation. I will also refer throughout to the following diagram by Apollon, which maps the logic of the perverse demonstration.[12]

The diagram starts with the position of the pervert in the lower left-hand corner, and can be read as follows: The perverse subject, in an unconscious pact with the Mother, offers to the partner a contract that requires him or her to occupy a specific role or position. This contract, which may or may not be formalized in speech or in writing, undergirds the staging of a scenario whose aim is the production of a specific jouissance. This jouissance, produced in the partner according to a mechanical, action-reaction logic, is offered up to the Mother, the absent witness or implied addressee of the demonstration, to show her that it is not necessary to pass through the signifier of the Other's (the father's) desire.

Serge André, "Dany, or the Choice of Masochism"

André reports that Dany, a young man of twenty, was driven to analysis by anxiety attacks and by a nagging question: "was he or was he not a 'transsexual'"?[13] He was inclined to say that he was, since he felt more like a girl than a boy. However, he also recoiled from the logical conclusion to which that statement seemed to lead. He was unable to commit to a sex change operation, since "surgical castration inspired only horror in him." For more than two years, he had postponed the moment of "cutting," as he put it, instead contenting himself with a hormonal treatment that had given his body some curves.

At the time the analysis began, Dany had been married for about a year to a colleague from work, who he described as a simple but honest person. The great sadness of his existence was the death of his mother, which happened unexpectedly when he was sixteen. After her death, he lived with his father under very strange circumstances, although their peculiarity was not apparent to him until the analyst pointed it out. The day after his mother's death, Dany's father proposed that his son start sleeping with him in the bed he had previously shared with his wife, explaining that he wanted to convert Dany's bedroom into a shrine to the deceased woman where all of the objects belonging to her would be gathered. "In this way," André observes, "the young man effectively came to occupy the place of his mother, while his symbolic locus (his bedroom) was transformed into a sanctuary where the remains of the deceased (notably all of her clothing) were offered as a spectacle."[14] Despite the intimacy of this arrangement, Dany's father was completely unaware of his son's transvestism, which had been established in his childhood and cultivated with the complicity of his mother. Now that her entire wardrobe was arrayed in his former bedroom, Dany could dress up in her clothing as often as he liked without his father suspecting anything.

As a young man, Dany "maintained and even accentuated this cleavage in his life." During the day, he felt he had to "play the man" [*faire l'homme*] at work and in society; but when he returned home at the end of the day, he could finally remove this "virile mask."[15] He would put on makeup, dress as a woman, and busy himself washing dishes, cooking, knitting, and sewing. However, Dany had no desire to exhibit himself as a transvestite or to frequent transvestite clubs, which filled him with horror. Nevertheless, and although he lived with the constant fear of being found out, Dany occasionally showed up at work dressed in a pair of stockings or women's underwear concealed under his pants.[16]

This brief synopsis immediately raises a question. If Dany feels that he is a woman, then why does he have to hide his feminine undergarments? Why must he "play the man" in public? What is at stake in this dissimulation?

A first observation I want to make is that it is not Dany's possible transsexualism that identifies him as a pervert, but rather the rigorous separation he maintains between the public and private spheres. This is not a matter of fearing the reactions or the judgments of other people, as it might be for a neurotic. Instead, it is as if the pervert refuses to articulate what is at stake in eroticism and desire to the social sphere. The refusal of this articulation is the first way in which the disavowal of castration is made manifest. The pervert wants to avoid the need to find a place for desire in the social sphere, and this is frequently what creates an impasse in his life. Dany's secrecy and dissimulation, his adoption of different "masks" and "roles," are linked to this avoidance. If he were to articulate these two spaces, he would have to take responsibility for that articulation. Hence, it is significant that what brings Dany into analysis is his inability to commit to undergoing sex reassignment surgery, despite feeling that he is more a girl than a boy.

The Pact with the Mother

First, however, we have to ask: what is at stake in this secret femininity? What is the nature of his fidelity to it, and why must it be veiled or hidden from others? Apollon's diagram places at the heart of the perverse demonstration an unconscious PACT between the pervert and the Mother (Fig. 7.1). André's case history offers an excellent example of such a pact, which accounts both for Dany's feeling of being a girl and his need to dissimulate that femininity from others.

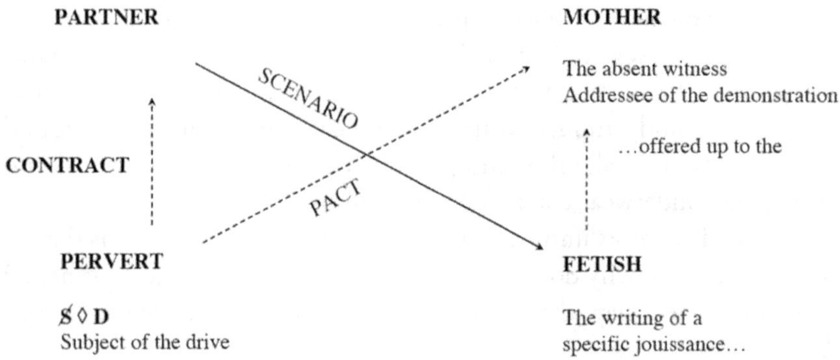

Fig. 7.1 The perverse demonstration

Dany, André writes, "claimed that he had always felt like someone of the feminine sex."[17] As he describes the circumstances of his childhood, however, Dany cannot see what is obvious to the analyst: that his own wish to change his sex is in fact dictated by the desire of his mother. "Dany's mother wanted a daughter and only a daughter," writes André.

> During her pregnancy, she had planned and prepared everything in view of this wish, as if she did not doubt that it would come true. When she learned from the doctor that she had just given birth to a boy, she refused to see or to touch him for two days.[18]

Eventually, Dany's mother seemed to resign herself to her fate. However, the name she gave her son at birth was in fact only the diminutive of the name she had chosen for the little girl she was expecting. From Dany's earliest childhood, she "took pleasure in dressing her son as a girl and teaching him what one generally transmits to little girls: playing with dolls, knitting, sewing, etc."[19] At the age of twelve, Dany required surgery for a symptom that demonstrated how thoroughly his development had been shaped by the mother's desire. His testicles had "stayed inside," as he put it, and an operation was needed to bring them down. Dany underwent the procedure reluctantly, however, since by this time, André notes, "he was already perfectly adapted to his imaginary status as a girl."[20]

Dany's transvestite practices started around the age of six, when he began to steal stockings from his mother's armoire. One day, he was standing in front of the mirror dressed up in a bra, underwear, and stockings when his mother walked in. She looked at him, then turned around and left without saying a word. Dany felt deeply ashamed, and quickly returned the stolen clothing to his mother's armoire. That night, however, he found that the pair of stockings had been placed under his pillow in what André describes as "a tacit display of attention from a mother thrilled with the feminine habits of her son."[21] From that moment, an unspoken complicity was established between Dany and his mother, of which the father was completely ignorant. Dany would put on a pair of stockings when he came home from school and keep them on until the hour when his father returned from work. When they heard his key turning in the lock, his mother would simply turn to Dany and say: "go change."[22] In this configuration, André writes, the father was "systematically deceived, cuckolded by the couple formed by the mother and her son":[23] a situation that continued, as we've already seen, even well after the mother's death.

André's case history brings into relief a number of elements that are central to the logic of the perverse demonstration. A crucial element of the scene of transvestism at age six is the fact that that *no words are exchanged* between mother and child: nothing is named or spoken about, and the nature of the tacit complicity established by the gift of the stockings remains out of language. (In Fig. 7.1, the dotted line that links the pervert to the mother indicates that this pact is unconscious—which means both that the pervert is not conscious of it and that it is not expressed in language.)

The perverse child has invariably had certain decisive experiences in his childhood, in which the discourse of his mother—at least from the perspective of the child—seemed to deny the value for her of the signifier of the father's desire. The child experiences a complicity with the mother that seems to say, "your father is nothing to me." This is not necessarily what the mother believes in fact, but it could be—since there is often some support in reality for the attitude the perverse child attributes to or discerns in the mother. Often the pervert says he was the confidant of the mother, a privileged witness to this repudiation of the father. For example, she complained to the child of being unfulfilled by her husband, that he doesn't understand her, that the marriage gives her no happiness, and so forth. The perverse child who is confronted with such a discourse may feel not only that his mother demands or needs something from him—a perception that is shared by many neurotics as well—but that he has what the mother wants, or at least the ability to give her what the father was powerless to provide. It isn't just that the pervert disavows the mother's castration or lack, however; frequently there is also a disavowal of castration on the mother's part: as if she had found a privileged address in the child, and thus a way of denying the defect in language.

Lucie Cantin observes that the pervert "tends to claim a central and particular relationship to the mother, a relation of complicity that supports the setting aside of the father's desire in the maternal universe."[24] The subject is bound to the mother by a genuine contract, which has a double significance. "Under its terms," Cantin writes, "the subject is first bound to the jouissance and/or suffering of the mother, to her will, to her *bon plaisir*."[25] In this case, Dany's mother she makes her child into a kind of doll, a thing subject to her whims: he is reduced to being nothing more than the instrument of her jouissance, and not a subject in his own right. In this way, she refuses to acknowledge that her desire remains unsatisfied or that her demand encounters a limit: including the limit represented by the subjectivity of the child himself, as a being who has his own desires. With his transvestism, the child offers the mother another way to realize her frustrated desires, which unfolds outside of language and bypasses the obstacles she encounters in reality. In Cantin's words, "the mother-child contract conspires to stage and demonstrate the uselessness of the paternal phallus"—the signifier of the father's desire—"for the mother."[26]

At the same time, however, the child's own life is completely overdetermined by the law of the Other's desire—in this case, the Mother's desire—but in a way that *entirely escapes his notice*. Dany doesn't seem to recognize that "his" experience of femininity, his desire to be a woman, is in fact conditioned by his mother's frustrated desire. He is aware of his mother's wishes and is able to speak about them clearly and at length, but he seems to make no connection between this narrative and his own feeling of being a girl: as if he is completely unaware that he's enacting a script that has been dictated—however tacitly—by the mother.

Dany's transvestism, however, attests to the extent to which the mother's desire has very literally scripted the terms of his erotic life. We see this in the words his mother addresses to him at the moment his father's key turns in the lock: "go change." In context, the words alert him to need to hide his transvestism from the father. But in French, the formula uses a reflexive verb: *Va te changer*, literally "go change yourself" (implicitly, "go change yourself *into a girl*"). Without being aware of it, the child experiences this formula as an imperative that he change his sex, which binds him to his mother's unsatisfied demand.

There is thus a contradiction: the demonstration serves the mother, by proving that the signifier of the Other's desire is both impotent and unnecessary, and yet his own life is completely conditioned by that signifier. This contradiction is what gives disavowal its dual dimension. The same act simultaneously avows or acknowledges the primacy of the Other's desire *and* disavows or denies it—in both cases unconsciously. Even as there is an implicit recognition of the subject's subordination to the signifier—to the script of the mother's desire—both the cause of the demonstration and its true address will need to be veiled, to remain hidden, in order to maintain the subject's ignorance about his own submission to what Cantin calls the Law of the Other's desire. This is the role of the SCENARIO, which makes use of a partner—and more specifically the partner's *body*—to stage the disavowal of castration for the benefit of an *absent witness* who is not present in the scenario, but who directs it from elsewhere.

The Scenario

André reports that many months into the analysis, Dany admitted that there were still certain things that he had never dared to tell the analyst. He then revealed "the most important and most secret part of his perverse practices."[27] These consisted of elaborate scenes of masochism, which he spent much of his time imagining and attempting to execute in reality. At least once a month, Dany had to be humiliated, bound, and beaten by a woman, in a very precise manner. First, he had to put on makeup and dress as a woman, wearing skin-tight latex clothing. Next, while he walked around the room pretending to do household chores, his partner had to "insult him, berate him about how poorly he kept the house, and order him to perform some particularly humiliating task."[28] Then, she had to attach him to the bedpost and "pull energetically on the strap so that he was bound very tightly, in such a way that the cords or chains left marks on his skin and he could barely breathe."[29] On several occasions, his neck had been squeezed to the point of strangulation, producing in him a "peculiar enjoyment" [*une jouissance particulière*]. Finally, "he had to be whipped very hard and sworn at until he reached orgasm."[30]

In order for this scene really to satisfy him, however, an essential condition had to be met: his partner had to "truly derive enjoyment [*jouir*] from whipping and humiliating him."[31] This condition was rarely fulfilled, however, since Dany "had quite a bit of difficulty finding partners who were ready to sign this type of contract and above all to honor it to the end."[32] Although he knew some "specialized prostitutes" who were willing to satisfy his requirements to the letter, "he was pretty sure that they didn't really get off from it."[33] In hopes of "discovering a woman who would submit to his desires out of pure pleasure," Dany spent innumerable hours combing through the personal ads in SM magazines and drafting announcements that he himself placed in these publications. Every time he had answered an ad, however—or someone else had responded to his—he had come away disappointed: "either no one came to the appointment, or the partner quit halfway through."[34]

Despite these difficulties, however, Dany was fortunate to have a wife who quickly accepted his transvestite habits and even seemed to find them entertaining. Even better, she was willing to humiliate and belittle him while he dressed up as a woman and attended to household chores.[35] Little by little, Dany was even able to convince his wife to take on the role of the partner, or at least some of its features. For example, she agreed to pinch his nipples until they bled, or to push pebbles up his anus, to help him reach orgasm. Occasionally she would agree to tie his hands behind his back, or squeeze his chest with a chain. However, she "categorically refused to beat him or cause him real harm."[36] And since Dany was more and more insistent that she do so, his wife was given increasingly to "fits of crying and anxiety attacks, and begged her husband not to ask of her such horrible things, since they filled her with fear."[37]

The Contract

At this juncture, we have to ask: why does the pervert need a partner in the first place? Why can't he simply fantasize about these scenes or masturbate to them? And why must the partner's function and reaction be codified to this extent? In André's case, a first observation is that Dany requires the partner to play a highly specified role. No deviation from this script is tolerable, even when the performance of that role causes the partner to quit or to feel anxiety and distress, as with his wife. The ads that Dany places in SM magazines can thus be understood the offer of a true CONTRACT (Fig. 7.1), which stipulates the precise traits, gestures, and actions that are required of the partner: the domineering and demeaning attitude, the wielding of the whip, and the bondage and humiliation. Of course, the partner is not necessarily aware of entering into a contract. For the pervert, however, this element is crucial. At stake is not merely an erotic scene, but a demonstration whose aim is twofold: first, to evacuate the Other and render useless the passage through demand by means of the contract; and second, to trigger a drive response through a scenario that unfolds in reality, which shows that we do not need the desire of the Other, to provoke a jouissance in her.

The first aim may seem inherently contradictory. If the pervert's objective is to show that words and speech are not necessary, that one does not have to address the other person or obtain her consent, then why write up a contract? In fact, the contract demonstrates very well the twofold movement of (dis)avowal. The contract is an agreement expressed in language that paradoxically functions to annul its intersubjective character and the lack or mediation it implies, by eliminating the risk represented by the partner's power of consent or refusal. On the one hand, the contract formalizes the subject's submission to another person and total dependence on her whims (in this case, the submission of Dany to the domineering woman). On the other, however, it empties out the place of the Other by reducing the other person to a series of traits, gestures, and attitudes: she becomes nothing more than the woman who wields the whip, and her own desires, motivations, and needs are irrelevant. Cantin explains this dual aim as follows:

> the contract regulates, defines, and formalizes the relation to the other. Things are said before they are done. The signifier compels and one must abide by it. At the same time, however, in this very situation, the other is evacuated. The contract effectively erases both Demand and the subjection to the Law of the other implied in it. The pact…renders useless the passage through the demand, just as it regulates, with the other's complicity and free consent—the evacuation of the other. Once the contract is signed, the other as a subject is abolished, along with her desire and freedom.[38]

The anonymity of the personal ads that Dany places in SM magazines offer a caricature of this abolishing of the subject, who is reduced to the characteristics required to trigger the repetition of the scenario. The contract evacuates the locus of the other precisely by constituting it as a series of positions, gesture, or traits that take precedence over the subjects who are conceived merely as "occupying" those positions or animating those traits. The eradication of the Other that Cantin describes thus has two faces: the effacement of the other person as a speaking subject or subject of desire, and in and through this, the eradication of the intersubjective dimension of speech and the address, which mediates and therefore compromises the question for satisfaction. "It is as if what must be erased," she writes, "is the signifier's initial determination by the Other. The signifiers must be reduced to a series of traces of jouissance that must be discovered, revived, or embodied in anyone who proposes to occupy one of the possible positions in the scenario."[39]

We've already seen that Dany disavows the extent to which his own feeling of being a woman is scripted by his mother's demand. This disavowal is even more apparent, however, in the way Dany accounts for the origin of his masochistic practices, and in particular, the requirement of being humiliated, beaten, and bound to the point of strangulation. One day Dany recounts to André that when he was seven years old, he used to play "Cowboys and Indians" with a little neighbor girl. In the role of the cowboy, he would capture the Indian (the little girl) and then tie her to a tree in the garden that the children had christened the "torture pole." One day when they exchanged roles, however, Dany found himself bound to the torture pole and abandoned there by the neighbor girl, who left him tied up and went home.[40] Dany recalled the terrible fright he had experienced at that moment, his frantic tears and cries for help, but also the sudden and unexpected transformation of his state. "After several minutes of panic and despair," writes André, "he had suddenly felt an extraordinary feeling of happiness and well-being coursing through his whole body. From that day on, he said, he had known that his jouissance was there, and that its condition was this bondage and a pitiless woman."[41]

As Dany tells it, the structure of the masochistic scenario is prompted by a *memory*, something that took place "in reality." This element is crucial to the demonstration. The memory seems to have a primordial status, as if this is where the masochism "begins" more or less out of the blue: as if the jouissance experienced here were a spontaneous manifestation not determined by anything else in the subject's history. Dany tells the analyst that this scene took place when he was seven years old. But we've already learned that his transvestite practices began at the age of *six*, along with the tacit contract he develops with his mother to conceal that scene from his father.

In other words, whether or not the childhood scene took place in reality exactly as he remembers it, it should be understood as a mental representation, a fantasy, that accounts for the child's subjective positioning with respect to the Mother's desire. The "memory" sutures the mental staging dictated by the fantasy to something in reality that the subject seems to have stumbled upon by accident, as if to suggest that he has merely discovered his predilection for masochism on his own. The event recalled in memory is not the formative instance, therefore, but a (re) staging that puts in play the signifiers coming from the Other even as it causes the connection between those signifiers and the staging to be lost. It offers itself as a construction or representation of something that the pervert chooses to keep veiled or to remain ignorant of.

What he discovers through this childhood game is not the origin of his perversion, therefore, but both a *particular staging of the fantasy that binds him to the mother* and a *technique for managing the jouissance it provokes* (namely, a way to produce jouissance mechanically). Dany is not aware of the first, only the second: a way to take control of that jouissance and master it, and thus a particular way of disavowing castration. The "memory" furnishes the structure of the scenario by establishing a series of positions and the precise linkages between them, and above all by determining in advance how the scenario will unfold and how it will end: with the eruption of the "peculiar jouissance" that comes over him as he stands alone and abandoned, tied to the torture pole. In this way, the origin of the fantasy in speech, in the Other, is disavowed in favor of a practice, a ritual, that is reduced to a limited number of actions and gestures.

The Fetish

This childhood recollection illustrates very well how the ritual formalized by the contract not only empties out the locus of the Other but also provides a way to manage the free drive and to take control of jouissance and the anxiety it provokes. Returning to the diagram of Willy Apollon in Fig. 7.1, we see that the "scenario" the pervert proposes to his partner produces—or at aims to produce—the FETISH: the manifestation of a specific jouissance in the partner. In the scene of humiliation described earlier, Dany explicitly seeks a sign from his partner that would prove that she really enjoys binding and whipping him (which might be revealed by an expression on her face, for example). The reaction of his wife is just as important, however. When he presses her to cause him injury or bind him to the point of suffocation, she not only cannot do it but also breaks down crying and is seized with anxiety attacks. These are also examples of a jouissance produced in the body of the partner, even if they aren't the enjoyment that he seems to be looking for. Importantly, the French word *jouissance*—especially as used by Lacan—does not denote only enjoyment, but can describe any bodily or emotional response that attests to the person in question being affected in a way that exceeds her control: for example fascination, excitement, anxiety, suffering, or revulsion. What is important in each case is the pervert's ability to trigger something in the partner, or even to *trigger* her in the sense we give to that term today.

Why then is he driven to produce this jouissance in his partner? What does it have to do with the unconscious pact with the mother and the disavowal of castration? And why, in Apollon's diagram, is it identified with the fetish? Freud, in his essay on fetishism, emphasizes that the concreteness and visibility of the fetish, its status as an object or image (a braid, a shoe, a "shine on the nose"), is intimately linked to the fetish's role in upholding the reality of the maternal phallus—as if this object whose existence were not confirmed by the senses were being forced into reality by the object that upholds and proves its realness. In Apollon's diagram, however, the fetish is described as the "writing of a specific jouissance." What is crucial in each case, I would argue, is the dimension of *verification.* Just as the fetish object attests to the reality of the maternal phallus that is not found in the field of perception, the response of the partner's body to the scenario functions to verify that the pervert has managed to trigger something in the body of the other person without requiring her consent or agreement.

One analysand was driven to tickle all of the women with whom he established a certain level of intimacy. He eventually recognized that what was essential for him was to be able to trigger an involuntary reaction in the other person. Whether she wanted to or not—and regardless of whether she actually enjoyed the experience—she would react with laughter and convulsive movements over which she had no control. It's not the same when someone approaches another person at a party and attempts to seduce them: their words may or may not have any effect, and the other person may or may not be interested.

The pervert positions himself as the agent of the drive (in Lacan's notation, $ ◇ D). More specifically, he wants to maintain a confusion between the drive and the instinct. In Cantin's words, "the pervert's position consists in denying the effect of the signifier as the source of the drive. The perverse denial seeks to equate the energy of the drive with that of the organism or the instinct, and thus to reduce the effect of the signifier to the logic of the organ."[42] That is, the aim of the demonstration is to trigger the manifestation of the drive, but in order to reduce it to an organ logic or to something instinctual or quasi-instinctual. When he convinces a woman to whip him, a jouissance will appear in her: enjoyment, anxiety, an expression of panic.

In the case of Dany, Serge André writes that "what he wanted, in searching for the ideal partner"—one who would truly enjoy what the scenario called on her to do—"was to prove that his fantasy was, in reality, a woman's fantasy."[43] But how should we understand this insight, and how does it relate to the "organ logic" Cantin describes? The aim of the demonstration, as we've seen, is to prove that the jouissance is not produced by a mental representation, a fantasy, because it can be triggered by a mechanical production. If this is true, then she is *exactly like him*: they are the same in their relation to jouissance, which can be produced mechanically in a way that is not mediated by the singular and irreducible fantasy of a subject, which is unlike any other. And if that is true, then there is no (sexual) difference, no Other. This observation clarifies why the disavowal of castration, in perversion, is invariably also a disavowal of sexual difference. Nevertheless, it is important to keep in mind what drives this disavowal. At issue is a particular way of dealing with jouissance and the anxiety it causes: namely, the demonstration that jouissance can be reduced to a constant.

In Dany's case, however—as in most cases of perversion—the demonstration encounters an obstacle that interferes with its aim. If Dany invariably fails to find a partner who would truly experience jouissance in occupying the place he assigns her in the scenario, it is because no two people share the same fantasy: it's not possible. To assume that two people could experience jouissance in the same way—or from the same scenario—is to assume that the scenario is not a fantasy, a mental construction specific to a given subject, but instead a mere mechanism or occasion for the manifestation of an instinct. It is to treat a human being as if he or she were an animal, a creature of pure instinct.

When members of the same animal species are faced with a given situation, they all react in the same way. We can think here of the response of a housecat to the jerky, irregular movement of a toy, which mimics the movement of a mouse or bird: every cat is triggered by the same thing, and responds instinctually to the prey profile. It's not the same for the human being. Each of us acts and reacts in a way that is completely unique, determined by a fantasy that no one else shares. This is precisely why speech and language must be rigorously controlled and evacuated by the contract and the staging. In choosing his partners for the same traits, or requiring that they behave in exactly the same way, the pervert is acting as if both he and the partner were like animals, responding to the promptings of an instinctual constitution. This is why the scenario is often experienced by the partner as painful, violent, or dehumanizing: it excludes and even abolishes her position as a subject.

The Absent Witness, Addressee of the Demonstration

This point makes clear that the production of jouissance is orchestrated not for the benefit of the partner, or even for himself, but for the MOTHER: she is the absent witness for whose benefit the scenario is staged. Willy Apollon, in his elucidation of the diagram I've been referring to throughout this chapter, states that the pervert's drive is "to answer the desire of the 'missing eye,' but without his partner (the father) knowing what is going on."[44]

In its completed form, then, the diagram underscores something we might not appreciate at first: that the partner always stands in the place of the *father*. In showing that we don't need words to trigger jouissance, the scenario demonstrates for the mother the uselessness of the signifier of the father's desire. The scenario is addressed to his mother, offered to her as a kind of gift, which shows that the pervert is able to provide what the father could not: while the father offered only his defective words, *he* is able to control the manifestation of jouissance (Fig. 7.2).

At this point, we can say that there are really two elements to the staging in Dany's case: the scene where he stands in front of a mirror wearing feminine undergarments (the childhood memory from age 6), and the scenario in which he is bound to the pole, humiliated, and whipped to the point of orgasm (in the childhood memory from age 7, but also in the

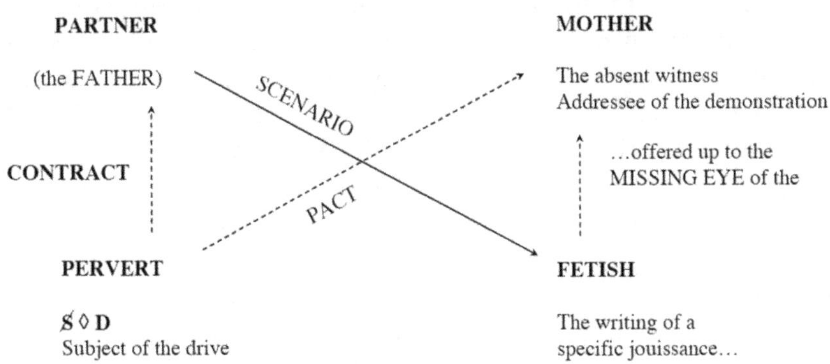

Fig. 7.2 The complete perverse demonstration

staging repeated with later partners). How can we understand the relationship between them?

When the child stands in front of a mirror wearing feminine clothing, we can say on one level that he is giving his mother the girl she always wanted to have. But why does he have to do it in front of a mirror? So as to *produce* and to *reproduce* the image of the phallic mother. When he looks at himself in the mirror, it is obvious that there is something in his underwear—whose contribution to the mirror image of the woman is key. Put another way, it is not just a girl that he sees in the mirror, but a *phallic girl*. He offers up his own penis to complete the (mirror stage of) the mother, to deny the dissatisfaction or lack of fulfillment that are attested by her complaint, as if to say: the mother is not a woman.

In this staging, therefore, Dany is reduced to being nothing more than the bearer of the penis that he offers up to the mother. We could also think about the role of bondage from this point of view. When he bound to the bedpost so tightly that he cannot breathe, it is as if he becomes one with the maternal phallus. Bondage is thus a means to satisfy the unstated maternal demand, but also and more importantly to assuage the anxiety it induces in him. It is a specific way of dealing with the "unbound" or free drive, an attempt to bind or cathect it in some way. Here, the staging literalizes this quest: as if the binding or cathexis did not need to entail the signifier or speech, but could be effected by a rope or a strap.

These different ways of producing and reproducing the maternal phallus are essential, because they show that he supports the maternal phallus in order to erase the feminine. What motivates Dany, in other words, is not the liberation or affirmation of his own innate femininity—as he believes at the moment he enters analysis—but rather the control and even the negating of that femininity: in the mother, but more importantly in *himself*. Feminine jouissance that finds no limit is a source of anxiety for the pervert. In creating a scenario that pretends to trigger—and so control—something in the Other, he is really trying to find a way to control that thing *in him*. In the staging, it is the partner (his wife) who feels anxiety. But in the scene from childhood, *he* is the one who experiences terror and anxiety while tied to the tree, before it transforms into an exquisite sensation of jouissance. This memory makes clear that it is really *his* anxiety that he is trying to control through the contract and the staging of the scenario. (Here it is worth recalling that one of Dany's reasons for seeking treatment in the first place is that he suffers from severe anxiety attacks.) In the scripted scene, jouissance is triggered in a way that is predictable and constant and can be controlled; outside of the staging, however, it cannot be managed.

From the Suffocation of the Subject to the Advent of True Speech

In requiring that the partner bind him so tightly to the bed post that he nearly suffocates, the scenario—and the contract that regulates it—requires the sacrifice of the subject (of desire, of speech) to the mother's demand, to which he is bound as a slave. Recall that when Dany entered analysis, he told the analyst that he had postponed as long as possible the "moment of cutting," which he dreaded. In context, he is referring explicitly to the sex change operation and the removal of the penis. But we can also understand these words as referring to his relation to his mother, whose logic escapes him completely even as he is driven to restage it again and again in the most repetitive way. He is unable to make the "cut," unable to separate himself from her demands concerning him, even long after her death. In choosing (however unconsciously) to serve his mother as a slave, he is also choosing to remain ignorant of his own desire and to avoid taking responsibility for it. In the clinic of perversion the analyst has to appreciate that this is the impasse in which the perverse subject finds himself, and devise a way of handling the transference that will enable the pervert truly to speak for the first time, and so discover his own desire.

For a pervert to seek out analysis, he needs to have encountered significant obstacles with the demonstration. We've already seen that Dany has difficulty finding partners who are willing to go all the way, and as a result is always reformulating the ads that he places in SM publications in an attempt to find someone willing to sign on to the terms of the contract. The same dynamic is apparent in the relationship Dany tries to establish with the psychoanalyst. André notes that when Dany begins to recount the details of his masochistic practices to the analyst in the first part of the cure, he regularly interrupts his account with certain questions or doubts; for example: "Can I continue?", or, "I don't know if I should go any further" (38).

The pervert's way of addressing the other is often not a true dialogue or exchange, but a constant work of verification whose aim is to determine whether his interlocutor can be induced to occupy the place of the partner (the father). In the case of the analyst, who professes to offer a "talking cure," the pervert may seek to verify the extent of the analyst's commitment to speech. After all, the analyst is someone who listens to intimate and obscene confessions in the privacy of a soundproof room. The perverse analysand might logically wonder, therefore: is he there to uphold the signifier and speech? Or is he there because he's fascinated by that jouissance? Can he be persuaded that the signifier is not really necessary? The pervert will often presume the latter, and attempt to demonstrate it by putting the analyst in a position where he must commit himself.

It is difficult for a pervert to abandon the demonstration, for two reasons. First, he needs to play the part of a master with regard to jouissance. But second, and more importantly for the unfolding of an analysis, he needs to avoid the risk that true speech implies. Often the pervert will try to eliminate the risk of spontaneous or subjective speech by adopting a form of presentation that is highly structured, that deflects all questions or demands and that cannot be interrupted. For example he might present the potential partner (including the analyst) with a written text, or a video that must be watched all the way to the end. Or he might display the marks that have been left on his body by his masochistic practices: marks that "speak for themselves" and that seem to obviate in advance the need for subjective speech.

In this respect, the pervert presents a specific challenge to the frame of the analytic work. André illuminates this characteristic impasse, and his strategy for avoiding it, with a simple example. Rather than responding to Dany's questions or asking him to go on, André simply returns the question to the patient in a way that underlines its imperative dimension. When Dany asks "Can I go on?," André responds, "Can you do otherwise?"[45] In refusing to respond to the analysand's question, and instead underscoring its imperative or compulsory dimension, the analyst forces him to confront the fact that the scenario has a *logic*, that it is the fantasy of the subject himself and not simply a "machinery" that functions more or less autonomously. In this way, he can constrain the analysand to find the words that will allow him to become conscious of what is repeating outside of language, so that he can come to know something about his position as a subject and discover his *own* desire.

The effect of this maneuver on André's part is that Dany begins to speak, and not merely to reproduce a highly scripted offer or resort to a formulaic staging. This speech is very painful for him. André describes how faint and halting Dany's voice becomes when he finally speaks of his own experience, and how markedly it contrasts with the relish with which he approached the formulation of the contract in his personal ads. At stake are thus two very different relations to if the latter is precise, controlled, and stripped of subjectivity, the first is vulnerable, uncertain, and without guarantee. In true speech, there is no script.

The Termination of the Analysis and the Turn to Writing

André reports that Dany, reflecting one day on the ads he was constantly rewriting, recognized that he sought to achieve in them what he called a "tight style" [*un style serré*].[46] This "tightness" echos the importance of straps, cords, and chains in the scenario staging, where Dany sought to be bound so tightly that he could no longer move and squeezed by the throat to such an extent that he could no longer speak and struggled even to breathe. André observes that Dany "had often insisted on this point, which had remained mysterious until now, because for him it was a source of permanent dissatisfaction: he was 'never squeezed tightly enough,' he said."[47]

André writes that while he "could have interpreted that regret along an imaginary axis, as a wish to be confused with the pole to which he was tied, to become one with the phallus, ...that would have sent him down a dead-end street." He therefore "chose instead to underline the central importance of the 'impossible to say' that a tight style strives to locate in language."[48] A few months later, Dany announced that he had managed to write a series of masochistic scenes with which he was especially pleased, and that he planned eventually to publish as a book. "A voluntary prisoner of the bonds [*liens*] of style," writes André, Dany chose from that point onward to dedicate himself to the writing of his fantasy, and "to dream of a reader [*un lecteur*]—and more specifically of a female reader [*une lectrice*]—who would chain herself to his words."[49]

Dany decides to end the analysis at this point, satisfied with the new outlet he had found for the expression of his fantasy. From the analyst's perspective, however, the work of the analysis had only just begun: the scenario that enacts Dany's submission to his mother's desire remained very much in place, even if it was now recognized and claimed as his own fantasy.[50] Nevertheless, we can see that there has been an important modification of Dany's position with respect to the demonstration and the castration it seeks to disavow. First, he begins to take some distance with respect to the mother's demands by abandoning the project of undergoing a sex change operation: recognizing that this is not "his" desire, that is, but his mother's. And because he now dedicates himself to writing erotic texts, rather than seeking a partner who would animate the traits and gestures ordained by the contract, it is possible that he may even find a way to forego the "staging in the real" that is at the heart of the demonstration: that is, to no longer seek confirmation from the partner (in the form of a jouissance or anxiety the demonstration would elicit in her body) that the staging is able to produce and control jouissance. The reader may or may not read the text that he publishes, and may or may not experience jouissance as a result of reading—he has no control over that.

To write stories, and especially to publish them, is also to articulate the erotic space to the public sphere. There is also an aesthetic dimension to this work of writing that was not present in the scenario, despite its marked theatricality. It holds open the possibility that Dany might one day transcend the fantasmatic dream of fascinating or ensnaring a potential reader, since the writing of the masochistic scenario potentially allows Dany to express or make visible to others something that is otherwise unaddressable, and therefore to share something of the uniqueness of his own subjective experience rather than reducing it to an impersonal constant. If the staging snuffs out the subject and takes his breath away, the writing of fiction potentially provides an outlet not only for the subject and his speech, but for the aesthetic creation by which we recognize the subject of the unconscious.

Notes

1. Marquis de Sade, *Philosophy in the Bedroom*. In *Justine, Philosophy in the Bedroom, and Other Writings*, trans. Richard Seaver and Austryn Wainhouse (New York: Grove Press, 1965), 238.
2. Serge André, *L'imposture perverse* (Paris: Seuil, 1993), 24. All translations are my own.
3. Jacques Lacan, "Kant avec Sade." In *Écrits*, trnas. Bruce Fink (New York and London: W.W. Norton & Co., 2006), 778.
4. André, *L'imposture perverse*, 23–4.
5. Marquis de Sade, "Last Will and Testament." In *Justine, Philosophy in the Bedroom, and Other Writings*, 157.
6. Sigmund Freud, "Fetishism," in *Sexuality and the Psychology of Love*, ed. Philip Rieff (New York: Collier Books, 1963), 205.
7. Jacques Lacan, "The Mirror Stage as Formative of the I Function." In *Écrits* 75–81.
8. Lucie Cantin, "Perversion and Hysteria." In Willy Apollon, Danielle Bergeron, and Lucie Cantin, *After Lacan: Clinical Practice and the Subject of the Unconscious*, ed. Robert Hughes and Kareen Ror Malone (Albany: SUNY Press, 2002), 163.
9. Freud, "Fetishism," 206.
10. Ibid.
11. Cantin, "Perversion and Hysteria." In *After Lacan*, 156.
12. This diagram was used by Apollon in the course of a presentation during a training seminar, and is reproduced with the permission of the author.
13. André, *L'imposture perverse*, 32.
14. Ibid., 33.
15. Ibid., 35.
16. Ibid., 36.
17. Ibid., 34.
18. Ibid.

19. Ibid.
20. Ibid.
21. Ibid., 34–5.
22. Ibid., 35.
23. Ibid.
24. Cantin, "Perversion and Hysteria." In *After Lacan*, 159.
25. Ibid.
26. Ibid.
27. André, *L'imposture perverse*, 36.
28. Ibid.
29. Ibid., 37.
30. Ibid.
31. Ibid., 36.
32. Ibid., 37.
33. Ibid.
34. Ibid.
35. Ibid., 37–8.
36. Ibid., 38.
37. Ibid.
38. Lucie Cantin, "The Fate of Jouissance in the Pervert-Hysteric Couple." In *After Lacan*, 174.
39. Ibid., 177.
40. André, *L'imposture perverse*, 39.
41. Ibid.
42. Cantin, "Perversion and Hysteria." In *After Lacan*, 156.
43. André, *L'imposture perverse*, 37.
44. Willy Apollon, Annual Training Seminar in Lacanian Psychoanalysis, GIFRIC, Quebec City, Canada, June 1999.
45. André, *L'imposture perverse*, 38.
46. Ibid., 41.
47. Ibid.
48. Ibid.
49. Ibid., 42.
50. Ibid.

Bibliography

André, Serge. *L'imposture perverse*. Paris: Seuil, 1993.

Apollon, Willy, Danielle Bergeron, and Lucie Cantin. *After Lacan: Clinical Practice and the Subject of the Unconscious*. Edited by Robert Hughes and Kareen Ror Malone. Albany: SUNY Press, 2002.

Freud, Sigmund. "Fetishism." In *Sexuality and the Psychology of Love*. Edited by. Philip Rieff, 204–9. New York: Collier Books, 1963.

Lacan, Jacques. *Écrits*. Translated by Bruce Fink. New York and London: W.W. Norton & Co., 2006.

Sade, Marquis de. *Philosophy in the Bedroom*. In *Justine, Philosophy in the Bedroom, and Other Writings*. Translated by Richard Seaver and Austryn Wainhouse. New York: Grove Press, 1965.

8

"The Pornography of His Eyes": A Vignette of Perversion

Derek Hook and Benjamin Strosberg

Uses of the Vignette

What is the value of the vignette in psychoanalysis? Less developed than a series of session notes or set diagnostic speculations, such a "brief evocative description, account or episode" (to site an online definition), poses itself rather as a stand-out clinical event, an illustration of a given facet of psychoanalytic theory, or, perhaps, as an indicator of where the clinical work may be headed. It may also, to adopt Baldwin's evocative

Although this is a co-authored chapter, it is based on a narrative developed by the first author (Derek Hook) which stemmed from an event that occurred during his own trainee clinical work. So, while we have used the first author plural for the majority of the chapter, the vignette is included in the form in which it was originally written, that is, in the first person, in Derek's voice. A stylistic oddity has arisen: in commenting on the vignette and the first author's experiences, Derek—as is perhaps befitting his role as a character in the vignette—is referred to in the third person.

D. Hook (✉) • B. Strosberg
Department of Psychology, Duquesne University, Pittsburgh, PA, USA
e-mail: hookd@duq.edu; strosbergb@duq.edu

M. Lee (ed.), *Lacan's Cruelty*, The Palgrave Lacan Series,
https://doi.org/10.1007/978-3-031-06238-4_8

description, take the form of "a shard" possessed of "a fractal quality," which reflects "the entire matrix" of a given type of suffering or subjective structure.[1] Such a vignette may also serve—and here a prospective limitation comes to the fore—as a vehicle of the clinician's own imaginary experience as narrativized via the means of secondary elaboration. Despite the latter concern, the retelling of an "unfinished" vignette—like the revisiting of a reoccurring dream in the clinic—may well possesses something of considerable psychoanalytic value, even if this "something" exceeds what the teller of the vignette has in mind. Our hope in this chapter is that the following vignette does indeed have psychoanalytic value, as an introduction to, and exemplification of, a perverse act as it is understood by Lacanian theory, even if ultimately this vignette exceeds the explanatory role we have accorded it.

Given that the vignette takes on a special form—modulated as it has been via creative writing practice—we begin this chapter by describing both the initial context of the event (as experienced by the first author, Derek Hook) and how it came to be written up. We then offer the vignette as Derek described it, almost ten years ago, in a piece of autobiographical creative non-fiction (a narrative form which, admittedly, extends beyond the parameters of a strictly clinical vignette). In the last section of the chapter, we consider how this vignette might helpfully illuminate Lacan's most well-known formula pertaining to perverse structure ("The [perverse] subject makes himself the [object-] instrument of the Other's *jouissance*"), the key terms of which (Other, object-instrument, *jouissance*) each require careful qualification.[2]

South West London, 2012

We begin by offering a few comments that contextualize the following vignette. Doing so helps us to locate the event relative to the first author's experience as a trainee clinician and to remark upon the written form of the vignette. Perhaps the first thing worth noting here is the elusive nature of the event itself. It emerged only as a memory of something that had been forgotten, of something that had been inadvertently retrieved. This is curious, because the event itself had been repeated several times over, and it had been both anxiety-provoking and disconcerting each time it occurred. This is another way of saying that its impact was not fully registered at the time it occurred, or, differently put again, that it *had* been, but not in a way that Derek was prepared to fully realize or admit to himself. The event did not feature in clinical supervision, perhaps simply because the key protagonist involved was not someone that Derek was conducting clinical work with.

The memory returned as part of Derek's attempt to write a piece of creative non-fiction for a master of fine arts (MFA) course that he had enrolled in approximately 18 months after his volunteer work at the prison had come to an end. He had been thinking about which facets of his prison experience might form the basis of an autobiographical short story; it was only after dismissing a series of initial ideas that the event was recalled. In other words, the memory only resurfaced once permitted the guise of an imaginative exercise. There was something about the exploratory dimension of creative writing—as opposed to the analytical task of converting clinical notes into a detailed case formulation—that made its recollection possible. As Geneviève Morel has commented, the author of autobiography indulges in something "[a]kin to the practice of free-associating in a psychoanalytic session" offering "certain thoughts, the true significance of which…[they] sometimes ignore."[3]

The event the vignette is based on took place in 2012, in a men's prison in South West London. It occurred in a section of the prison referred to as the Vulnerable Prisoner's Unit (VPU) which was home to a number of sexual offenders and a variety of other inmates who were felt to be at risk in the broader prison population. Derek spent one day a week there over a two-year period offering one-to-one therapy sessions, typically to four inmates each day in addition to attending on-site group supervision.

It is worth noting that—so as to adequately contextualize the vignette—Derek found the prison depressing, and, more significantly yet, that he felt highly self-conscious when on site, as if he were being monitored, especially so when actually entering the VPU. This was not without reason—one of the other volunteer counsellors had been recently suspended from working at the prison for not abiding by strict security protocols. Added to this was the fact that anyone entering the VPU would invariably be scrutinized by officers and inmates alike. In an effective reversal of

Bentham's panopticon, the entire two-story population of this corridor of this prison had the opportunity—providing inmates were not in lockup—of sizing up anyone entering the building. This was particularly the case in the mornings, when prisoners had a brief period outside of their cells after overnight lockup, and again after lunch, prior to afternoon lockup. The self-conscious was not just the result of actually being observed. Derek's state of anxiety upon entering the prison stemmed also from a sense of being an outside, a university lecturer and volunteer counsellor who didn't really feel that he belonged there. Here then is Derek's description of the event, extracted from a longer autobiographical short story:

> *There he was, the same guy who'd been standing there the last few weeks. Such a strange-looking, leery man. He'd had black lines tattooed around his eyes, a type of permanent eye-shadow. It gave him a dusky, seductive, disconcertingly feminine quality that was totally at odds with his aging, mawkish masculinity. He had positioned himself between me and the circular stairwell that I needed to access to get the first floor of the prison. He made a point, I felt sure, of doing this every week, of situating himself here, waiting for me, knowing that I would be re-entering the prison after lunch. That way he could fix that look on me, that gaze that lingered, that forced its way into my eyes. This was his thing: lecherous gazing. His modus operandi was—I guessed—to picture the most obscene scenario he could imagine, and then lock eyes with you, while this appalling peep-show was running through his mind. His satisfaction came by not looking away, by forcing that intrusive stare upon you, until something of the pornography of his eyes passed into you.*
>
> *One look at him and you were tempted to believe the old language of sexual degeneracy. There was something—it felt to me in that moment—that was wrong in him, in his body, something wrong in his biology. There was no natural sexuality in him. His life was a perpetual state of tacit arousal. Everyone was game. The smallest of social interactions could provide what he craved: to set off other people. For him there was a whole spectrum of pleasures to be had in sparking off unease in others, and in letting them know that he would always be willing to take it one step further. He seemed to combine different incompatible sexualities in the same ill-fitting body. The pretty eyes of a ten-year old girl; the unknowing innocence of the prepubescent; the brash, coquettish sexuality of a prostitute who had done it all before; the jaded eyes of an unshaven, dishevelled and aging pervert (the "dirty old man"); all of these were comingled in a gaze that fairly leaked with obscene intent. If he could rape you with his eyes,*

he would. That, it dawned on me, was exactly what he was trying to do: to fuck you—me—through his gaze.[4]

Retroactive Diagnosis

What then can we learn from this vignette, bearing in mind its somewhat "corrupted" form (filtered as it has been through the creative writing process)? An initial question might be whether it has any real clinical value, given that it resembles more a subjective reflection than a detached piece of clinical observation? Our first general point here would be to troubles this distinction (between subjective reflection and clinical detachment). In retrospect, the writing up of this vignette was, in an odd way, a part of the experience itself, a belated extension of an experience which had very clearly left its (suppressed) mark. As we have already suggested, the creative process enabled a kind of thinking about—indeed a *processing* of—the event that may not otherwise have been available. In fact, it was only via such an imaginative re-elaboration—the creative equivalent of a type of free association—that the perverse core of the event was revealed.

We could go so far as to suggest that a retrospective diagnosis of the event was made possible via the act of writing. Of course, there is no real way of knowing what was going through the mind of the inmate who gazed with such apparently prurient intent.[5] And yet the belated intuition—influenced, admittedly, by a novice reading of Lacanian theory—struck Derek with the force of a delayed realization when he finally committed it to paper. The *deferred* nature of this "insight" (if our guess as to the underlying dynamic of the situation is to be credited as such) is perhaps unsurprising, as is the degree to which the memory had been suppressed. Why so? Here it pays to recall the neurotic's tendency to avoid—or in this case, to simply deny and forget—any situation in which they feel they might be made the object of the Other's *jouissance*. It was perhaps due to his lack of clinical experience at the time that Derek did not think to apply the rudimentary Lacanian diagnostic indicator: if someone repeatedly and deliberately incurs anxiety in you, and *enjoys* doing so, one should consider the possibility of perverse structure. (This diagnostic indicator is to be differentiated from an interpretative technique which pivots on the notion of projective identification, and which is used by clinicians trained in the object-relations tradition, namely, the making of specific verbal interpretations about a patient based on the "evidence" of the clinician's own current emotional state.)[6]

A Perverse Choice of Partner

Foregrounding the first author's subjective experience, as we clearly have done here, begs an important question: What role did this subjectivity played in the event? Jean Clavreul's paper "The perverse couple"—a touchstone in much of the Lacanian literature on perversion—emphasizes the *subjective disparity* of the perverse subject's choice of partners ("we find the athlete linked with a puny little kid…the immoral alcoholic with a saint, the vicious dirty old man with the prepubescent adolescent."[7] By way of introducing this point, Clavreul offers the comment—a helpful rearticulation of the Lacanian formula of the pervert as object of the Other's *jouissance*—that in perversion, "erotic excitation…comes from the contemplation of the other's discomfort or suffering," adding that this excitation "sustains itself in…[the] certitude…that the *other* is innocent."[8] He clarifies:

> The pervert is not indifferent to his choice of partner. Of importance about the other are his activity, his commitments, the insignia that he bears, the virtues that he possesses. The crossing of two paths, let us say, of two ways that are profoundly differently…this the pervert seems not only to submit to but to seek. Perverse eroticism is most certain to be sustained if one of the partners defends himself in the name of certain values and thus precipitates himself even more quickly into the other's game, first as a participant, then as an accomplice.[9]

How does this relate to the vignette offered above? Well, it suggests that Derek's discomfort and self-consciousness at being in the prison, his own (perhaps undeclared) intent of "doing some good" (as a volunteer counsellor), and his (presumed or relative) sense of innocence all made him an excellent choice as a prospective "partner" for the perverse subject. Indeed, the very attempt to defend one's self "in the name of certain values" (a dedication to the clinical work, the rehabilitative ideals of the institution, etc.) would only heighten one's suitability as a prospective candidate for perverse attentions.[10]

This casts a somewhat critical light on the foregoing narrative and, for that matter, the contextualizing information we have used to frame it. For as much as Derek might claim naivete, lack of clinical experience, or neurotic defensiveness, it would seem important that any clinician avoid sleepwalking into a participating role in such an insidious erotic game. The shift from the role of (unwitting) participant to effective accomplice is one we will return to below. It is worth highlighting already here as it speaks to a feature of structural importance within perversion, namely the imperative to defile, to degrade, or in some way despoil the Other. Henry Bond's *Lacan at the Scene*, which draws on Lacanian theory to interpret a series of (perverse, psychotic, neurotic) crime scenes, offers a wonderfully accessible example, that of graffiti, to introduce this idea of the Other:

> graffiti is not designed to be looked at by a specific individual; the audience for obscene graffiti is precisely an unknown and implied Other: an Other who cannot avoid (does not chose to view) some provocative image or statement, and is corrupted by it.[11]

This helpful description, which nicely foregrounds the generalized anonymity of the Other as point of fantasized public reception, should be kept in mind as we continue, especially given Lacan's insistence that in perversion "The Other is absolutely essential."[12]

Phallic Eyes, or The Exhibitionism of the Gaze

Before expanding on this crucial idea (the role of the Other in perversion), we should address the most striking feature of the vignette: the factor of the perverse gaze. The Freudian/Lacanian concept of the scopic drive seems obviously central here (although, upon reflection, it is worth wondering to what extent other trainee counsellors working in different [existential, humanistic, cognitive-behavioral] therapeutic modalities would have picked up on the sexual dimension of this event without the benefit of this Freudian concept). Clavreul tells us that "The true partner of the pervert will always be [the] eye, which…lets itself be seduced and fascinated."[13] For the perverse subject, he continues, the eye assumes the place that "neurotic subjects…reserve for the phallus and loved object."[14] This poses a question. "Is the eye there to see, to look, to jouir, or better yet, to seduce?" Clavreul asks—to which we might respond, in light of the foregoing vignette, very possibly, *all of the above*—before going on to reiterate that "It is always there [that is, by means of the eyes] that the pervert will have to employ his charms."[15] Clavreul's description is particularly apt. Not only does it help us foreground the complexity of the gaze (as simultaneously a means of enticement, seduction, enjoyment, intrusion, and violation). It also highlights how the eyes can be *phallic*, an assertion which, in turn, implies that the gaze can *itself be an instrument of exhibitionism*. This, admittedly, is a departure from how exhibitionism is typically defined (as an act of indecent exposure centered on the *genitals*). Yet given a Lacanian understanding, which stresses that various partial objects (excrement, the breast, the phallus, the voice, and the gaze) can assume the position of the *object a* of the drive, such a suggestion seems credible. Given the fact of the prison context, furthermore, where such an act of genital exposure would immediately have been met with a heavy disciplinary penalty, it seems very likely that the prisoner may have sought an alternative means of exhibitionism.

We can supplement this developing account by referring to Stephanie Swales' book-length study of perversion. Swales affirms that the primary drive for the exhibitionist is the *scopic* drive and emphasizes also—a fact of particular pertinence—that the gaze in exhibitionism takes the place of *touch*. She explains that

> the primacy of the gaze [is typically] paired with the other highly controlled aspects of the exhibitionist's act (including choosing for his victim a stranger and choosing for his venue a public place where his victim's surprise is ensured)…the exhibitionist tries to ensure his control over the scenario by catching the Other off guard and by not giving [them]…the opportunity to consent.[16]

Swales' account perfectly fits the lived experience described in the vignette. We see here just how much the exhibitionist depends upon the presence of audience in the execution of the perverse act. In an additional passage, worth quoting in full, Swales further elaborates on the function of the gaze in respect of the role of the Other. During the act of exhibitionism, she says:

> the exhibitionist's interest is centered upon the Other and…[their] reaction to his display. He gazes at the expression in…[their] eyes and on…[their] face and also listens for a possible vocal response. The exhibitionist's aim is to provide the Other with jouissance in the form of a shock or feelings of shame, anxiety, or horror…The epiphanic moment of the exhibitionist acts occurs when the gaze appears in the Other: The shocked, horrified, repulsed and anxiety-filled reaction of the victim is important insofar as it is the sign that [he or] she is experiencing the gaze in [him or] herself…In addition to the gaze of the victim and the gaze of the exhibitionist, then, there is a third gaze which is the imagined gaze of [a] third party.[17]

There is much that is crucial here. Firstly, the accuracy—phenomenologically speaking—of Swales' account of how the victim's reaction shows that they are "experiencing the gaze in [him or] herself." This chimes powerfully with several features of the vignette, particularly the description of how "the pornography of his eyes passed into you" and, the belated conclusion that "what he was trying to do [was]…to fuck you…through his gaze." The intensity of this forced and intimate over-proximity suggests, counter-intuitively, that a form of "empathy" might be at apparent in the perverse or anti-social act (i.e. precisely where we would least expect to find it). Consider the following scene in Ian McEwan's *Machines Like Me*, in which the narrator, Charlie, and his partner, Miranda, confront a man named Gorringe who had raped Miranda's friend Mariam. As Charlie considers Gorringe's mental state during the act, he comes to a disturbing realization:

> He suffered the failure of imagination that afflicted and enabled all rapists. When his weight was on Mariam, when she was pinned to the grass…he failed to imagine her fear. Even as he saw and heard and smelled it. The

> lifting curve of his arousal was not troubled by the idea of her terror. At that moment, she may as well have been a sex doll, a device, or a machine. Or—I had Gorringe completely wrong. I had the mirror image of the truth. I was the one with the failed imagination: Gorringe knew the state of mind of his victim all too well. He entered his misery and thrilled to it, and it was precisely this triumph of imagining, of frenzied empathy, that drove his excitement into an exalted form of sexual hatred.[18]

Now while we should be clear that not all forms of perversion need be criminal, anti-social or even pathological—the notion of perverse structure in Lacanian theory carries no pejorative or moralizing connotations and is inclusive of non-pathological instances of what we might call "everyday perversion"—the above example is worth including because it suggests that a type of empathy might underlie certain forms of perverse gratification (even if admittedly, it is empathy as the term is typically understood).

Which Other? Whose *Jouissance*?

We need now return to Swales' description of exhibitionism, and more particularly, the emphasis she places on the idea of the "third gaze," a topic which connects back to the role of the Other in perversion, and, accordingly, Lacan's related formula ("The [perverse] subject makes himself the instrument of the Other's *jouissance*").[19] While this might seem obvious to readers familiar with Lacanian theory, it is worth noting the ambiguity inherent in this formula. Who exactly does "the Other" refer to here? It seems useful here to cite Bowie's qualification that the notion of the Other in Lacanian theory has both short- and long-range referents, designating as it does both "one member of the dialectical [subject-other] couple, and…the [trans-subjective] field…in which both members find themselves."[20] In our vignette, the "Other's *jouissance*" seems, at first glance, to apply to the anxiety-filled reaction provoked in the narrator (i.e. to the negative affect elicited in Derek by the lascivious gaze). This seems to be corroborated by Swales' account (and the extract from McEwan's *Machines Like Me*) in which the perverse subject carefully monitors the facial expressions and reactions of their victim. And yet, as Bond's account of the reactions elicited by obscene graffiti suggests, this is assuredly not the only vector of *jouissance* involved.[21] There is also the *jouissance* of that Other for whom the "perverse ceremonial" is in effect being staged.[22] This is the Other as the implicit (if not always obvious) third-party witness to what is being performed, the Other as a point of appeal and/or authority beyond the delimited frame of any intersubjective encounter.

In the vignette, the Other (for whom the perverse act was staged) seems, at first glance, to be the other prisoners who were able to witness the enactment of the prurient gaze, to enjoy the possible humiliation of the naïve volunteer counsellor. Now while there is an important sense in which such a reading is warranted—the dimension of the Other is, after all, invoked in the instantiation of any public scene or spectacle—we should bear in mind that the Lacanian big Other also typically entails a presumption of authority (the Other as locus of truth, as standpoint of Law, as "the subject supposed to know"). This suggests that the Other in the above scenario refers also—and perhaps more significantly—to the *prison officers* precisely as stand-ins for the Law. These representatives of the Law, moreover, were both being potentially provoked by this behaviour (which presumably they had seen before) and shown to be impotent. Indeed, they were shown up as powerless to act (in directing his intrusive gaze at newcomers, the prisoner was, after all, technically "doing nothing wrong").

Bond's analysis of crime scene photographs chimes with the above description, and helps us differentiate between these two intersecting dimensions of the Other (Other as social witness, broadly defined, and Other-*as-Law*). Bond demonstrates how the body of the murdered victim in perverse crime scenes is often arranged—in contrast to the hidden, secreted away bodies of those killed by obsessionals—in very explicit, highly public and/or staged ways, so as to horrify or titillate whoever might go on to discover the body. Such scenes, he says, have "been carried out—acted, played out—…constructed primarily in relation to an audience…it is *their* expectations/reactions that were privileged [in the construction]."[23] The Other in this respect corresponds to an envisaged series of spectators, to—as above—the level of the public scene or spectacle

(Other as social witness). Importantly, this dimension of the Other entails a fantasmatic aspect, which is to say that it necessarily involves a fantasized sense of *how such a scene might be apprehended*, of *what distressing affects* will be induced in those who encounter the scene, and so on. Incidentally, this aspect of fantasy rumination can serve as a vital differential-diagnostic consideration. Whereas a neurotic subject would feel considerable shame or guilt if some compromising fact of their private sexual life were publicly revealed, a perverse subject would not only feel considerably less by way of shame and guilt but would typically be far more preoccupied with *the Other's scandalized reaction* to such a revelation.[24]

Back though Bond's analysis of crime scene photographs and to how we might understand the Other-as-Law. Bond makes mention of the unfortunate fact that in some instances, investigating officials found themselves to be aroused by the scenes they were investigating. This echoes what we noted above regards the importance of a legal dimension to the Other. The sadistic criminal, says Bond, is aware that the crime scene "will be inevitably scrutinized by the investigating officer, the evidence gatherers", gatherers, furthermore, who will "carefully record what they find, treat all with great care" (p. 58). Such witnesses, Bond continues will be "tricked—or, perhaps more accurately, seduced—into making a series of obscene photograph, and thus also becoming unwitting collaborators, accomplices" (p. 58).[25] Here we see again not only how the Other is invoked by the perverse act, but how the Other-*as-Law* is simultaneously *appealed to* and yet *discredited*, performed for yet mocked, instantiated and also subverted. This sheds some light on a series of postulates that we often find reiterated in the Lacanian literature, such as the idea that the pervert "displaces division onto the Other"[26] and the notion that the quintessential perverse manoeuvre involves "turn[ing] symbolic authority into derision by reducing it…to a façade."[27] Likewise pertinent here is Dor's assertion that "[b]y constantly provoking the law, the pervert assures himself that it is still there"[28] and Eyers' insistence that "the pervert will orient his desire around the attempt to transgress the Law and in so doing reinforce its bounds."[29] We have thus—in Eyers' words—a double structure "of the immanence of the Law's constitution and [its] dissolution, of the coincidence of…transgression with the setting of the

Law."[30] In Lacan's own words: "in perversion…subversion of the law…is in fact truly and verily the support of a law."[31]

God's Anxiety

Having noted the importance of law (indeed, of the Other-*as-Law*) in the perverse act and perverse structure, we should now offer a few qualifications that will hopefully reiterate and refine the arguments advanced above. In *Seminar X*, Lacan offers a variation on his formula of perversion by stressing that the pervert maintains a "fantasy of being the object of a *jouissance* of the Other."[32] He goes on to emphasize that a very *particular response* is sought out in this Other (not merely that of *jouissance*), but that of *anxiety*. This adds two crucial pieces to the puzzle. Firstly, the formula of perversion refers not simply to a perverse act but to something far more significant and foundational, namely, the *organizing fantasy* that underlies and precedes the act (it is worth stressing that Lacan's matheme of perversion, that is, *object a* in relation to the barred subject (a <> $) is precisely matheme of perverse *fantasy*). Secondly, Lacan is telling us that while the *jouissance* of the Other is indeed what is in question in perverse fantasy, *anxiety* is the more precise analytical term—as opposed to an open-ended reference to *jouissance*—in grasping the Other's *response* as elicited in the perverse act.[33]

It is worth highlighting just how emphatic Lacan is in highlighting this (anxiety/*jouissance*) distinction in *Seminar X*. "It is said that the masochist aims at the Other's *jouissance*," he remarks, before adding "what is concealed by this idea is that he aims in fact at the ultimate term, at the Other's anxiety."[34] Lest we think this prioritization of the *Other's anxiety* holds only for masochism and not for sadism (as a distinct substructure of perversion), Lacan immediately offers "an analogous remark" regards sadism: "It is patent that the sadist seeks the Other's anxiety. What is thereby masked is the Other's *jouissance*."[35] We might say then that anxiety is the prelude, the *preliminary* affect that covers over, obscures (or, in Lacan's own words, *masks*) a less differentiated condition of *jouissance* that it may, in due course, lead to.

There are, no doubt, many reasons for Lacan's reiteration of this distinction—aside from the more refined diagnostic sensibility that it presumably brings about. One such prospective reason, which proves illuminating in respect of our vignette, is that a state of anxiety can be sustained—*endured*—for a far longer period than a pronounced experience of *jouissance*. A condition of anxiety may entail a far more subtle and surreptitious state than a condition of pained *jouissance*, (our vignette, and our account of the associated events came to be remembered, seem particularly telling in this respect). A subtle, "slow-burn" state of anxiety can insidiously get under one's skin—and be borne in a less than fully conscious capacity—for a considerable period. Engendering anxiety is a more enticing strategy if the intended target of perverse attentions is neurotic, given that the neurotic is likely to immediately flee any situation in which they perceive themselves as being the object of the Other's *jouissance*. The slow-dawning realization of anxiety will surely keep them in place longer than the more immediate and dramatic provocation of a state of enjoyment.

Let us stay with Lacan's account in *Seminar X*, however, for much of what he offers corroborates our foregoing discussion (particularly in respect of the role of the Other):

> Where is the Other at issue here? This is precisely why the third term in this range has been given, which is always present in perverse *jouissance*. We are meeting…the profound ambiguity in which an apparent dyadic relation is located.…[W]e might say…that this anxiety, which is the…[pervert's] blind aim…[is] in real terms, what we might call God's anxiety.[36]

It would be hard to think of a better exemplar of the Other (as the ultimate third-party witness, locus of authority, instantiation of Law, or "subject supposed to know") than God Himself. Lacan's discussion of God opens up a series of additional perspectives on perversion. It provides a segue way to the most famous of Lacan's literary references, namely the perversity of the Marquis de Sade, or perhaps more accurately yet, the perversity of Sade's *written works*, which seem so evidently aimed not only at the Other of a historical beyond (i.e. the generations of future readers who will discover and be titillated and/or appalled by his texts) but also at God as arbiter of Law. As Lacan stresses: "a relation with God…[is] everywhere in Sade's text. Sade cannot take a single step…without it turning out…that God is the one involved."[37] In the final analysis, Sade's "essential act of putting the Other [as God] to the question" works to "simulate…the exigencies of moral law" which would not otherwise function (at least for Sade).[38]

The reference to God brings a further implication to the fore. The marked asymmetry and disproportionality of the man-to-God relation underscores the "instrumental character to which the function of [the perverse] agent is reduced."[39] This perhaps comes as something of a surprise when we have foregrounded the pervert's own prospective enjoyment in their acts (as is implicitly the case in our vignette). And yet, to return once more to the formula we have focused on so much in this chapter, the perverse subject's position is that of the *object*. And so, while the pervert presumably feels some *jouissance*—or, as is perhaps a pronounced *relief of anxiety*—in the perverse act, the accent in Lacan's formula is squarely on the Other's *jouissance*. For Lacan, the perverse subject remains, in a very significant sense, "oblivious to the way this [the Other's *jouissance*] functions," even as they "offer [themselves] loyally" to it.[40]

We miss the point, then, if we focalize the enjoyment of the perverse subject. "[T]he pervert doesn't [essentially] know what *jouissance* he is serving in exercising his activity," Lacan observes, adding that in the final analysis this activity is not "in the service of his own *jouissance*."[41] A question emerges: what does this position of being the object (of the Other's *jouissance*) conceal? Lacan's answer? It "mask[s] over…the fact of…[the perverse subject's] positing [of] himself in the function of the human wreck, the poor bodily scrap."[42] This suggests then that the pervert's actions should not be read as securing the status of a subject. Such acts are not, in other words, primarily about attaining a somehow elevated subjectivity—about prioritizing their *jouissance* at the cost of all others, for example, about gratifying their narcissism, or leaving an indelible imprint of their historical presence and thereby demonstrating to the world (as the obsessional wishes to do) that they are always necessarily subject as opposed to object. To be reduced to a "bodily scrap," a piece of human wreckage, means precisely that one's subject status is in a significant sense surrendered relative to the role of being precisely *an object* of the Other.[43] This reduced position has, moreover, a protective function:

> If we know something now about the pervert, it is that what appears from the outside to be an unbounded satisfaction is actually a defence and an implementation of a law inasmuch as it curbs, suspends, and halts the subject on a path to *jouissance*.[44]

What is so crucial about Lacan's position here is that it implies that the prevailing discourse that emerges in response to instances of perversion—a moralizing discourse of punishment, retribution and condemnation—is, in a way, itself perverse. How so? Well, it presumably aims—even if in an unadmitted capacity—to engender anxiety and *jouissance* in the perverse culprit who is seen as deserving of punishment. To this, we can add the obvious—if once again unadmitted—factor of sadistic enjoyment in the prospect of this punishment. In an odd way, we could maintain that this punitive aim is more perverse that perverse structure itself. Whereas the latter desperately attempts to shore-up and re-instantiate a law that isn't functioning as such, discourse of retribution entail the libidinal gratifications of unleashing a furious superegoic *jouissance* that goes the bounds of the formal symbolic law.

Conclusion

In Patricia Gherovici's description of the historical conditions underlying the emergence of the Puerto Rican Syndrome, she makes note of how "[i]n medical practice, a diagnostic category may appear as an objective description of a clinical fact that only affects those experience…problems."[45] In other words, in conventional medicine, the diagnostic pronouncement applies only to the person who is thus afflicted and who suffers, to the person whom the diagnostic label seems most obviously directed. Gherovici continues, though, to point out that "However, the clinician is not only implicated in understanding and engaging the patient; since the clinician provides an account [of the ailment, the area of suffering]…he or she is not just an observer but also a participant."[46]

In the introduction to this chapter, we quoted Morel's comments on creative writing, highlighting her point that "the author of an autobiography offers us certain thoughts, the true significance of which he sometimes ignores and which illuminate his life."[47] There is a convergence of sorts between Gherovici's comments and Morel's: the clinician, like the author, is not—as much as he or she might like to believe it—ever separable from the material—clinical or autobiographical—they reflect upon.

Reviewing a draft version of this chapter, we were struck by the degree to which our own writing approach was in some way itself indicative of a perverse orientation. Much within the psychoanalytic vocabulary of perversion could be said to apply to this piece of writing. We have in mind here not only the ostensibly fetishistic use of the vignette (which arguably functions to provoke or to titillate an audience, to engender a form of anxiety) but also the "exhibitionistic" nature of the content, that is, the exposure of a revealing and in some ways prurient experience which—in displaying something of the discomfort involved—could, in addition, be considered masochistically satisfying. This brief autocritique is worth noting not only inasmuch as it points to how diagnostic language might be turned against those who typically wield it, but also so as to question the very idea of perversion as warranting its own distinct diagnostic structure. Dany Nobus, for example, has argued that "[w]henever Lacan examined the eroto-sexual dynamics of fetishism, sadism and masochism, he did not hesitate to do so under the banner of perversion, yet this in itself does not warrant the identification of a separate structure of perversion in Lacan's theory."[48]

Whether we agree with Nobus' position or not—and there is much above which seems to support his claim that perversion is often "a counter-transference diagnosis which serves the purpose of alleviating the anxiety of the analyst, when the analysand…triggers anxiety and threatens to destabilize his or her professional comfort"[49]—we can note that work with perversion brings distinct challenges. The first of these includes knowing how to deal with being made a target or destination—via the vehicle of the perverse subject—of the Other's *jouissance*. In other words, to work with perversion is to be made a participant. A second challenge involves having a sense of which of one's own perversions one might find while conducting the work.

Notes

1. Yael Baldwin, *The Talking Cure: Lacanian Tales of Love, Sex, and Other Catastrophes* (London: Karnac, 2016), 10.
2. Jacques Lacan, *Écrits: A Selection*, trans. Alan Sheridan (London: Tavistock, 1977), 320.
3. Geneviève Morel, "Susan Stern: *Sham*." In *On Psychoanalysis and Violence: Contemporary Lacanian Perspectives*, eds. Vanessa Sinclair and Manya Steinkoler (London and New York: Routledge, 2019), 166.
4. We have opted to include here certain comments that we would otherwise distance ourselves from (the problematic reference to the notion of degeneracy, the idea that someone might have "something wrong in his biology," the heteronormative assertion "There was no natural sexuality in him"). While these ideas obviously deserve to be critiqued, we felt it necessary to reproduce the narrative as it was written. It seemed important, furthermore—and certainly in line with a psychoanalytic approach—not to censor Derek's frank admission of the prejudices that passed through his mind at the time (or at the time of writing).
5. We were interested to find, in Rachel Cusk's (2021), *Second Place*, a fictional example of the type of thing Derek had experienced (the conviction, after looking into someone else's eyes, that they were picturing an explicit sexual scenario involving you, the person they were looking at). The novel's narrator relates a scene in which she meets a beautiful, rich, young woman. This character glances towards the narrator's partner Tony, and gives him a starkly appraising look ("she…gave him the most frankly assessing, up-and-down look I had ever seen in my life!" [Cusk 2021, p. 46]) before turning her attention to the narrator. The narrator puts it this way: "Then she…gave me the same look, and I saw that she was imagining me and Tony together sexually" (p. 46). While obviously different in key respects—the scene depicted does not seem perverse as such, even though it could be said to involve a vaguely voyeuristic aspect—it was nonetheless helpful to have another example (albeit of a fictional sort) of the odd experience of viewing 'the pornography of [another's] eyes.'
6. The idea here—repudiated by Lacanians—is that the clinician's emotional state is itself a clinical instrument, a receiver of unconscious communications (that have projected upon, or in more Kleinian terms, 'put into' the figure of the analyst) by the patient.

7. Jean Clavreul, "The Perverse Couple," in *Returning to Freud: Clinical Psychoanalysis in the School of Lacan*, ed and trans. Stuart Schneiderman (New Haven, NJ and London: Yale University Press, 1980), 219–20.
8. Ibid., 220.
9. Ibid.
10. Ibid.
11. Henry Bond, *Lacan at the Scene* (Cambridge, MA: MIT Press, 2009), 57.
12. Jacques Lacan, *The Seminar of Jacques Lacan Book X: Anxiety*, ed. Jacques-Allain Miller, trans. A. R. Price (Cambridge: Polity Press, 2014), 164.
13. Clarveul, "The Perverse Couple," 223.
14. Ibid., 226.
15. Ibid.
16. Stephanie Swales, *Perversion: A Lacanian Psychoanalytic Approach to the Subject* (London and New York: Routledge, 2012), 135.
17. Ibid., 133–4.
18. Ian McEwan. *Machines Like Us* (London and New York: Penguin, 2019), 260.
19. Lacan, *Écrits*, 320.
20. Malcolm Bowie, *Lacan* (Cambridge: Harvard University Press, 1991), 83.
21. Bond, *Lacan at the Scene.*
22. Clavreul, "The Perverse Couple," 222.
23. Bond, *Lacan at the Scene*, 42.
24. Another diagnostic indicator is worth mentioning here. Whereas the neurotic subject's accounts of how they attain *jouissance* are likely to be obscured by uncertainty, embarrassment, inhibition, or avoidance, what we often observe in perverse subjects is a remarkable degree of clarity regards what gives *jouissance.* Rather than this being a topic clouded by repression or evasion, causes of *jouissance* can be plainly stated. The first author learned this in one of the first sessions he offered in the context of his prison work. A sexual offender in his sixties sat down, and entered an account of his various crimes which he spoke of in a direct and detailed manner without the faintest hint of shame. There was none of the neurotic self-consciousness stemming from an attempt to prepare a self-exculpating narrative or to present himself as somehow likable before an unknown interlocuter, just a straightforward cataloguing of events. While provoking anxiety in those he recounted his crimes in such a frank way to, may have been a factor for him, there was another sense in which any potential interlocutor was irrelevant. His own *jouissance* was neither

shameful nor in any way problematic to him, and no interlocutor was likely to induce such a questioning or guilt in this respect.

25. Bond, *Lacan at the Scene*, 58.
26. Slavoj Žižek, *How to Read Lacan* (London: Granta, 2006), 110.
27. Serge André, "The Structure of Perversion: A Lacanian Perspective." In *Perversion: Psychoanalytic Perspectives/Perspectives on Psychoanalysis*, eds. Danny Nobus and Lisa Downing (London and New York: Routledge, 2006), 111.
28. Joël Dor. *The Clinical Lacan* (New York: Other Press, 1999), 44.
29. Tom Eyers. *Lacan and the Concept of the 'Real'* (London and New York: Palgrave, 2012), 104.
30. Ibid.
31. Lacan, *Seminar X*, 150.
32. Ibid., 163.
33. This qualification is worth underscoring, particularly in light of recent calls to be more precise in applying the notion of *jouissance* as a viable analytical (as opposed to merely *descriptive*) term in both clinical psychoanalysis (Leader 2021) and in Lacanian social theory (Hook 2018).
34. Lacan, *Seminar X*, 177.
35. Ibid.
36. Ibid., 163.
37. Ibid., 165.
38. Ibid., 164.
39. Ibid., 165.
40. Ibid., 49.
41. Ibid., 150.
42. Ibid., 162.
43. It would be hard to find a better cinematic example of how the pervert (or, in the context of the film itself, a 'sex-addict') is reduced to the status of an object in positioning themselves as instrument of the Other's *jouissance* than Steve McQueen's (2011) *Shame*. Many thanks to Stephanie Swales for suggesting this film as an illustration of perverse structure.
44. Lacan, *Seminar X*, 150. We were reminded in this respect of a view expressed by our colleague Kristen Hennesy in relation to clinical work with perverse subjects. The tendency of perverse subjects to gravitate to uncomfortable positions of over-proximity and to stimulate *jouissance* in others, she suggested, arises (at least in part) because they need to know "what to do with it" (i.e. excesses of anxious *jouissance*).

45. Patricia Gherovici, *The Puerto Rican Syndrome* (New York: Other Press, 2003), 35.
46. Ibid.
47. Morel, *The Law of the Mother*, 166.
48. Danny Nobus, "Perversion in the 21st Century: A Psychoanalytic Conundrum." In *Perversion Now!*, eds. Diana Caine and Colin Wright (London and New York: Palgrave, 2017), 103, (emphasis ours). Nobus goes on to argue, with numerous references to Lacan's early seminars, that "Lacan argued in favor of a continuity between perversion and neurosis" (p. 103).
49. Ibid., 106. We could extend Nobus' argument in the following way. If the majority of analysts tend to be neurotic, and if it is indeed the case that neurotics have a virtually allergic reaction to being made the object of the Other's *jouissance* (Fink 1997), then it is not hard to understand why there might be a profound *psychical* basis for the emergence of perversity as a separate diagnostic structure. Those with neurotic structure, in other words, are predisposed to treat any subject who elicits their anxiety in such a way, as categorically and thereby diagnostically different. As such, the diagnosis of perversion very possibly tells us as much about who is being diagnosed as about who is doing the diagnosis (which is, admittedly, very much Nobus' point).

Bibliography

André, Serge. "The Structure of Perversion: A Lacanian Perspective." In *Perversion: Psychoanalytic Perspectives/Perspectives on Psychoanalysis*. Translated by Danny Nobus and Lisa Downing. London and New York: Routledge, 2006a.

———. "The Structure of Perversion: A Lacanian Perspective." In *Perversion: Psychoanalytic Perspectives/Perspectives on Psychoanalysis*, edited by Danny Nobus and Lisa Downing. London and New York: Routledge, 2006b.

Baldwin, Yael. *Let's Keep Talking: Lacanian Tales of Love, Sex, and Other Catastrophes*. London: Karnac, 2016.

Bond, Henry. *Lacan at the Scene*. Cambridge: MIT Press, 2009.

Bowie, Malcolm. *Lacan*. London: Fontana, 1991.

Clavreul, Jean. "The Perverse Couple." In *Returning to Freud: Clinical Psychoanalysis in the School of Lacan*. Edited and Translated by Stuart Schneiderman. New Haven, NJ and London: Yale University Press, 1980.

Cusk, Rachel. *Second Place*. New York: Farrar, Straus & Giroux, 2021.

Dor, Joël. *The Clinical Lacan*. New York: Other Press, 1999.
Eyers, Tom. *Lacan and the Concept of the 'Real'*. London and New York: Palgrave Macmillan, 2012.
Fink, Bruce. *A Clinical Introduction to Lacanian Psychoanalysis: Theory and Technique*. Cambridge: Harvard University Press, 1997.
Gessert, Astrid. "Exploring Transgression from a Lacanian Perspective." In *Perversion Now!*. Edited by Diana Caine and Colin Wright. London and New York: Palgrave Macmillan, 2017.
Gherovici, Patricia. *The Puerto Rican Syndrome*. New York: Other Press, 2003.
Hook, Derek. "Racism and Jouissance: Evaluating the 'Racism as (the theft of) Enjoyment' Hypothesis." *Psychoanalysis, Culture and Society* 23, no. 3 (2018): 244–66.
Lacan, Jacques. *Écrits: A Selection*. Translated by Alan Sheridan. London: Tavistock, 1977.
———. *The Seminar of Jacques Lacan Book X: Anxiety*. Edited by Jacques-Allain Miller and Translated by A. R. Price. Cambridge: Polity Press, 2014.
Leader, Darian. *Jouissance: Sexuality, Suffering and Satisfaction*. Cambridge and Medford: Polity, 2021.
McEwan, Ian. *Machines Like Us*. London and New York: Penguin, 2019.
McQueen, Steve, director. *Shame*. London: Film4/UK Film Council, 2011. 1 hr., 41 min.
Morel, Geneviève. "Susan Stern: *Sham*." In *On Psychoanalysis and Violence: Contemporary Lacanian Perspectives*. Edited by Vanessa Sinclair and Manya Steinkoler. London and New York: Routledge, 2019.
Swales, Stephanie. *Perversion: A Lacanian Psychoanalytic Approach to the Subject*. London and New York: Routledge, 2012
Žižek, Slavoj. *How to Read Lacan*. London: Granta, 2006.

9

Neoliberalism and Liminality: Perverse Cruelties in the Age of the Capitalist Discourse

Stephanie Swales

In this chapter, I will take up a number of Lacan's conceptions of perversion to shed light on the perverse cruelty at the heart of neoliberalism. Seen through the lens of Lacan's discourse of the capitalist, neoliberalism is a perverse discourse insofar as it reduces desire to demand and disavows the lack in the Other. Instead of the promised satisfaction that accompanies each new product or experience, what results for the subject is an endless cycle of the production of painful surplus-jouissance (*plus-de-jouir*). Further perverse cruelties can be seen in the ways in which the *parlêtre*, the speaking being under neoliberalism, is marked by liminality at the level of identity. A type of subjective position that Carol Owens and I see as rapidly proliferating in our neoliberal age is what we call a "liminal creature" or a "liminal being." Liminal creatures are those who are shaped by the capitalistic superegoic command to "Enjoy!," interpreting it at the level of identity in an ideal of endless becoming in pursuit of

S. Swales (✉)
Department of Psychology, University of Dallas, Irving, TX, USA
e-mail: sswales@udallas.edu

M. Lee (ed.), *Lacan's Cruelty*, The Palgrave Lacan Series,
https://doi.org/10.1007/978-3-031-06238-4_9

one's own brand of jouissance. Far from achieving the imagined pleasures associated with meeting the contemporary ideal of "you doing/being you," such liminal beings are instead beholden to the ravages of the drive. This chapter has three main sections. First, the cruelties inherent in neoliberalism are explained and explored via Lacan's discourse of the capitalist. Second, the liminal being is shown to exemplify a certain type of suffering associated with late capitalism, one that is in some ways paradigmatic. YouTubers and posthuman transhumanists are given as examples of liminal beings. Third, the discourse of the analyst is posited as a way out of the suffering produced by engaging in the capitalist discourse; however, as Lacan pointed out, this solution is only for some.

Neoliberalism and the Capitalist Discourse

Neoliberalism, referring to the current phase of capitalism, comprises a set of ideological practices which are applied both to the market and to social life. As such, it has profoundly affected and shaped both the social sphere and the individual. Neoliberalism began as a set of financial policies in response to the economic turmoil of the 1970s, when governments shifted away from intervention in the market by governments seeking to promote the welfare of its people and toward a radically free market in which competition is maximized. Reaganism and Thatcherism are paradigmatic examples of the promotion of neoliberal policies and ideology. For instance, during Margaret Thatcher's terms as Prime Minister from 1979 to 1990, her attempts to revive the U.K.'s economy resulted in a dramatic increase in poverty rates—increases that correspond to her opinions about the "dependency culture" she saw as having been fostered by governmental welfare which she opposed.[1] Thatcher is infamous for her radically individualist statement, "There is no such thing as society."[2] Correspondingly, neoliberal ideology defines individuals as consumers who compete for resources and who are rewarded for hard work or ingenuity and punished for the lack thereof. The deregulated market supposedly ensures that each individual receives what she or he deserves, positing that inequality is due to the presence or absence of individual merits rather than problems with the system of late capitalism itself. In other words, in perverse fashion, the neoliberal symbolic order is one that disavows castration and ensures the suffering associated with increased inequality as well as the guilt accompanying failure to live up to its ideals.

In the name of ideal of individualism and the supposedly equal opportunities available via neoliberalism, indifference to the welfare of others proliferates. Although, of course, the diagnoses of psychopath and antisocial personality disorder bear little resemblance to psychoanalytic conceptions of perversion, they do capture something of essence of the cruel indifference or coldness that Gilles Deleuze highlighted in his study of Masoch in *Masochism: Coldness and Cruelty.*[3] As such, it is notable that a 2019 article in *Forbes* cites psychologist Kevin Dutton as maintaining that, along with "attorney, media personality and salesperson," one of the most common career choices for psychopaths includes Chief Executive Officer of a company.

Our social sphere, currently marked by neoliberalism, shapes individuals in particular fashions such that the speaking being of today's time does not navigate the sexual non-rapport and structural division in the same ways as those of Freud's time. We therefore see different sorts of complaints in the clinic corresponding to the ways those under capitalism deal with *das Unbehagen*, their discontents or their suffering. Patients today suffer not so much from guilt or shame about jouissance as from commanded jouissance, or from a societal superegoic imperative to follow one's jouissance rather than to pursue one's desire. Correspondingly, the newer versions of the DSM have added disorders related to such an imperative, including diagnoses like "Gambling Use Disorder" and "Binge Eating Disorder." In true neoliberal fashion, rather than taking a critical look at the social structure that breeds such difficulties, those diagnosed with such disorders are seen as failing at a moral level, as lacking in "impulse control."

Although Lacan's most substantive discussion of the capitalist discourse was given in 1972 ("The Discourse of Jacques Lacan at the University of Milan"),[4] his comments provide important insights about the social bond under neoliberalism that was to take root more firmly by the end of the 1970s. For Lacan, a discourse is a structural system of relations that regulates interactions between its elements, and it is thus what makes a particular social bond operate. By way of the capitalist discourse, we can understand that there is a particular social link that predominates in our age of neoliberalism, although other discourses and social links are also possible. Lacan presented the bulk of his discourse theory in 1969–1970 via his seventeenth seminar, *The Other Side of Psychoanalysis*,[5] when he spoke of the four discourses: the discourses of the hysteric, master, university, and analyst. Because the sexual relationship is real or "that which doesn't stop…being written,"[6] we must use speech in order to form bonds between people. Accordingly, each of the four discourses is a mode of dealing with the sexual non-rapport—the absence of fixed rules and laws regulating social relationships. Because a full explication of Lacanian discourse theory and the capitalist discourse are outside of the scope of this chapter, I will limit my comments to those most essential to understanding the neoliberal social bond as perverse or fetishistic and resulting in perverse cruelties.

Because Lacan's original four discourses utilized a fixed structure, wherein there were only four possible variations, the capitalist discourse is what Lacan designated as the contemporary substitute for the master's discourse.[7] Whereas the master's discourse is initiated by the S1 in the position of agent/semblance,[8] through someone playing the role of an authority who makes commandments, the capitalist discourse is initiated when someone plays the role of the split subject, demanding the resolution of the lack inherent to subjectivity. While it may not be immediately apparent why Lacan considered the capitalist discourse to be so closely related to the master's discourse—apart from each serving as the dominant discourse for their respective epochs—what is evident is that although the figure of the master is hidden from the position of agent, the master in the form of the structure of neoliberalism is that which silently pulls the strings. In other words, in neoliberal society, we believe we have the freedom to order this or that product or to choose this or that lifestyle, but yet neoliberalism is inescapably powerful, being constitutive of our very selves.

In his designation of the capitalist discourse as the substitute for the master's discourse, Lacan suggested that the social structure reflective of the discourse of the master, the age of the traditional authoritarian Other, had declined and was beginning to be replaced by the capitalist discourse.

Insofar as psychoanalysis had long since commented on the symptoms associated with the decline of the traditional figure of the father, Lacan said, "the crisis, not of the master discourse, but of capitalist discourse, which is its substitute, is overt (*ouverte*)."[9] What is this crisis that Lacan foresaw?

The answer is evident in the formula for the capitalist discourse provided by Lacan in 1972, which can be written via the master's discourse but with three key alterations:

1. The horizontal arrow on the top row pointing from the position of agent/semblance to the position of other/jouissance is removed.
2. The arrow on the left-hand side which points vertically up from the position of truth to the position of agent/semblance becomes an arrow pointing downwards, rendering the previously inaccessible position of truth now accessible to the agent.
3. S1 is replaced by $.

The three alterations represent several important features of our current age of consumerism under capitalism: the decline of the social bond, the changing position of truth, and that the agent who runs the show is a subject attempting to deny the non-rapport and engaging in the perverse disavowal of castration.

Correspondingly, consider Lacan's main comments about the capitalist discourse:

> it is the cleverest discourse that we have made. It is no less headed for a blowout. This is because it is untenable. It is untenable … in a thing that I could explain to you … because capitalist discourse is here, you see … [*indicates the formula on the board*] … a little inversion simply between the S1 and the S… which is the subject … it suffices so that that goes on casters (*ça marche comme sur des roulettes*), indeed that cannot go better, but that goes too fast, that consumes itself, that consumes itself so that is consumed (*ça se consomme, ça se consomme si bien que ça se consume*).[10]

The capitalist discourse is supported by casters, endlessly racing around, because it supposes itself to have found a way around the non-rapport. In the original four discourses, the non-rapport is maintained by the inaccessibility of the position of truth and by the positions of agent and other being influenced by two other positions that are not mutually related. The capitalist discourse, by contrast, utilizes an arrow that arrives at all four of the positions, creating an endless closed circuit of movement. In Lacan's comment that this discourse "goes too fast, that consumes itself," we can see an allusion to the consumer culture of capitalism in contemporary times. Moreover, it consumes itself because of the loss of distance between the split subject and the object *a* (on account of the inversion of $ and S1) which results in the split subject being plagued by the bodily tension inherent in surplus-jouissance—since the object *a* here occupies the position of surplus-jouissance.

The capitalist discourse can be considered perverse from several angles. In the perverse subject's placement of himself in the position of object *a* as object-cause of the Other's jouissance (citation), he tries "himself compensate for the flaw of the Other."[11] Lacan saw the mechanism of disavowal as being constitutive of the subjectivity of the pervert, with the foundational disavowal being that of the Other's castration. The capitalist discourse can correspondingly be considered perverse as it manufactures a belief in the existence of a solution to lack. As such, the capitalist discourse revolves around a disavowal, which might be stated as "I know very well that the next S1 won't bring me the promised state of satisfaction, but all the same I prefer to believe that upon obtaining it I will feel complete." S1 thus functions as a sort of fetish object to make up for lack.

Under the capitalist discourse, the split subject disavows castration through its attempt to aim directly at what it supposes to be the root of the problem: the lack of a particular S1, seen as a certain product or experience that could be achieved in reality. In so doing, the capitalist discourse erodes the social bond, because the agent/semblance in the original four discourses makes an appeal to the other (as indicated by the horizontal arrow starting from the position of the agent/semblance and pointing at the other—an arrow which is only absent in the capitalist discourse). For instance, in the discourse of the hysteric, which also begins with the split subject, the suffering corresponding to the subject's lack is addressed to an authority in the hope that the authority will provide answers that will quell the suffering. In contrast, in the capitalist discourse, that suffering is presumed to have a direct answer in S1 (occupying the position of truth which is inaccessible to the agent/semblance in the original four discourses). As such, the social relation, speaking beings addressing one another, is passed over in favor of aiming directly at an answer, at an S1 that will get rid of the subject's *Unbehagen*. Lacan thus said in Television in 1974: "capitalism, that was its starting point: getting rid of sex."[12] The resulting social changes such as neighbors hardly knowing one another and people choosing technology over socialization abound.

In its reach toward an S1, the capitalist discourse disavows that the discontents resulting from subjective division are structural and irremediable. The capitalist discourse emphasizes subjective discontents and manufactures demands for S1s, which supposedly remedy those very discontents. The advertising industry is the most obvious way in which this is achieved, as it is the science of how to create consumer demand for specific products. A successful advertising campaign targets a certain type of individual, making an educated guess at what might approximate the object *a*, and then trying to convince such a person that the product will bring them complete satisfaction. For example, some might be persuaded that a gold Rolex watch, if only they could save enough money for its purchase, would perfectly complement their lack, enabling them to have finally "made it" or to really be able to enjoy themselves. With its emphasis on self-responsibility for one's sufferings, neoliberal ideology even promotes S1s, which are touted to treat the sufferings created by the very excess in jouissance commanded by neoliberalism: for instance, meditation practices, anti-depressant medications, the newest diet regime, and self-help programs such as Marie Kondo's organizing method that encourages consumers to minimize their possessions and throw out everything that does not "spark joy"—while at the same time offering products for purchase "that will spark joy for years to come!"[13]

Capitalist Discourse and Surplus-Jouissance

The perversity of the capitalist discourse hinges upon its disavowal of lack. The perverse cruelty at the heart of neoliberalism can be found in the subject's relation to surplus-jouissance. Unlike jouissance, surplus-jouissance is not related to the law but instead to the failure of discourse itself. In Lacan's discussion of surplus-jouissance at the beginning of Seminar XVII,[14] he continued the comparison he made in his prior seminar with the Marxist conception of surplus value, wherein the aim of capitalism is making a profit through the sale of fetishized products. In Seminar XVI, Lacan pointed out that that using discourse creates a fetishistic relationship to surplus-jouissance.[15] As Samo Tomšič[16,17] lucidly describes it, whereas the product of capitalism is a commodity while the product of discourse is language, both of these systems create a fetishistic relation to their products. At the same time, there is a loss at the center of both capitalism and discourse. The lack and loss around which discourse revolves is why in Seminar XIX Lacan designates surplus-jouissance as the product of each of the discourses.[18] By using language to address the lack of jouissance at the center of subjectivity, language invariably falls short, as Lacan expressed in Seminar XVII when he said that surplus-jouissance is at the center of the experience of "the entire dialectic of frustration in analysis."[19] In other words, when language or discourse is utilized, the result is a painful bodily experience of frustration: surplus-jouissance, as external to discourse. Surplus-jouissance, as an unsettling bodily tension, is therefore part and parcel of our alienation in language, but it has an especially disturbing status in its placement in the capitalist discourse.

The heart of the perverse cruelty of the capitalist discourse is the split subject's discontents being in object *a* in the position of surplus-jouissance. To underscore the point, it is the only discourse in which the split subject is directly affected by the object *a* (on account of the diagonal arrow beginning at the object *a* in the position of product or surplus-jouissance and pointing at the split subject in the position of agent or semblant). Whereas in the four discourses, the suffering linked to surplus-jouissance is managed by making an appeal to an other via the social bond, in the capitalist discourse, the subject's solution is the endless search for a better, truer, S1. As soon as the split subject as consumer obtains the S1, S1 loses its veil and becomes just another product to be used and discarded, just another experience to undergo, just another signifier. With the object *a* in the position of surplus-jouissance, this disappointing realization elicits the painful feeling of loss and desire, which is characteristic of surplus-jouissance. Nevertheless, instead of realizing the jig is up, the subject in the capitalist discourse is further fueled by the surplus-jouissance of its renewed discontents, and begins the cycle of consumption anew through the appointment of a new signifier to the status of S1. That is why Lacan remarks upon the continuous loop on which the capitalist's discourse runs that burns the subject out.

As previously stated, Lacan dubbed the capitalist discourse the contemporary substitute for the master's discourse in the wake of the decline of the authoritarian father figure. Correspondingly, in *Television*, given in 1973, the year after Lacan's presentation at the University of Milan of the formula for the capitalist discourse, he remarked upon the loss of an authority who could tell us who and how to be in the way of identity and jouissance. In the age of the capitalist discourse, Lacan said that we instead take our "bearings from the ideal of an overcoming [*plus-de-jouir*]."[20] Back in 1960 in "The Subversion of the Subject and the Dialectic of Desire in the Freudian Unconscious," Lacan had said that the perverse structure is connected to the subject's attempt to "pursue jouissance as far as possible,"[21] and so we can see that the capitalist discourse invites subjects as consumers to pursue jouissance as far as possible, to push past the limits of the pleasure principle. It was in this vein that Lacan remarked that "capitalism is the extensive, hence insatiable production of a lack in jouissance."[22]

Because neoliberalism does nothing to set limits on the drive—in fact, it does quite the opposite—contemporary subjects suffer its perverse cruelties through the transgression of the pleasure principle at the level of jouissance, linking jouissance to the cruel superego. As Lacan has argued, the superego itself is essentially an imperative to jouissance as the Other's "will-to-jouissance,"[23] remarking that "nothing forces anyone to enjoy (*jouir*) except the superego."[24] Instead of producing pleasurable enjoyment, the superego ensures jouissance experienced as suffering. An update to Lacan's capitalist discourse is in order regarding how it revolves around the perverse neoliberal superegoic injunction "Enjoy!"—to "pursue jouissance as far as possible."[25] In this regard, there is a doubling of the perverse cruelty in the capitalist discourse, in the sense that it compounds the suffering already associated with the superego by way of the neoliberal ideology of the pursuit of enjoyment. The pervert himself suffers on account of his excess in jouissance, and in fact the unconscious aim of a perverse act is to set limits to jouissance and bolster the paternal function.[26] When, via the imperative of neoliberalism, the neurotic subject attempts to realize him or herself the fantasy of the pervert's pursuit of jouissance to the limit or the neurotic's "dream of being [perverse],"[27] the reality is shown to be rife with painful surplus-jouissance. Along these lines, Lacan remarked "'That's not it' is the very cry by which the jouissance obtained is distinguished from the jouissance expected."[28,29] At best, the semblance of the promised jouissance of S1 falls short of the mark of the fullness of jouissance expected. Under neoliberalism, the experience of pleasurable enjoyment is often restricted to the expected jouissance of the S1, from the enjoyment of hitting the "order now" button on a website.

Whether the jouissance in question via the capitalist discourse is that of jouissance expected or the disturbing surplus-jouissance that is actually obtained, Lacan has indicated that jouissance is in direct opposition with desire.[30] Consequently, the split subject's reach for the S1 cannot be situated within the axis of desire. Far from employing the subject's desire in its reach for each successive S1, the capitalist discourse operates to flatten desire to the level of demand. This is reminiscent, of course, of the pervert's reduction of the Other's desire to demand in seeing himself as the answer to the question of what the Other wants. Capitalist discourse mobilizes the reduction of desire to demand through the treatment of each pang of the subject's discontent as if there were an S1, a perfect complement, to address it. In clinical work in the age of neoliberalism, it is therefore especially challenging to hystericize the patient's desire through the transformation of the initial demand for something like "coping skills" to a radical questioning of oneself at the level of the unconscious. In therapeutic modalities such as cognitive-behavioral therapy (CBT), the demand for coping skills as an S1 inevitably produces renewed discontents. What burns out in the capitalist discourse is the subject's desire, the demand for satisfaction at the expense of desire only serving to increase the perverse cruelty of the discourse. Although there is no such thing in our society as escaping from the structure of capitalism, clinical work that operates in accordance with the discourse of the analyst—whether with neurotic or perverse subjects[31]—can serve as an antidote to many of the discontents suffered under the primacy of the capitalist discourse. In analysis, what is curative is the mobilization of the analysand's desire to explore the unconscious as well as the subject's eventual assumption of responsibility for desire.

In another take on how capitalism is a perverse discourse, we could consider capitalism itself as a form of perversion from the standpoint of capitalist discourse making itself the instrument for the Other's jouissance. More specifically, the capitalist discourse bears the most resemblance to the operations of the sadist. As I have pointed out in my book on perversion,[32] in the perverse act the sadist plays the role of the lawgiving Other—an entity in whom the pervert only holds a tenuous belief—and humiliates and elicits anxiety from his victim. In playacting castration, the sadist brings the voice into the scenario and enunciates a law—or rather, the Other's desire or will which serves as a substitution for the sadist. This enunciation isolates that which embodies the object *a* for his victim, eliciting anxiety by threatening its loss, with the anxiety serving as proof of its status as the treasured object *a*. Through bringing into being the object *a* to which the law corresponds, the sadist makes the Other exist.

For the present purpose, it is noteworthy that the sadist utilizes the voice to enact a law in the form of his will, given that the capitalist discourse, as a discourse, uses language and moreover enunciates a certain moral law via neoliberal ideology. We might say that the mobilization of the capitalist discourse mirrors the sadistic act to achieve its unconscious aim of propping up the societal Other shaped by neoliberalism. At a fundamental level, capitalist discourse as sadistic targets all individuals, and it is perhaps no accident that in our times anxiety disorders abound. Under capitalism, the individual imagines itself to be a free agent making choices in pursuit of its own version of happiness, but the individual is actually a slave to the invisible master figure of neoliberalism. In fact, the individual's personal version of happiness is formed in relation to neoliberal ideology, and so it might embody what Derek Hook catchily describes as a "libidinal treasure" or an object *a* which is emblematic of a social group.[33] The sadistic capitalist structure operates by threatening the loss or seeming impossibility of attaining the S1 which elicits the individual's anxiety, brings forth the object *a*, and props up the Other of capitalism. The enunciation of the law of neoliberalism leaves the individual in a state of anxiety that he or she lacks the moral qualities necessary to succeed, worrying either that someone will wrest the object away or that obtaining the S1 might not be possible. In the U.S., for instance, the individual is endlessly caught up in working to realize the American dream, and this translates to not only labor but, of course, also consumeristic behavior, which solidify the symbolic order of the U.S. as undergirded by neoliberalism.

In another important sense, sadistic capitalist discourse isolates object *a* by fueling fantasies, which revolve around xenophobia. For example, in the U.S., the racialized other and the undocumented immigrant are discursively figured as either stealing or having stolen the nation's libidinal treasures. The xenophobe—in this light appearing as the "victim" of the sadism of the capitalist discourse—experiences the anxiety of castration in relation to seeing the target of xenophobia as having perpetrated or threatening to perpetrate the loss. Marginalized groups are, of course, seen through the lens of neoliberal ideology as enjoying too much and working too little, such that their modes of jouissance are fantasied to be destructive to the country's libidinal treasures and to the happiness of supposedly more deserving citizens of the neoliberal order. Capitalist discourse thus enunciates the moral law that disenfranchises marginalized groups (e.g., ensuring that racialized others are overrepresented in the prison system and are more likely to work for minimum wage and lack health insurance)—while disavowing responsibility for so doing—and also brings the object *a* into being through the creation of anxiety in the xenophobic individual.

Liminal Beings in an Age of Commanded Jouissance

In his book *What About Me? The Struggle for Identity in a Market-Based Society*, Paul Verhaeghe argued that neoliberalism's focus on achievement and happiness operates to destabilize one's identity. Referring to sociologist Zygmunt Bauman's notion of contemporary society as "liquid modernity,"[34] Verhaeghe remarked, "a kind of 'liquid identity' has come into being."[35] Liquid identity, I would argue, corresponds to the notion of the liminal insofar as someone in a liminal state of being is in-between psychosocial positions and occupied with transition or change. The figure of the "borderline" (i.e. someone diagnosed with borderline personality disorder, BPD) is thus perhaps the most commonly recognized type of being who suffers from identity instability under neoliberalism; of course, the illness is seen as reflective of the failures of the borderline himself or herself rather than of the structure of neoliberalism. Of note is the borderline individual's characteristic and paradoxical cathexis to the label of BPD, revealing an enjoyment in claiming the signifier of "borderline" as speaking to their identity despite it typically being used in a derogatory fashion.

The liquid identity prominent under neoliberalism can be seen as paired with what Arpad Szakolczai has dubbed "permanent liminality." With "liquid identity" and "permanent liminality" in mind, Carol Owens and I have commented upon a neoliberal ideal of ceaseless liminality, which shapes a certain type of speaking being—who strives toward ceaseless reinvention at the level of identity. Owens and I call those to aspire to this state "liminal creatures" or "liminal beings."

The liminal being is one who takes the neoliberal dictate "to thine own jouissance be true"[36] seriously, prizing the value of constant innovation that enables standing out amongst rivals, and endlessly strives for a better, more authentically enjoying self. Although this chapter's focus is on the individual person as a liminal being, it is perhaps no accident that under capitalist discourse, companies prioritize the ideal of innovation; in a recent BCG survey, 75% of companies reported innovation as a top-three priority.[37] The neoliberal value of innovation as a character trait—whether in reference to a person or a company (to the degree to which neoliberalism considers there to be a meaningful difference)—speaks to ideal of perpetual transformation in a liminal identity.

The liminal as an identity destination is a path which ensures the experience of several facets of the perverse cruelty at the heart of neoliberalism. First, a perpetual process of becoming creates its own unending source of guilt for the inevitable failure to reach and maintain the status of authentically enjoying and reinventing oneself. Second, the liminal is a response to experiences of transition, passage, disruption, or loss, and as such involves suffering.[38] To tarry in the liminal as an identity destination associated with an ideal of "to thine own jouissance be true" is to be unsettled and disturbed by the jouissance that corresponds to the drives running wild. Third, for a liminal being, the S1 is figured as an enjoyable object, experience, or identity label, and the attainment of the S1 is often fantasied to ensure an experience of or identity related to being true to their jouissance. Although the disappointments and false promises of the S1 correspond to the prototypical way in which the capitalist discourse adds fuel to the fire of the subject's painful surplus-jouissance, discussion of the fantasied S1s of the liminal being illuminates this type of subjectivity.

One identity label which might serve as an S1 affixed to the ideal of permanent liminality is "social media star," because it promises constant transformation so as to reap the rewards associated with maintaining and attracting followers. One platform that makes this clear is BitClout. Essentially, BitClout is a social media platform in which users earn revenue and derive jouissance from being true to their jouissance. Earning the nickname of "social-media stock market,"[39] by way of the site's native currency, BitClout, users can invest in someone's "creator coin" if they believe her or his popularity will rise. A quick perusal of BitClout's list of top-valued "creators" showed numerous social media stars, such as YouTuber MrBeast (at #25 on the list), with the vast majority of the top creators having recognizably large social media followings—an index that is included in the Top 100 chart.[40] Someone is called a "creator" if they have created or otherwise claimed their profile. Regarding these so-called BitClout "creators," it is useful to recall Michel Foucault's comment that in our age of neoliberalism, the individual is "an entrepreneur of himself."[41] The ideal of entrepreneurship is to be self-directed, self-employed, and make lots of money. Often, it is paired with creativity and constant innovation so as to be on the cutting edge of the tastes of consumers, perhaps even creating something consumers did not previously know they craved. Wedding the value of creativity with the economy of late capitalism, each BitCoin creator is an entrepreneur of the self. What BitClout renders apparent is the neoliberal ideology of the liminal being as one that propagates the injunction to enjoy.

Through Foucault's claim that the neoliberal subject is an entrepreneur of the self, he points out that what had been the self's relatively immutable feature—the body—has now become possible to transform. Practices of transforming the body include such things as Lasik eye correction, plastic surgery, cool sculpt, as well as a litany of different diets to fit desired associated identities (e.g., Paleo diet, slim fast, Nutrisystem, flexitarian, Eco Atkins, Supercharged Hormone, and vegan). Such methods of bodily transformation aimed at increasing social capital promote at the same time an ideology of liminality. Including and extending beyond physical transformation is a so-called philosophy that rose to prominence under neoliberalism: transhumanism.

Liminal beings adhering to transhumanism pursue the neoliberal ideal of ceaseless liminality through a search for technologies that improve the human species. Enhancements are sought for problems related to human limitations in the way of decelerating the aging process and increasing longevity, increasing physical capabilities, and improving cognition, psychological capacities, and mood. The sciences behind bioengineering, genetic engineering, cybernetics, and digital technology are employed towards these ends. It is no accident that the transhumanist movement began at the same time as neoliberalism. Not only do transhumanist liminal beings seek to go beyond the limits of the human condition, but they also believe that doing so is possible. (Accordingly, some transhumanist liminal beings might very well be psychotic in structure if this belief is at the level of delusion.) As such, transhumanism mobilizes science to disavow the Other's castration through a denial that the human species is irrevocably limited and lacking.

Liminal beings who follow transhumanism believe that they occupy liminal identities between human and technology, between human and posthuman, and are forever striving to transform to the next level of human being. In 2018, photographer Matthieu Gafsou created a series of photographs of transhumanists entitled "H+," bringing to mind human plus, as something beyond or better than human.[42] Gafsou's photographs feature the likes of Lukas Zpira, who wrote the "Body Hacktivism Manifesto"[43] and Julien Deceroi, who implanted a magnet into his middle finger to give himself another sense perception—that of the perception of magnetic fields.[44] This type of liminal being seeks to make a reality out of the fantasy of the cyborg, which is a common trope in science fiction on the page and on the screen (e.g., *Robocop*). Each augmentation and reinvention of the self functions as an S1.

At the extreme, posthuman transhumanists believe that even death can be conquered.[45] To somehow remove from the equation humanity's being-towards-death (to allude to Heidegger) would create a different type of being, a posthuman being. Plugging up the ultimate lack in human beings is an immensely popular fantasy in the neoliberal age as reflected on the screen. The achievement of digital immortality is depicted in *Upload* by way of uploading one's consciousness to a data cloud, while immortality is achieved in *Altered Carbon* via uploading one's consciousness to a synthetic body called a "sleeve"—as though a body were simply clothing to be traded in, changed, and augmented as one pleases. Even if both series serve in some ways as cautionary tales, they nevertheless depict access to an enjoyment beyond the limits of the human species. To call this enjoyment "superhuman" would not be accidental, given the explosion of popularity in the figure of the superhero—which itself is another type of transhuman fantasy—evident in the proliferation of on the screen stories of the genre in the age of neoliberalism.

Alcor is a company that offers cryogenic suspension or "pausing the dying process," and as of June 13, 2021, had 1353 "members" who pay a monthly subscription fee in order to be cryogenically preserved at some later date.[46] One such Alcor member was notable transhumanist FM-2030, who on July 8, 2000, died from pancreatic cancer and was vitrified. Reflecting his belief in the eventuality of digital immortality and the transportation of the mind through outer space, FM-2030 was born—or "launched" as he called it on October 15, 1930[47]—as Fereidoun M. Esfandiary. He explained that he changed his name in the mid-1970s for two primary reasons. First, the "2030" part of his self-nomination demonstrated his belief that he would live to the age of 100 and that in "2030 we will be ageless and everyone will have an excellent chance to live forever."[48] Second, he saw FM-2030 as a way to break out of the restrictive conventions of names. On this account, he said, "Conventional names define a person's past: ancestry, ethnicity, nationality, religion. I am not who I was ten years ago and certainly not who I will be in twenty years."[49] There are thus several forms of protest encompassed in his chosen name. Adding to the protest against the limit of death, he took issue with a name that would bind him to his past, further revealing him as a liminal being operating under the neoliberal ideal of ceaseless reinvention of the self. FM-2030 also took a stand against various forms of xenophobia and divisiveness, but perhaps more centrally his conflict had to do with any identity imposed upon him by the Other.

Similarly, FM-2030 disliked answering questions about his nationality or his age,[50] which he may have viewed as pinning him down into one static identity. In terms of the question of his age, according to his obituary in the *New York Times* "his latest artificial hip was only two years old, making the question, in his view, meaningless."[51] Regarding his nationality, he saw himself as a "global citizen, and said there were no illegal immigrants, just irrelevant borders,"[52] eschewing even the limits or demarcations of a nation's identity. Because FM-2030's father had been an Iranian diplomat, by the age of 11, he had lived in 17 different countries.[53] FM-2030's insistence upon seeing even typically fixed identities such as age and nationality as fluid speaks to his dogged pursuit of the neoliberal ideals of constant self-reinvention.

In his teaching and writings, the work life of FM-2030 largely focused on futurist and transhuman themes. From 1979 to 1991, FM-2030 taught a seminar at the University of California Los Angeles (UCLA) Extension School entitled "Major Transformations: The Next 20 Years,"[54] and his unpublished works during that same period include titles such as "Countdown to Immortality."[55] As an entrepreneur of the self, FM-2030 was known for his book, *Are You a Transhuman?: Monitoring and Stimulating Your Personal Rate of Growth in a Rapidly Changing World*.[56] Evident in the title's use of "rate of growth" is the facet of neoliberal ideology that renders everything and everyone calculable. The phrase "monitoring and stimulating your personal rate of growth" could apply equally as well to funds invested in the stock market. Liminal states associated with personal change and transformation are therefore flattened under the rubric of an investment in the value of the self as well as commanded in perpetuity to grow and improve. "Monitoring and stimulating" also speak to a kind of science behind the ideal of endless growth in a "rapidly changing world" or Other, which itself occupies a ceaselessly liminal identity. The perverse cruelty at the root of the promises of this title certainly involves the endless source of guilt produced by its readers for their failure to transform fast enough and completely enough to achieve their ideal selves.

Other speculations as to the signification of the "FM" in FM-2030's chosen name include "Future Man", "Future Modular", and "Future Marvel."[57] Regardless of whether or not it is only the "2030" or also the "FM" in his chosen name that indicates his perpetual reach toward the future, these signifiers would further tie him to the neoliberal ideal of ceaseless liminality. Some of FM-2030's S1s would undoubtedly have been those that promised him a closer relationship to a better future, both for humanity and for himself. On his side, FM-2030 itself may have functioned at one time as an S1 and proved inevitably disappointing. So too would cryogenic suspension have operated as an S1, with its great allure being the promise of enabling eternal life (once his physical ailments could be cured and then upon the achievement of digital immortality). It is only through his death that he could exit from the capitalist discourse—and, of course from all discourse—because his final S1 would not have the opportunity to disappoint him and create further discontents. FM-2030's S1s for the sake of humanity (with himself included in the human species, of course) included a "Santa Claus machine [that] would produce three-dimensional objects in the manner of copying machines. This, combined with free energy from the sun, would produce limitless resources and eliminate competition."[58] As an S1, the Santa Clause machine operated to prop up a perverse belief in the uncastrated Other. FM-2030, then, not only disavowed his own lack but also the lack in the Other.

It is, of course, rather ironic that in the capitalist discourse versions of the fantasied, uncastrated Other would include limitless resources and the elimination of competition! It is worth highlighting that common disavowals of the lack in the Other occurring in our time include such beliefs in the eradication of the very competition, pollution, and racism that are clearly exacerbated and even commanded under neoliberalism. For instance, during a U.S. House hearing in early June of 2021, Texan Republican Louie Gohmert proposed an interesting solution to the climate change crisis by way of a request to Jennifer Eberlien, associate deputy chief of the Forest Service. Referencing recent significant solar storm activity, Gohmert said,

> I was informed by the past director of NASA that they have found that the moon's orbit is changing slightly and so has the Earth's orbit around the sun… Is there anything that the national Forest Service or [Bureau of Land Management] can do to change the course of the moon's orbit or the Earth's orbit around the sun? Obviously, that would have profound effects on our climate.[59]

Reducing fossil fuel use and increasing renewable energy sources was clearly not on the table. Instead, amusingly evocative of the significance of the Copernican revolution, the patently absurd idea of changing the orbit of the Earth or the moon—and by the U.S. Forest Service, no less!—reflects a disavowal of the lack in the Other of science in order to continue enjoying destructively and cruelly. Because Gohmert was speaking as a representative of the U.S., his position was also that of the split subject in the capitalist discourse who sought to deny the castration of the U.S. through the S1 of altering the orbit of the Earth or moon.

Conclusion

To review, including a harmful indifference to the environment and global welfare, there are a number of ways in which neoliberalism enacts perverse cruelties upon the speaking being, society, and even the Earth itself. The discourse of the capitalist can be considered to be perverse in a generalized way insofar as it ensures suffering through a disavowal of lack. It does so through the false promises of the S1 in the position of truth as well as through propping up a belief in eventual perfection of science. Upon obtaining an S1, it loses its value, and the agent in its disappointment is plagued with surplus-jouissance. In an endless circuit, the renewed discontents provokes the agent to reach yet again for another, different S1. This guarantee of the production of unsettling surplus-jouissance is at the perverse core of the capitalist discourse. This core relates to how speaking beings suffer from commanded jouissance and a lack of the installation of desire in the capitalist discourse's perverse reduction of desire to demand. The drives are left to run wild and the primal father as cruel superegoic jouisseur reigns. Liminal beings, as one type of subjective position common under neoliberalism, suffer on all of these accounts. What is more, in their pursuit of ceaseless innovation at the level of identity, they experience the pain associated with liminal states of becoming alongside the inevitable failure to be true to their jouissance and transform as they would wish. The approach used by liminal beings to handling their singular experiences of psychical disruption and transition is therefore in opposition with the construction of and identification with a sinthome. While S1 is just another signifier, the sinthome is a knotting together of real, symbolic, and imaginary and is thereby beyond meaning. The sinthome allows the speaking being to live through providing a singular organization of jouissance. In their perpetual drive to reinvent themselves by way of the capitalist discourse, they work against the sinthomatic solution of knotting to hold the speaking being in place.

In the construction of the neologism "sinthome" in Lacan's 23rd seminar,[60] Lacan made use of his interpretation of the figure of the *saint homme*, holy man or saint, and it is no accident that by way of comparing the analyst with the saint that Lacan provides an answer to the crises caused by the capitalist discourse. On this account, in *Television*, Lacan said, "The more saints, the more laughter; that's my principle, to wit, the way out of capitalist discourse—which will not constitute progress, if it happens only for some."[61] Lacan compares the analyst to figure of the saint because the saint's "business… is not *caritas*"[62] and thus is not about acting for someone's Good. Instead, the saint "acts as trash [déchet]; his business being *trashitas* [*il décharite*]."[63] In being *trashitas*, the analyst is situated outside of what is "in demand" under the consumeristic logic of capitalism, and this allows him to occupy the role of the object *a* as "cause of the subject's own desire."[64]

The discourse of the analyst then is ultimately the antidote to the discourse of the capitalist. Whereas in the capitalist discourse, the speaking being does not address an other in its search for a solution to its discontents, in the analyst's discourse, a connection is forged between the agent and other, between the split subject and the object *a* or between the analysand and the analyst. Although in the capitalist discourse, there is also a direct relationship with the object *a*, in that discourse, it plagues the speaking being, fueling its discontents anew, only operating to motivate the subject to find yet another S1 as though the S1 really were the lost object that could be recovered. Instead, in playing the role of object *a* as *trashitas* what the analyst installs is the desire of the speaking being that is so notably missing in the discourse of the analyst. This involves the articulation of the lack of the speaking being rather than its disavowal. In addressing the problem of its suffering to the analyst, the analysand's desire is mobilized in arriving not at the fantasmatic solution of the S1 but instead toward a savoir-faire regarding its surplus-jouissance through identification with the sinthome. This is indicated by the S1 as the master signifier occupying the end position of the discourse which Lacan later designated that of surplus-jouissance.

As Lacan commented, the way out of the perverse cruelties of the capitalist discourse is "only for some."[65] Unfortunately, the alternative path of the discourse of the analyst is accessible only to those who engage in psychoanalysis. It should go without saying that in times of neoliberalism, psychoanalysis is not sought out or practiced nearly as often as other forms of the talking cure, including cognitive-behavioral therapy and speaking to a priest (or other religious authority). What is more, the practice of psychoanalysis does not affect transformation of the structural inequalities promoted by neoliberalism in the name of individualism and freedom nor does it ameliorate harm done to the Earth itself.

Notes

1. According to the Institute for Fiscal Studies, in 1979, 13.4% of the population lived below 60% of median incomes before housing costs. By 1990, it had risen to 22.2%, or 12.2 million people, with huge rises in the mid-1980s. https://www.ifs.org.uk/tools_and_resources/incomes_in_uk. Accessed June 15, 2021.
2. Margaret Thatcher, "Interview for Woman's Own ("no such thing as society")." https://www.margaretthatcher.org/document/106689. Accessed June 15, 2021.
3. Gilles Deleuze, *Masochism: Coldness and Cruelty*, trans. Jean McNeil (New York: Zone Books, 1991).

4. Jacques Lacan, "Discours de Jacques Lacan à l'université de Milan." *Lacan in Italia* (1972): 32–55.
5. Jacques Lacan, *The Seminar of Jacques Lacan, Book XVII: The Other Side of Psychoanalysis*, ed. Jacques-Alain Miller, trans. Russell Grigg (New York: W.W. Norton & Co., 2007).
6. Jacques Lacan, *The Seminar of Jacques Lacan, Book XX: On Feminine Sexuality, the Limits of Love and Knowledge, 1972–1973*, ed. Jacques-Alain Miller, trans. Bruce Fink (New York: W. W. Norton, 1999), 59.
7. For an excellent thorough explication of the capitalist discourse, see Stijn Vanheule, Stijn, "Capitalist Discourse, Subjectivity and Lacanian Psychoanalysis." *Frontiers in Psychology 7*, article 1948 (2016): 1–14.
8. In *Seminars XVIII* and *XIX*, Lacan (e.g., Jacques Lacan, *The Seminar of Jacques Lacan, Book XIX: …or Worse*, ed. Jacques-Alain Miller, trans. Adrian Price (Cambridge: Polity, 2018), 169) reformulated the discursive positions of agent, other, and product. In the position that in Seminar XVII, Lacan had designated as that of the agent, he placed the function of the *semblant* or semblance. Likewise, for the position of other, he substituted "jouissance", and he replaced the position of product with "surplus-jouissance."
9. Jacques Lacan, "Discours de Jacques Lacan à l'université de Milan (The Capitalist Discourse)" (1972), trans. Jack Stone, 20. https://freud2lacan.b-cdn.net/DISCOURSE_OF_CAPITALISM-bilingual.pdf. Accessed June 15, 2021.
10. Ibid., 20.
11. Jacques Lacan, *Le Séminaire Livre XVI: D'un Autre à l'Autre*, ed. Jacques-Alain Miller (Paris: Éditions du Seuil, 2006), 265 (my translation).
12. Lacan, *Television*, 34.
13. https://shop.konmari.com/. Accessed June 15, 2021.
14. Lacan, *Seminar XVII*, 19–20.
15. Lacan, *Le Séminaire Livre XVI*, 45.
16. Samo Tomšič, "Homology: Marx and Lacan." *S J. Jan Van Eyck Circle Lacanian Ideol. Crit.* 5 (2012): 98–113.
17. Samo Tomšič, *The Capitalist Unconscious, Marx, and Lacan* (London and New York: Verso, 2015).
18. Lacan, *Seminar XIX*, 193.
19. Lacan, *Seminar XVII*, 19.
20. Lacan, *Television*, 32.

21. Jacques Lacan, "The Subversion of the Subject and the Dialectic of Desire in the Freudian Unconscious." In *Ecrits: The First Complete Edition in English*, trans. Bruce Fink (New York: W. W. Norton, 2006), 700.
22. Jacques Lacan, "Radiophonie." *Scilicet* 2/3, (1970): 55–99. English translation from www.lacantokyo.org/img/Radiophonie_tr_en.pdf, trans. Jack Stone, p. 22. Accessed June 15, 2021.
23. Jacques Lacan, "Kant with Sade." In *Ecrits: The First Complete Edition in English*, trans. Bruce Fink (New York: W. W. Norton, 2006), 652.
24. Lacan, *Seminar XX*, 3.
25. Lacan, "The Subversion of the Subject," 700.
26. Stephanie Swales, *Perversion: A Lacanian Psychoanalytic Approach to the Subject* (New York and London: Routledge, 2012).
27. Lacan, *Seminar XX*, 80.
28. Ibid., 111.
29. For an excellent explication of this point, see also Adrian Johnston, "The Forced Choice of Enjoyment: *Jouissance* Between Anticipation and Actualization," *Lacanian Ink: The Symptom*, 2 (2002, Spring/Summer): http://www.lacan.com/forcedf.htm.
30. Lacan, "The Subversion of the Subject," 700.
31. Swales, *Perversion.*
32. Ibid., 169–70.
33. Derek Hook, "Racism and *jouissance*: Evaluating the "Racism as (the theft of) Enjoyment" Hypothesis." *Psychoanalysis, Culture & Society* 5, no. 3 (2018).
34. Zygmunt Bauman, *In Search of Politics* (Stanford: Stanford University Press, 1999).
35. Paul Verhaeghe, *What About Me? The Struggle for Identity in a Market-Based Society*, trans. Jane Hedley-Prôle (London: Scribe, 2014), 33.
36. Stephanie Swales and Carol Owens, *Psychoanalysing Ambivalence with Freud and Lacan: On and Off the Couch* (New York and London: Routledge, 2019), 86–7.
37. Boston Consulting Group, "Overcoming the Innovation Readiness Gap: Most Innovative Companies 2021." https://www.bcg.com/publications/2021/most-innovative-companies-overview. Accessed June 15, 2021.
38. Bjorn Thomasson, "Revising Liminality: The Danger of Empty Spaces". In *Liminal Landscapes: Travel, Experience and Places in-Between*, eds.

Hazel Andrews and Les Roberts (New York and London: Routledge, 2017).

39. "The Dark Democratizing Power of the Social Media Stock Market" is an Article from the New Yorker magazine. https://www.newyorker.com/tech/annals-of-technology/the-dark-democratizing-power-of-the-social-media-stock-market. Accessed June 15, 2021.
40. https://bitcloutlist.com/. Accessed June 10, 2021.
41. Foucault, *The Birth of Biopolitics*, 226.
42. https://www.mapsimages.com/works/h/. Accessed June 15, 2021.
43. "Meet the Transhumanists Turning Themselves Into Cyborgs" is an article from Wired! Magazine. https://www.wired.com/story/transhumanism-cyborg-photo-gallery/. Accessed June 15, 2021.
44. https://we-make-money-not-art.com/h-we-are-all-transhumanists-now/. Accessed June 15, 2021.
45. Nick Bostrom, "A History of Transhumanist Thought." In *Academic Writing Across the Disciplines*, eds. Michael Rectenwald and Lisa Carl (New York: Pearson Longman, 2011).
46. https://www.alcor.org/. Accessed June 15, 2021.
47. "Futurist Known as FM-2030 is Dead at 69" is an article from the New York Times. https://www.nytimes.com/2000/07/11/us/futurist-known-as-fm-2030-is-dead-at-69.html. Accessed June 15, 2021.
48. "FM-2030" is a radio clip from National Public Radio. https://www.npr.org/2000/07/11/1076532/fm-2030. Accessed June 15, 2021.
49. Ibid.
50. "Futurist Known as FM-2030 is Dead at 69" is an article from the New York Times. https://www.nytimes.com/2000/07/11/us/futurist-known-as-fm-2030-is-dead-at-69.html. Accessed June 15, 2021.
51. Ibid.
52. Ibid.
53. Ibid.
54. http://archives.nypl.org/mss/4846. Accessed June 15, 2021.
55. Ibid.
56. FM-2030, *Are You a Transhuman?: Monitoring and Stimulating Your Personal Rate of Growth in a Rapidly Changing World* (New York: Grand Central Publishing, 1989).
57. Ibid.
58. Ibid.

59. "Rep. Louie Gohmert Asks if Forest Service can Shift Earth's or Moon's Orbit to Fight Climate Change" is an article from the *Dallas Morning News*. https://www.dallasnews.com/news/politics/2021/06/09/rep-louie-gohmert-wants-forest-service-to-shift-earth-or-moons-orbit-to-fight-climate-change. Accessed June 15, 2021.
60. Jacques Lacan, *The Seminar of Jacques Lacan, Book XXIII: The Sinthome*, ed. Jacques-Alain Miller, trans. Adrian Price (Cambridge: Polity, 2016).
61. Lacan, *Television*, 16.
62. Ibid., 15.
63. Ibid., 15.
64. Ibid., 15.
65. Ibid., 16.

Bibliography

Bauman, Zygmunt. *In Search of Politics*. Stanford: Stanford University Press, 1999.

Boston Consulting Group. "Overcoming the Innovation Readiness Gap: Most Innovative Companies 2021": https://www.bcg.com/publications/2021/most-innovative-companies-overview. Accessed June 15, 2021.

Bostrom, Nick. "A History of Transhumanist Thought." In *Academic Writing Across the Disciplines*. Edited by Michael Rectenwald and Lisa Carl. New York: Pearson Longman, 2011.

Deleuze, Gilles. *Masochism: Coldness and Cruelty*. Translated by Jean McNeil. New York: Zone Books, 1991.

FM-2030. *Are You a Transhuman?: Monitoring and Stimulating Your Personal Rate of Growth in a Rapidly Changing World*. New York: Grand Central Publishing, 1989.

Foucault, Michel. *The Birth of Biopolitics: Lectures at the Collège de France, 1978–1979 (Lectures at the College de France)*. Translated by Graham Burchell. New York, NY: Picador, 2010.

Hardy, Michael. "Meet the Transhumanists Turning Themselves Into Cyborgs." *Wired!* (September 17, 2018): https://www.wired.com/story/transhumanism-cyborg-photo-gallery/. Accessed June 15, 2021.

Hook, Derek. "Racism and *jouissance*: Evaluating the "Racism as (the theft of) Enjoyment" Hypothesis." *Psychoanalysis, Culture & Society* 5, no. 3 (2018).

https://www.alcor.org/. Accessed June 15, 2021.

http://archives.nypl.org/mss/4846. Accessed June 15, 2021.

https://bitcloutlist.com/. Accessed June 10, 2021.

https://www.mapsimages.com/works/h/. Accessed June 15, 2021.

https://shop.konmari.com/. Accessed June 15, 2021.

https://we-make-money-not-art.com/h-we-are-all-transhumanists-now/. Accessed June 15, 2021.

Institute of Fiscal Studies. *Living Standards, Poverty and Inequality in the UK*: https://www.ifs.org.uk/tools_and_resources/incomes_in_uk. Accessed June 15, 2021.

Johnston, Adrian. "The Forced Choice of Enjoyment: *Jouissance* Between Anticipation and Actualization," *Lacanian Ink: The Symptom*, no. 2 (2002, Spring/Summer): http://www.lacan.com/forcedf.htm.

Justin, Raga. "Rep. Louie Gohmert asks if Forest Service can shift Earth's or moon's orbit to fight climate change." *Dallas Morning News* (June 9, 2021): https://www.dallasnews.com/news/politics/2021/06/09/rep-louie-gohmert-wants-forest-service-to-shift-earth-or-moons-orbit-to-fight-climate-change. Accessed June 15, 2021.

Lacan, Jacques. "Discours de Jacques Lacan à l'université de Milan." *Lacan in Italia* (1972): 32–55.

———. "Kant with Sade." In *Ecrits: The First Complete Edition in English*. Translated by Bruce Fink, 645–668. New York: W. W. Norton, 2006a.

———. *Le Séminaire Livre XVI: D'un Autre à l'Autre*. Edited by Jacques-Alain Miller. Paris: Éditions du Seuil, 2006b.

———. "Radiophonie." *Scilicet* 2/3 (1970): 55–99.

———. *The Seminar of Jacques Lacan, Book VII: The Ethics of Psychoanalysis, 1959–1960*. Edited by Jacques-Alain Miller. Translated by Dennis Porter. New York: W. W. Norton, 1992.

———. *The Seminar of Jacques Lacan, Book XVII: The Other Side of Psychoanalysis, 1969–1970*. Edited by Jacques-Alain Miller. Translated by Russell Grigg. New York: W. W. Norton, 2007.

———. *The Seminar of Jacques Lacan, Book XIX: …or Worse*. Edited by Jacques-Alain Miller. Translated by Adrian Price. Cambridge: Polity, 2018.

———. *The Seminar of Jacques Lacan, Book XX: On Feminine Sexuality, the Limits of Love and Knowledge, 1972–1973*. Edited by Jacques-Alain Miller. Translated by Bruce Fink. New York: W. W. Norton, 1999.

———. *The Seminar of Jacques Lacan, Book XXIII: The Sinthome*. Edited by Jacques-Alain Miller. Translated by Adrian Price. Cambridge: Polity, 2016.

———. "The Subversion of the Subject and the Dialectic of Desire in the Freudian Unconscious." In *Ecrits: The First Complete Edition in English*. Translated by Bruce Fink, 671–702. New York: W. W. Norton, 2006c.

———. *Television*. Translated by Denis Hollier, Rosalind Krauss, and Annette Michelson. New York: W.W. Norton & Co., 1990.

Lester, Caroline. "The Dark Democratizing Power of the Social Media Stock Market." *The New Yorker* (June 9, 2021): https://www.newyorker.com/tech/annals-of-technology/the-dark-democratizing-power-of-the-social-media-stock-market. Accessed June 15, 2021.

Martin, Douglas. "Futurist Known as FM-2030 is Dead at 69." *New York Times* (July 11, 2000): https://www.nytimes.com/2000/07/11/us/futurist-known-as-fm-2030-is-dead-at-69.html. Accessed June 15, 2021.

National Public Radio. "FM-2030" (June 11, 2000): https://www.npr.org/2000/07/11/1076532/fm-2030. Accessed June 15, 2021.

Supran, Geoffrey and Oreskes, Naomi. "Rhetoric and Frame Analysis of ExxonMobil's Climate Change Communications." *One Earth* 4 (2021): 696–719.

Swales, Stephanie. *Perversion: A Lacanian Psychoanalytic Approach to the Subject*. New York and London: Routledge, 2012.

Swales, Stephanie and Owens, C. *Psychoanalysing Ambivalence with Freud and Lacan: On and Off the Couch*. New York and London: Routledge, 2019.

Thatcher, Margaret. *Interview for Woman's Own ("no such thing as society")*: https://www.margaretthatcher.org/document/106689. Accessed June 15, 2021.

Thomasson, Bjorn. "Revising Liminality: The Danger of Empty Spaces." In *Liminal Landscapes: Travel, Experience and Places in-Between*. Edited by Hazel Andrews and Les Roberts, 21–35. New York and London: Routledge, 2017.

Tomšič, Samo. "Homology: Marx and Lacan." *S J. Jan Van Eyck Circle Lacanian Ideol. Crit.* 5 (2012): 98–113.

———. *The Capitalist Unconscious, Marx, and Lacan*. London and New York: Verso, 2015.

Vanheule, Stijn. "Capitalist Discourse, Subjectivity and Lacanian Psychoanalysis." *Frontiers in Psychology* 7, article 1948 (2016): 1–14.

Verhaeghe, Paul. *What About Me? The Struggle for Identity in a Market-Based Society*. Translated by Jane Hedley-Prôle. London: Scribe, 2014.

Index[1]

[1] Note: Page numbers followed by 'n' refer to notes.

M. Lee (ed.), *Lacan's Cruelty*, The Palgrave Lacan Series,
https://doi.org/10.1007/978-3-031-06238-4

U

W

Z

GPSR Compliance
The European Union's (EU) General Product Safety Regulation (GPSR) is a set of rules that requires consumer products to be safe and our obligations to ensure this.

If you have any concerns about our products, you can contact us on

ProductSafety@springernature.com

In case Publisher is established outside the EU, the EU authorized representative is:

Springer Nature Customer Service Center GmbH
Europaplatz 3
69115 Heidelberg, Germany

www.ingramcontent.com/pod-product-compliance
Lightning Source LLC
Chambersburg PA
CBHW071923160226
39777CB00005B/358
9783031062377